Populist Seduction in Latin America

T0385781

This series of publications on Africa, Latin America, Southeast Asia, and Global and Comparative Studies is designed to present significant research, translation, and opinion to area specialists and to a wide community of persons interested in world affairs. The editor seeks manuscripts of quality on any subject and can usually make a decision regarding publication within three months of receipt of the original work. Production methods generally permit a work to appear within one year of acceptance. The editor works closely with authors to produce a high-quality book. The series appears in a paperback format and is distributed worldwide. For more information, contact the executive editor at Ohio University Press, 19 Circle Drive, The Ridges, Athens, Ohio 45701.

Executive editor: Gillian Berchowitz
AREA CONSULTANTS
Africa: Diane M. Ciekawy
Latin America: Brad Jokisch, Patrick Barr-Melej, and Rafael Obregon
Southeast Asia: William H. Frederick

The Ohio University Research in International Studies series is published for the Center for International Studies by Ohio University Press. The views expressed in individual volumes are those of the authors and should not be considered to represent the policies or beliefs of the Center for International Studies, Ohio University Press, or Ohio University.

Populist Seduction in Latin America

Second Edition

Carlos de la Torre

Ohio University Research in International Studies
Latin America Series No. 50
Ohio University Press
Athens

First edition published as *Populist Seduction in Latin America:
The Ecuadorian Experience* by Ohio University Press.
©2000 by the Center for International Studies, Ohio University

Printed in the United States of America
The books in the Ohio University Research in International Studies Series
are printed on acid-free paper ∞ ™

18 17 16 15 14 13 12 11 10   5 4 3 2 1

Library of Congress Cataloging-in-Publication

Torre, Carlos de la.
  Populist seduction in Latin America / Carlos de la Torre. — 2nd ed.
    p. cm. — (Ohio university research in international studies, latin america series
; No. 50)
  Includes bibliographical references and index.
  ISBN 978-0-89680-279-7 (pb : alk. paper) — ISBN 978-0-89680-474-6 (electronic)
  1. Populism—Ecuador—History—20th century. 2. Ecuador—Politics and govern-
ment—20th century. 3. Velasco Ibarra, José María, 1893–1979. 4. Bucaram Ortiz,
Abdalá, 1952–5. Populism—Latin America—History—20th century. 6. Political
culture—Ecuador. 7. Political culture—Latin America. I. Title.
  JL3081.T67 2010
  320.9866—dc22
                        2010000620

Contents

Preface to the Second Edition

Since the publication of *Populist Seduction in Latin America* in 2000 there has been a renaissance of scholarship on populism.[1] The term has also traveled from academia to the media and policy circuits. *Populism* currently is used to describe the left-wing and nationalist governments of Hugo Chávez, Rafael Correa, and Evo Morales, which claim their legitimacy through winning elections, but which also follow certain authoritarian practices. Critics have charged these regimes with not respecting the separation of powers, the rule of law, the rights of the opposition, or the independence of the media. Critics also claim that their ultranationalist and statist economic policies cannot last and are viable only because of the current high prices of mineral resources. In these rentier states, for example, oil accounts for 75 percent of Venezuela's exports and for 64 percent of Ecuador's; in Bolivia natural gas accounts for 52 percent of all exports (Weyland 2009, 151). Contrary to these pessimistic and sobering assessments, Chávez, Correa, and Morales claim to be leading post-neoliberal regimes that have enhanced rights and that are experimenting with new forms of democratic politics. Their supporters consider these regimes as creative experiments of hope that can show to the left in the West the possibility for novel post-neoliberal social and economic policies. These experiments, they argue, can rejuvenate and reinvigorate democracy.

These contradictory assessments about the state of democracy in Latin America, and about its relationship with populism, are based on how the word *democracy* has been understood through three democratizing traditions. The first is the liberal-republican democratic tradition, with its emphasis on individual freedoms, pluralism, procedural politics, accountability, and institutional designs aimed at maintaining checks and balances between the different branches of government. The second tradition, rooted in Marxism, emphasizes social justice and has advocated direct forms of democratic representation and participation in pyramidal citizen councils where delegates can be recalled (Held 1987, 105–39). Populism represents the third democratizing tradition. Populist leaders have constructed politics as an ethical and moral confrontation between the people and the oligarchy. They have sought direct forms of representation and have understood democracy as the occupation of public spaces in the name of a leader constructed as the symbolic representation of the excluded populace.

These three traditions have worked as ideologies that appeal both to logic and to passion. They depict what democracy ought to be and have been used as political myths that have mobilized and inspired people to participate in politics. Even though many scholars argue that the liberal-republican model can accommodate many of the demands of the other traditions, others, drawing on Marxism and populism, claim that it does not allow for the direct expression of popular sovereignty or for genuine democratic representation. Radical substantive models have been presented as alternatives that can fulfill the unmet expectations of genuine participation and decision making in the affairs of the collectivity. Populists and Marxists advocate for direct forms of participation and representation of the people's sovereignty. Contrary to liberals, who argue that in a differentiated society with a plurality of interests, the will of the people cannot be conceived as one and homogeneous, populists and Marxists have understood the people as having one will (Abts and Rummens 2007; Lefort 1986). Populists and Marxists also contrast a politics of the will, where crowds directly express their sovereignty, to the legal procedures, mediations, and compromises of liberal politics. Marxists and populists share Schmittian understandings of politics as a struggle between enemies (see Schmitt 2007). The interests of the people are as potentially antagonistic to those of the oligarchy as the interests of the proletariat are to the interests of the bourgeoisie.

This book explores the tensions between these democratic traditions. It aims to depart from essentialist and ideological defenses or condemnations of populism and to explore their ambiguous relationship with liberal democracy. Liberal democracy is built on the uneasy coexistence of a liberal constitutionalist emphasis on pluralism and individual rights with democratic demands for equality and for people's sovereignty (Mouffe 2005a, 52–53). "Democratic systems are characterized by an intrinsic tension between the power of the people on the one hand (the popular/populist will), and, on the other, the constitutionalist provisions which protect citizens from the power of government, and from the arbitrary exercise of power" (Mény and Surel 2002a, 7).

Latin American populists have appealed to the principles of equality and sovereignty. Historically they have given priority to social and political rights at the cost of civil rights. Understanding sovereignty as a function of free and open elections, populists have also expanded the franchise, incorporating previously excluded groups (Peruzzotti 2008). But populists have not valued the liberal traditions of civil rights and pluralism. Populists' lack of regard for political liberalism can be explained by the fact that, unlike the contractual bases of authority based on the individual, they have advocated for organic and holistic conceptions of community (Zanatta 2008). These views allow populist leaders to claim to embody the voices of undifferentiated communities that share the same identities and interests. Even though populists have searched for alternatives to liberal democracy, they have not totally abandoned all the instruments of representative democracy. "Populism rejects parties but usually organizes itself as a political movement; it is highly critical of political elites, but runs for elections; it advocates the power of the people, yet relies on seduction by a charismatic leader" (Mény and Surel 2002a, 17).

The tensions between pluralism and civil rights on the one hand and sovereignty and equality on the other can be further explored as the conflict between what Margaret Canovan (1999, 2005) has argued are the two phases of democracy.

From a pragmatic point of view, corresponding to the ordinary, everyday diversity of people-as-population, modern democracy is a complex set of institutions that allow us to coexist with other people and their divergent interests with as little coercion as possible. But democracy is also a repository of one of the redemptive visions (characteristic of modernity) that promises salvation through politics. The promised savior is "the people," a mysterious collectivity somehow composed of us, ordinary people, and yet capable of transfiguration into an authoritative entity that can make dramatic and redeeming political appearances. (2005, 89–90)

The inherent tension between these two phases of democracy explains why populism continues to reappear. Whenever citizens feel that politicians have appropriated their will, they can demand to get it back. Populism, however, does not have the same effects in different institutional settings. In institutionalized political systems, "populism can be read as a fever warning which signals that problems are not being dealt with effectively, or point to the malfunctioning of the linkages between citizens and governing elites" (Mény and Surel 2002a, 15). In poorly institutionalized systems, "populist fever" can run out of control, and may not necessarily lead to an improvement of democratic governance and accountability. "[Populism] is far more deleterious in newer democracies where the 'rules of the game' are more contested and constraints on populist actors are weaker: here populism's association with charismatic leadership and organizational de-institutionalization has a natural tendency toward messianic leadership" (March 2007, 73).

As Margaret Canovan maintains, the term *the people* "is not only the source of political legitimacy, but can sometimes appear to redeem politics from oppression, corruption, and banality" (2005, 125). Populists distrust views of democracy as accommodation and compromise. Instead, they advocate democracy "as the politics of the will" (Canovan 2002, 34), where the people express their sovereignty directly and without intermediaries. Over the past ten years Bolivia,

Ecuador, and Venezuela have experienced intense political mobilizations and insurrections carried out in the name of popular sovereignty
and democracy. Supporters and opponents of Chávez have polarized
Venezuela, using collective action as a means of expressing their
views in the streets. In 2002 the military briefly ousted and then restored Chávez to power, arguing they were fulfilling the will of the
masses marching both for and against the president (López 2005).
Between 2000 and 2006 Bolivia experienced intense collective action
and political instability. Scholars have debated whether or not that
nation went through a revolutionary epoch (Dunkerley 2007; García
Linera 2004; Hylton and Thomson 2007; Webber 2008). In Ecuador
since 1996 three elected presidents have had their terms cut short by
constitutional coups carried out under the excuse of implementing
what the people had willed in the streets.

Many analysts have interpreted recent Andean rebellions as populist
resurrections; "the people," without intermediaries, took their political destinies into their own hands. Since the heyday of Latin American
populism, in the 1940s, when the excluded masses became incorporated into politics, democracy has been lived and experienced as the
occupation of public spaces in the name of a leader exalted as the
embodiment of poor people's aspirations. In Argentina, workers'
demonstrations to rescue Gen. Juan Perón from military arrest in
1945 became enshrined as Loyalty Day and a part of Peronist myths
and rituals (Torre 1995). José María Velasco Ibarra, five-time president of Ecuador, eloquently constructed the notion of democracy as
the occupation of public spaces: "the streets and plazas are for citizens to express their aspirations and yearnings, not for slaves to rattle
their chains" (de la Torre 1993, 160).

Populism is based on a Manichaean rhetoric of us versus them. In
Latin America, this antagonism has been constructed as that of the
people against the oligarchy. Under populism, all social, economic,
and ethnic differentiations and oppressions fall into two irreconcilable poles: the people, who constitute both the nation and *lo popular*,

versus the foreign-led oligarchy, which has illegally appropriated the will of the people. The notion of the popular incorporates the Marxist idea of class, understood as antagonistic conflict between two groups, with the romantic view of the purity of the people. As a result, the popular has been imagined as an undifferentiated, unified, and homogenous entity (Avritzer 2002, 72). Marxists share the populist emphasis on reducing the complexity of social struggles to a Manichaean struggle between two antagonistic camps. Both Marxist and populist traditions disdain liberal mediated politics, seeking instead for radical substantive democracy based on the direct enactment of sovereignty, and as direct representation. These two traditions, however, disagree as to the roles to be given to different actors. Whereas Marxists give normative and theoretical priority to the proletariat, populists search for the vaguer category the people. Given the similarities of the two traditions, it is not a surprise that a few Marxist academics, despite the bad reputation of the term *populism,* have searched for a combination of populism and socialism (Laclau 1977, 2005a, 2006; Raby 2006).

This new expanded and revised edition of *Populist Seduction* explores the tensions between democratization and charismatic-plebiscitarian leadership. It includes three new chapters. The first of these, "The Resurgence of Radical Populism in Latin America" (chapter 5), analyzes the regimes of Hugo Chávez, Evo Morales, and Rafael Correa. It explores not only the continuities of these regimes with existing populist cultural and discursive traditions but also their innovations. It focuses on Marxist and Indianist scholarly critiques of liberal democracy. It also explores the tensions between radical participatory democracy and charismatic leadership in the new institutions created in Venezuela to improve and transcend liberal forms. Chapter 5 explores different constructions of the category the people and the resulting levels of polarization in different populist experiences. It critiques the commonly held view of the politics of the informal sectors as disorganized masses and shows why the poor continue to endorse populist leaders.

The ambiguities of Rafael Correa's project for a post-neoliberal citizens' revolution are explored in chapter 6. It studies the 2006 presidential campaign in Ecuador, contrasting the rhetoric and style of Correa with that of Álvaro Noboa. It shows how traditional ways of campaigning have merged and have become hybridized with modern uses of television. The chapter analyzes Correa's style of governing through permanent political campaigns and explores the contested meanings of democracy and the prospects of democratizing society under his administration.

This new edition also follows Abdalá Bucaram's saga, from self-imposed exile in Panama in 1997 to his triumphant return to Guayaquil in 2005. Bucaram's return to Ecuador in 2005 provoked different reactions, including the overthrow of President Lucio Gutiérrez, in April 2005. It helped further delegitimize political institutions and political parties and clear the path for the election of Rafael Correa, who ran as an outsider, promising to overhaul the country's economic and political systems.

Finally, the conclusion, "Between Authoritarianism and Democracy," outlines the challenges of radical populism for newly established democracies. This chapter explores the similarities and differences between what the literature describes as classical populism, neoliberal neopopulism, and radical left-wing populism. These populist experiences are examined in case studies of Ecuadorian politics that focus on José María Velasco Ibarra, Abdalá Bucaram, and Rafael Correa. The book also compares different Latin American experiences during these three surges of Latin American populism.

My understanding of populism follows recent work that has uncoupled politics from economics and that has departed from the views of populism as a phase in the history of Latin America linked to specific economic policies (Roberts 1995; Weyland 1996, 2001, 2003). Populist regimes have followed nationalist, Keynesian, and redistributive policies, as well as their opposites—neoliberal market economy policies. Unlike the market reform policies of Alberto Fujimori or

Carlos Menem, the current wave of radical populists is following classical populist nationalist and redistributive principles nowadays branded as socialism of the twenty-first century (Weyland 2009).

Populism is better understood as a discourse that dichotomizes politics as a struggle between two irreconcilable and antagonistic camps: the people against the oligarchy. Under populism the name of a leader becomes an empty signifier that incorporates a series of unmet demands that cannot be processed within the existing institutional and hegemonic order (Laclau 2005a; Panizza 2008). Since populism is based on a rhetoric that pits the people against the oligarchy, the level of polarization and confrontation that populism entails has varied. Radical populists such as Hugo Chávez are politicizing existing inequalities and confronting society in political, socioeconomic, and ethnic terms (Roberts 2003). Chávez, Morales, and Correa use discourses that are similar to other national radical populists, such as Juan Perón, Jorge Eliécer Gaitán, and the young Víctor Raúl Haya de la Torre, whom the literature has labeled classical populists. The discourse of other leaders, such as Velasco and Fujimori, provoked political polarization but not the same level of class and ethnic confrontation as the aforementioned experiences.

Populism is also a strategy to get elected and to govern based on this Manichaean discourse. Populist leaders aim to have a direct, but not necessarily institutionalized, relationship with their followers. Populism is a strategy of top-down mobilization (Roberts 2008) that clashes with the autonomous demands of social movement organizations. Populist glorification of common people and their attacks on elites could open spaces for common people to press for their agendas and the redress of their grievances (Ellner 2005, 2008). The tension between top-down mobilization and autonomous mobilization from below is characteristic of populism.

Under populism new political and economic elites have replaced well-established elites. The so-called classical populist regimes allowed industrial elites to share power with or replace agrarian elites, or both. The replacement of elites is one of populism's democratizing features (Weyland 2003). Even though populism as lived is profoundly democratic, it has simultaneously built a leader into the embodiment of an undifferentiated vox populi. Hence populists have simultaneously democratized their nations by expanding the franchise and by incorporating formerly excluded people, while leaders have been created as the personification of the people's democratic aspirations and as the authorized interpreters of their will. Populism has created not only new social orders but novel social pacts. Populists have destroyed institutions while promising to build a new society from the ashes of the old regimes. Yet the new institutions and new rules sometimes clash with the authoritarian conception of leaders as being above procedures, norms, and institutions.

This book aims to understand the redeeming dimensions of populist politics, as well as the dangers of "fantasies of salvation" to pluralism and to civil and human rights (Tismaneanu 1998). It explores how populism is a recurrent feature in societies marked by deep structural inequalities and with weak institutional channels to process social conflicts. It explains how populist appeals work in contexts where people are economically and legally poor, and where discourses of democracy are used to silence and to exclude the poor and the nonwhite. Even though populism as lived is liberating and empowers the poor and the nonwhite as the essence of a nation, it continues to rely on plebiscitary acclamation and on the appropriation of the will of the people by charismatic saviors.

Several institutions and people helped me in preparing this new edition of *Populist Seduction in Latin America*. I thank Gillian Berchowitz at Ohio University Press for her continuous support. I wrote the new material for the book at the Woodrow Wilson International Center for Scholars, where I was a fellow during the 2008–9 academic year. The center gave me the time and a stimulating environment to work on this project. I thank the staff and scholars of the center for their support, in particular the Program for Latin American Studies and its director, Cynthia Arnson. I also thank Taylor Jardno for her help as research assistant at the Wilson Center. A version of chapter 5 was published in *Constellations,*[2] and I thank Andrew Arato and Martin Plotke for their comments and suggestions. Chapter 6 builds on my collaborative work with Catherine Conaghan, a friend and mentor who deeply influenced my work. I also thank my colleagues and students at the Facultad Latinoamericana de Ciencias Sociales Sede Ecuador (FLACSO-Ecuador) for their continuous engagement with my work and for their suggestions on how to improve my arguments. Julio Aibar, Enrique Peruzzotti, Mauro Porto, Kenneth Roberts, Kurt Weyland, and Loris Zanatta have commented on my work. Finally, Carmen Martínez has always been there for me, challenging my ideas and supporting my endeavors.

Preface to the First Edition

Books tend to reflect, to a large extent, the obsessions and life histories of their authors. This volume is a result of my ambiguous feelings toward, and intellectual fascination with, Latin American populism. I remember as a child how my family life was affected by the passions stirred by populist leader José María Velasco Ibarra. Some of my uncles and aunts were passionate *Velasquistas*. They had supported the caudillo in his five presidencies (1934–35, 1944–47, 1952–56, 1960–61, and 1968–72), and longed for him during his exiles. My father, the late Carlos de la Torre Reyes, who was the editor of *El tiempo*, a Quito newspaper, was an opponent of Velasco. As a liberal, my father was committed to a struggle for fundamental democratic freedoms that were not always respected by the populist caudillo, and faced many attacks by Velasco's supporters. For instance, *El tiempo* was at the forefront of the opposition against Velasco's *autogolpe* (self-inflicted coup d'état) in 1970. I remember watching how Velasco's nephew and minister of defense, Jorge Acosta Velasco, insulted and falsely accused my father on television and how my father's office in *El tiempo* was vandalized by Velasquista crowds. In this climate of political instability and lack of rights for the opposition, we were always ready to face my father's imprisonment. Fortunately that never occurred.

Reflections on the late 1960s and early 1970s also brings back memories of large crowds and collective action. I was impressed by the large crowds that Velasco attracted when giving public speeches. I also remember the traffic jams and the smell of tear gas left by police repression of student demonstrations against Velasco's regime.

Several years later, in 1988, as a student at the Graduate Faculty of the New School for Social Research, I returned to Ecuador to define my dissertation topic. I was surprised by the passion aroused by Abdalá Bucaram, a new populist caudillo. In this election he faced Rodrigo Borja, a moderate Social Democrat. Most scholars and journalists saw in Borja the promise of a social democratic modernity. After all, his party, Izquierda Democrática, was a modern political organization with a clear ideological platform. Borja was committed to the respect of human and civil rights and the reconciliation of the nation after the authoritarian excesses of León Febres Cordero's regime (1984–88). With the excuse of stopping "subversion," Febres Cordero had abused the human rights of his opponents. Several guerrilla members, including some of my friends, had been tortured and killed by the government. Conflicts between the executive and congress and the judiciary had plagued Febres Cordero's administration. He had also faced a military insurrection led by General Frank Vargas. After these years of political instability, most journalists and intellectuals saw the 1988 elections as a contest between a modern party with a concrete ideology and program of modernization and democratization and the populist politics of the past, represented by Abdalá Bucaram.

Journalists and social scientists constructed Bucaram as the embodiment of the rabble and a charlatan who charmed ignorant masses. They argued that poverty and lack of education explained poor people's support for Bucaram (Fernández and Ortiz 1988). He was seen as a corrupt demagogue and a danger to democracy. In spite of what the press and some academics were expressing, Bucaram's populist movement was obviously more than manipulation. Only middle-class prejudices could reduce his followers to ignorant masses misled by a charlatan. When, out of curiosity, I attended some of Bucaram's mass meetings, I was impressed. Bucaram drew on popular culture and humor to attack the well-established "white" elites and champion the dignity and self-worth of his supporters. During these mass meetings, Bucaram established a dialogue with the audience. He focused on everyday life to politicize the humiliations of common mestizo Ecuadorians. He transformed the servants, the poor, and the excluded into the essence of the real Ecuadorian nation, and their bosses into effeminate antinational oligarchies. I was also terrified to see how this self-appointed messiah saw himself as the embodiment of the people's will that stood above and beyond any democratic institution or procedure.

The tensions and ambiguities between the authoritarian appropriation of the people's will and the inclusion of previously excluded people into the political community that was so clearly revealed in Bucaram's populism are what attracted me to the study of these phenomena. I wanted to understand how populist leaders appealed to those they led without assuming manipulation by leaders, irrationality of followers, or the reduction of populism to models of instrumental rationality that explained politics by the exchange of votes for goods and services. I became determined to understand the complexities of populist seductions and explore the tensions between liberal democracies and populism.

The study of populism is certainly puzzling. In Latin America, populism is generally viewed in negative terms. For most it implies an abnormality, an anomaly, and a passing phenomenon that will eventually, and hopefully, go away. That is why most studies of populism begin by focusing on its negative characteristics, on what populism is not when it is compared with other political ideologies, parties, movements, or regimes. For instance, unlike liberalism or socialism, populism lacks an ideology. Populist movements are not the political expression of the economic interest of a particular social class. Nor can populism be specified as a type of political regime. Because of populism's negative characteristics, modernization theory, for example, considered it a temporary event, an aberration produced by abrupt processes of social change.

Populism is also associated with leaders who manipulate, followers who are betrayed, and overall backwardness. Modernization theorists, influenced by mass-society models, interpreted populist caudillos as charlatans who duped backward masses left in a state of anomie after sudden processes of social change. From the opposite ideological angle, orthodox Marxists have tried to explain the historical abnormalities that have not allowed the proletariat to discover its own class interests when it has been misled by populist leaders. José Álvarez Junco (1994, 16) illustrates how this orthodox Marxist thesis of the proletariat as a revolutionary class whose historical mission is the struggle against capitalism and bourgeois domination is based on erroneous assumptions that have substituted dogma for historical research. Álvarez Junco claims the thesis is based on a view that assigns a priori an essence to historical subjects even before their historical appearance. The proletariat has been constructed as a revolutionary subject whose historical mission has been predetermined by a teleological evolutionary theory of society.

Populism is not only viewed as a negative and ephemeral phenomenon, it is also a profoundly ambiguous category. In 1967 a leading group of scholars met at the London School of Economics to try to define the new specter haunting the world: populism. The result of this endeavor was not fully satisfactory because many and contradictory definitions of this term emerged. The editors of the volume based on this conference, Ghiţa Ionescu and Ernest Gellner, wrote, "There can, at present, be no doubt about the *importance* of populism. But no one is quite clear just what it *is*. As a doctrine or as movement, it is elusive and protean. It bobs up everywhere, but in many contradictory shapes. Does it have an underlying unity, or does one name cover a multitude of unconnected tendencies?" (1969, 1; emphasis in original).

Despite the increasing number of case studies of populist experiences and the efforts to develop a theory of populism, at present we are as perplexed as these scholars were almost thirty years ago. There is no underlying definition of the term or a convincing theory of populism. Moreover, there are so many objections to the use of the category populism that perhaps we should forget about it and abandon its study for good. What can another book on populism offer to the debate on a phenomenon that we cannot even define?

Margaret Canovan urges us to retain the term *populism,* arguing that at least "it provides a pointer, however shaky, to an interesting and largely unexplored area of political and social experience" (1981, 6). The term *populism,* as Felipe Burbano (1998) argues, continues to allow us to compare historical experiences by reflecting on key issues of political sociology such as the generation of political identities, the study of political discourses, the analysis of political cultures and clientelism, and the research of the particularities of citizenship and democracy in Latin America. Because the categories offered by the detractors of populism tend to be reductionist in that they squeeze these phenomena into the utilitarian exchange of political loyalty for material goods or the study of the economic policies of these regimes, the term *populism* at least allows for the study of the multidimensional aspects of these experiences.

I see populism as a modern political phenomenon that cannot be shortened to a historical phase in the history of Latin America or to specific economic policies. Contrary to the hypothesis of modernization theory, populism is not the anomalous result of rapid processes of political mobilization. Nor is it a phase in the history of the region closely linked to import substitution industrialization, as dependency theorists have argued. Populism has adapted itself to a new neoliberal conjuncture characterized by the privatization of state enterprises and the opening of the economy. Populism, old and new, is the product of a particular form of political incorporation of the popular sectors into politics—one based on strong rhetorical appeals to the people and to crowd action on behalf of a leader. As many authors have shown, citizenship is not strong in Latin America, and political and social rights have been given priority over civil rights. The poor whose rights are specified in constitutions and laws, do not have the power to exercise these rights. They have to rely on protectors who can help them to take advantage of their rights and who can defend them from the arbitrariness of the police and of the powerful. Politicians who have become such guardians have organized clientelist networks that have allowed their followers limited access to goods and services, not as rights but as concessions to interest groups. Personalized relations of domination based on unequal exchanges between leaders and led allow some politicians to present themselves as saviors of the underdog. Populist politicians have been successful in incarnating the demands of those at the bottom of society for symbolic and material dignity. Their authoritarian appropriation of the people's will has posed fundamental challenges to the institutionalization of democracy, and their movements, which have included previously excluded groups, have not always respected the norms of liberal democracies.

The essays and case studies in this book represent my attempt to understand Ecuadorian populism in a comparative perspective. My aim is to develop a research strategy to understand the social creation of political leaders. I want to examine how followers' actions produce certain leaders at particular conjunctures. With the study of political symbolism and discourse, I have incorporated the analysis of material exchanges emphasized by studies grounded in notions of instrumental rationality. Velasco's leadership in the 1940s, for instance, was based on political alliances between political parties and associations of civil society. They shared a discourse that personalized politics as the struggle between the Liberal oligarchy and the people, understood as citizens whose will has been mocked at the polls by Liberal electoral fraud. Velasco was not only successful in building his leadership on this shared populist discourse. He also became the embodiment of the democratic ideal. He presented the incarnation of a religiously based ascetic figure whose aim was to bring moral and social redemption to common people. Bucaram in the 1980s and 1990s politicized the experiences of humiliation of common mestizo Ecuadorians. He represented the world turned upside down. The well-established elites became the incarnation of foreign and effeminate lifestyles, and common people were portrayed as the incarnation of the real and authentic Ecuadorian nation to come, under the leadership of Bucaram, "the leader of the poor."

My engagement with populism is not just motivated by an almost masochistic intellectual interest in an object of study that defies precise categories and in a slippery and undertheorized concept that is regularly banned from the vocabulary of the social sciences. I am also politically committed to understand the appeal that so many populist leaders have had in Latin American politics since the 1940s and to explore their ambiguous impact on the construction and strengthening of democracy.

The study of populism is a privileged site to analyze the particularities of Latin American democracies. If Latin American populism was a fundamental democratizing force that marked the entrance of common people into the political community (Vilas 1995b), the specificity of this process of inclusion needs to be explained. Most social scientists have accepted Marshall's description (1963) of democratization in the West as the movement from civic to political to social rights. Charles Tilly argues that citizenship, defined as the "sense of rights and mutual obligations binding state agents and a category of persons defined by their legal attachment to the state," only became "a widespread phenomenon during the nineteenth century" in Europe (1995, 375). Unlike the Western pattern, common people in Latin America are not necessarily tied to the state by citizenship. Even though there is a legislation that guarantees and specifies citizenship rights, paternalistic relationships between powerful people—"patricians," who are above the power of laws—and their clients guarantee the access of the latter to state resources and legally recognized citizenship rights. Moreover, the civil rights of common people are not respected, and they live at the mercy of the arbitrariness of law enforcement agents (Chevigny 1995; Pinheiro 1994, 1997).

The differentiation between common people, whose rights are not recognized in their interactions in everyday life, and powerful people, who can use laws and citizenship rights to their convenience (Matta 1991), results from the incredible economic, social, ethnic, and status inequalities in Latin America. If citizenship is not the mechanism that binds common people and the state, it is not a surprise that liberal democratic institutions and the rule of law are not always respected. As Guillermo O'Donnell (1994) has argued, Latin American delegative democracies are different from representative democracies. Delegative democracies are based on the idea that those who win an election have the popular mandate to govern according to their interpretation of the people's will and interests. The president claims to embody the nation. He sees himself as the redeemer of the homeland. His policies, therefore, do not need to be linked to his promises during the campaign or with the agreements made with organizations and associations that supported his election. All the responsibility to rule the country falls to the president. He is perceived as the source of the country's ills or its successes. Because he feels that his duty is to "save the nation," he does not always have to respect democratic procedures or the rights of his political rivals.

Hence, democracy in Latin America has been constructed differently than in the West. Populist leaders have invoked forms of direct democracy against liberal models. Modernizing elites have also used discourses of democracy as tools to exclude common people from the political decision-making process. They have used paternalistic arguments to claim that ordinary people are not prepared for democracy. However, as in the West, common people have used the rhetoric of democracy to struggle for their rights. The fact that elites have to pay at least lip service to a discourse of rights, citizenship, and democracy attests that the struggle for a more equitable and participatory political system continues. It also implies that in the future democratic struggles might cease implementing a system based on the binding consultation of citizens, the equality of citizenship, the breadth of citizenship from civic to political to social rights, and the protection of common people from the arbitrary power of the state and law enforcement agents (Tilly 1995).

For the last ten years, I have been writing about the uneasy relationship between populism and democracy and the problem of populist leadership. Chapter 1 is a modified version of an essay first published in *Social Research* in 1992. This chapter reviews some works about what some scholars nowadays call classical populism. It develops a multidimensional approach to the study of populist leadership that goes beyond the binary options between rational choice and crowd psychology. I argue that to understand the social creation of populist leaders, economic and social structural processes must be analyzed together with cultural and political variables. Economic and social structural changes allowed for the emergence of populist politics. The transformations of oligarchic systems by capitalist development, urbanization, and the expansion of the state apparatus created social classes and groups that demanded their political inclusion. However, social and economic transformations do not explain why populism became the rhetoric and style of political mobilization that included previously marginalized sectors. To analyze the specificity of the populist relationship between leaders and led, all these variables must be studied. The personalistic charismatic relationship between leaders and followers must be examined together with the material and symbolic exchanges of clientelist networks and patronage relationships. The social history of populism and the autonomous expectations of the crowds need to be analyzed in conjunction with the Manichaean discourses of leaders.

Chapter 2 builds on my dissertation, and my book, *La seducción velasquista* (1993). In this chapter I study the emergence of mass politics in Ecuador in the late 1930s and 1940s and the transformation of Velasco Ibarra into the redeemer of the homeland. I analyze the patterns of collective violence in a populist civilian-military insurrection against the Liberal regime and in the name of a populist politician. The shared, if contested, frame of discourse that transformed the Liberals into the embodiment of sin and the lack of democracy and the simultaneous transformation of Velasco into the incarnation of the democratic ideal allow an understanding of the success of Velasco's leadership and the patterns of collective violence in the Gloriosa (May

1944), which destroyed the symbols of Liberal rule while respecting the property of the non-Liberal elites. Velasco's oratory and his ambiguous commitment to democracy are also explored.

While writing my dissertation, I began to study Abdalá Bucaram's political style. I attended several of Bucaram's mass meetings and those of his rival politicians in the 1992 presidential campaign and gathered their televised propaganda, flyers, and journalistic accounts. I returned to Ecuador in 1996 with Carmen Martínez to carry out ethnographic participant observation of Bucaram's presidential campaign. Chapter 3 is based on this data and builds on my book *¡Un sólo toque! Populismo y cultura política en Ecuador* (1996). This chapter analyzes the interrelationship between daily life, populism, and political culture in present-day Ecuador. This chapter examines how the figure of populist politician Abdalá Bucaram has allowed modernizing political and intellectual elites to constitute themselves as the incarnation of the democratic ideal, while representing the populist leader as the embodiment of the rabble and a threat not only to democracy but to civility. I explore two moments of collective effervescence to illustrate how everyday forms of domination and resistance have produced particular political cultures: the electoral rituals that transformed Bucaram into "the leader of the poor" and the demonstrations demanding his resignation that made him the "repugnant other" who had to leave the presidency and the country.

Chapter 4 reviews the recent literature on neopopulism, showing how previously unresolved research questions have reappeared in the literature. It suggests new lines for future research, and the chapter concludes with a reflection on the specificity of Latin American democracies and the paradoxes of populist politics for strengthening those regimes.

I have benefited from the support of many people and institutions. My research on *Velasquismo* was financed by an Alvin Johnson dissertation fellowship from the New School for Social Research (1990–91), and by a doctoral fellowship of FLACSO-Ecuador (1990–92). My

PREFACE TO THE FIRST EDITION

thanks to Amparo Menéndez-Carrión, former director of FLACSO-Ecuador, for her support. I did archival research at the Biblioteca de Autores Ecuatorianos Aurelio Espinosa Pólit. My gratitude to its director, Father Julián Bravo, and his staff—Wilson Vega, Martha Llumiquinga, and Elizabeth Villareal. I also thank Ramiro Ávila, curator of the Archivo Histórico del Banco Central. My research on Bucaram's populism was generously funded by the Centro Andino de Acción Popular and by a faculty research grant from Drew University. My gratitude to Francisco Rhon, director of the Centro Andino de Acción Popular, and to Paolo Cucchi, dean of the College of Liberal Arts at Drew University for their continued support. I also acknowledge Santiago Nieto Montoya, director of Informe Confidencial, for the public opinion surveys on Bucaram's image and popularity.

My dissertation committee—William Roseberry, Andrew Arato, José Casanova, and Charles Tilly—has encouraged me and helped me for several years. Preliminary versions of my analysis of how Bucaram got to power were presented at FLACSO-Ecuador in September and November 1996. I delivered a paper on the relationship between Bucaram and the mass media at the conference Media and the Politics of Democracy at the New School for Social Research, 6 March 1998. A version of chapter 3 was presented at the Workshop of Contentious Politics, Lazarsfeld Center for the Social Sciences, Columbia University, 16 November 1998. I am grateful to the participants in these seminars and workshops, in particular Andrew Arato, Javier Auyero, Jeff Goldfarb, Margot Olavarría, and Charles Tilly. I also thank Robert Dash and Kristen Anderson for comments on earlier versions of chapter 3. Some of the arguments of chapter 4 were presented in papers at Ohio University in April 1998 and the Consejo Superior de Investigaciones Científicas, Madrid, in June 1998. I thank Felipe Burbano, Carmen Martínez, César Montúfar, Ricardo Muratorio, and the anonymous reader of Ohio University Press for comments to earlier drafts of this book.

Finally, I express my gratitude to several people whose support continues to inspire me: my mother, Noemí Espinosa; my sister María Soledad; and my brother Felipe; Alberto Acosta, Francisco Rhon, and Felipe Burbano, with whom I published my first book on populism; José Álvarez Junco and Tom Walker, who encouraged me to organize this book. This book would not have been possible without the support and encouragement of Carmen Martínez. She postponed her dissertation research in 1996 to come to Ecuador to do the research of Bucaram with me and has been the most enthusiastic and critical reader. This book is for her and in memory of my father, whose passion for politics and intellectual work has always inspired me.

Abbreviations

ADE	Alianza Democrática Ecuatoriana (Ecuadorian Democratic Alliance)
AP	Alliance for a Proud and Sovereign Homeland
APRA	Alianza Popular Revolucionaria Americana
BAEP	Biblioteca Aurelio Espinosa Pólit, Cotocollao
CEDOC	Confederación Ecuatoriana de Obreros Católicos (Ecuadorian Confederation of Catholic Workers)
CFP	Concentración de Fuerzas Populares
CONAIE	(Confederation of Indigenous Nationalities of Ecuador)
COPEI	Christina Political Electoral Independent Organization
CTE	Confederación de Trabajadores del Ecuador
FEINE	Federation of Indigenous Evangelicals of Ecuador
FEV	Frente Electoral Velasquista
FLACSO	Facultad Latinoamericana de Ciencias Sociales
ISI	Import Substitution Industrialization
PRE	Partido Roldosista Ecuatoriano (Ecuadorian Roldosista Party)
PRIAN	Partido Renovador Institucional Acción Nacional
SIN	Servicio Nacional de Inteligencia

Populist Seduction in Latin America

Chapter 1

The Ambiguity of Latin American "Classical" Populism

THE STUDY OF Latin American populism has a long history. From the pioneering analyses of Gino Germani in the 1950s to the present, different paradigms have been proposed to explain these phenomena that simultaneously attract and repel social scientists. Certainly the main challenge in the study of populism lies in explaining the appeal of leaders for their followers, without reducing the latter's behavior to either manipulation or irrational and anomic action or to a utilitarian rationalism, which supposedly explains everything.

Using a discussion of case studies, this chapter presents a multidimensional approach to the study of what is currently called "classical" Latin American populism. It stresses the analysis of those mechanisms that explain, on the one hand, the appeal of populist leaders and, on the other, the expectations and actions of followers. The selection of case studies is not intended to present an overview of all populist experiences in Latin America nor to analyze all the existing literature. My interest, rather, is to review innovative works on Latin American populism for their conceptual and methodological advances, while examining particular characteristics of populism. In the course of the analysis, I make suggestions for further research.

Before presenting a new approach to the study of Latin American populism, let us examine the different uses of this concept in the existing literature. The term *populism* has been used to refer to all the following phenomena:

— forms of sociopolitical mobilization in which "backward masses" are manipulated by "demagogic" and "charismatic" leaders (Germani 1971, 1978);
— multiclass social movements with middle- or upper-class leadership and popular (working-class or peasant) bases (di Tella 1973; Ianni 1973);
— a historical phase in the region's dependent capitalist development or a stage in the transition to modernity (Germani 1978; Ianni 1975; Malloy 1977; O'Donnell 1973; Vilas 1992–93);
— redistributive, nationalist, and inclusionary state policies. These populist state policies are contrasted with exclusionary policies that benefit foreign capital, concentrate economic resources, and repress popular demands (Malloy 1987). In contrast, from a neoliberal perspective, populism is interpreted as "ill-conceived development strategies" that emphasize growth and income distribution via a strong intervention of the state, but that deemphasize the risks of inflation, deficit finance, and external constraints (Dornbusch and Edwards 1991);
— a type of political party with middle- or upper-class leadership, strong popular base, nationalistic rhetoric, charismatic leadership, and lacking a precise ideology (Angell 1968);
— a political discourse that divides society into antagonistic fields — the people *(el pueblo)* versus the oligarchy *(la oligarquía)* (Laclau 1977);
— attempts of Latin American nations to control foreign-led modernization processes through the state's taking a central role as defender of national identity and promoter of national integration through economic development (Touraine 1989);

2

—a political style that implies a close bond between political leaders and led, usually associated with periods of rapid mobilization and crisis, but that emerges in periods of exceptionality as
well as at other times (Knight 1998).

The previous enumeration of the uses of the concept of populism
seem to confirm Peter Wiles's observation that "to each his own definition of populism, according to the academic ax he grinds" (1969,
166). Given its many different uses and the variety of historical experiences to which it seemingly refers, authors such as Ian Roxborough
(1984) and Rafael Quintero (1980) have proposed eliminating the
concept from the vocabulary of the social sciences. They base their
arguments on case studies that show that populism is not a stage in
Latin American development linked to import substitution industrialization (Collier 1979; Roxborough 1984). They also argue that
views privileging the importance of charismatic leaders and anomic
and available masses have been replaced by interpretations emphasizing the rational utilitarian political behavior of popular sectors
(Menéndez-Carrión 1986), or by class analysis of specific populist
coalitions (Quintero 1980; Roxborough 1984). Finally, they question
the theoretical validity of a concept that refers equally to civilian and
military regimes in the region over a span of sixty years, which may,
but do not necessarily, espouse anti-imperialist ideologies and in
some cases apply distributive economic policies and in others policies that concentrate economic power. If we add to these objections
the generally negative attributes of the term, such as manipulation, or
a deviation from "normal politics," one might conclude (as did
Menéndez-Carrión) that the term *populism* has been "conceptually
exhausted" (1992, 200).

Contrary to the premature efforts to ban populism from the vocabulary of the social sciences, this book argues that, despite the misuses
and abuses of the term, it is worth preserving and redefining. The
phenomena that have been designated as populist have in common

certain characteristics that can be identified and compared by using this notion. Otherwise, "important empirical content can be lost when concepts are discarded prematurely as a result of ambiguity or an incomplete 'fit' across cases" (Roberts 1995, 88). As Laclau points out (1977), populism is not just a sociological concept, but rather an actual experience of people who have defined and do define their collective identities through populist participation as Peronists, *Cefepistas,* or *Gaitanistas.* Finally, authors who abandon the notion of populism in favor of objectivist categories for analyzing social reality cannot take into account realms of populist experience such as the formation of identity, ritual, myths, and the ambiguous meanings of populism for the actors involved.

I see populism as a style of political mobilization based on strong rhetorical appeals to the people and crowd action on behalf of a leader. Populist rhetoric radicalizes the emotional element common to all political discourses (Álvarez Junco 1987). It is a rhetoric that constructs politics as the moral and ethical struggle between el pueblo and the oligarchy. Populist discourse transmutes politics into a struggle for moral values without accepting compromise or dialogue with the opponent. Populist politics is based on crowd action. Crowds directly occupy public spaces to demand political participation and incorporation. At the same time, these crowds are used by their leaders to intimidate adversaries. Mass meetings become political dramas wherein people feel themselves to be true participants in the political scene. Populist politics includes all these characteristics. It is an interclass alliance based on charismatic political leadership; a Manichaean and moralistic discourse that divides society into *el pueblo* and oligarchy; clientelist networks that guarantee access to state resources; and forms of political participation in which public and massive demonstrations, the acclamation of leaders, and the occupation of public spaces in the name of a leader are perceived as more important than citizenship rights and the respect for liberal democratic procedures.

4

The Structural Preconditions of Populism

The first round of studies on Latin American populism, those of modernization and dependency theorists, tried to come to grips with the experiences of the major republics. In the 1930s and 1940s Argentina, Brazil, and Mexico endured processes of urbanization and import substitution industrialization associated with the emergence of the populist politics of Peronism, Varguism, and Cardenism. Hence Gino Germani (1971), for example, presented the hypothesis that populism is a phase in the transition to modernity. Developing an alternative explanation, authors working within the dependency perspective criticized the teleological assumptions of modernization theory and offered a structuralist argument that linked populism with import substitution industrialization (O'Donnell 1973; Malloy 1977).

Recent scholarship has demonstrated that the fit between populism and import substitution, even in the major republics, is not that neat (Perruci and Sanderson 1989, 34–35). For example, Ian Roxborough (1984) shows that, whereas import substitution industrialization started in Brazil before the 1930s, populist politics was inaugurated in the late 1940s and during Vargas's second term in office (1950–54). Moreover, in countries such as Peru and Ecuador, there is no fit between populism and import substitution. Populist movements emerged long before import substitution industrialization. Nevertheless and in general terms, populism is associated with dependent capitalist development and of the resulting emergence of popular sectors demanding an expansion of closed political systems (Collier 1979; Drake 1982). In this context, I will examine the social conditions that allowed the emergence of *Sanchezcerrismo* and *Aprismo* in Peru in the 1920s and 1930s, *Gaitanismo* in Colombia in the mid-1940s, and Velasquismo in Ecuador in the 1940s in this chapter.

The oligarchical social order typical of Latin America in the late nineteenth and early twentieth centuries had been characterized by a combination of "liberal-inspired constitutions (division of the three powers, elections, and so on) with patrimonial practices and values polarized around a *cacique, patrón, gamonal, coronel,* or *caudillo"* (Ianni 1975, 79). These estate-based societies excluded the majority of the population from political decision making and had relations of domination and subordination characterized by unequal reciprocity. Alexis de Tocqueville's analysis (1961) of how socioeconomic differentiation between rich and poor in traditional societies appeared as naturalized relations of inequality between masters and servants is relevant here. Tocqueville points out that a fixed hierarchical social order is constituted in which generations pass without any change in position. "There are two societies superimposed, always distinct but governed by analogous principles. . . . Certain permanent notions of justice and injustice are generated between them. . . . Fixed rules are recognized and, in the absence of a law, there are common prejudices that direct them; between them reign certain determined habits, a morality" (Tocqueville 1961, 152).

In his study of the 1931 Peruvian elections in which APRA (Alianza Popular Revolucionaria Americana) was defeated by Luis Sánchez Cerro's populist movement, Steve Stein (1980) analyzes the changes in socioeconomic and political structures during the 1920s and 1930s that brought to an end the so-called República Aristocrática. They included a greater integration into the world market through an increase in mineral and agricultural exports—primarily sugar—and an increasing presence of foreign capital from the United States, which modified the class structure. The state was modernized. The number of public employees increased from 975 in 1920 to 6,285 in 1931, an increase of 545 percent (Stein 1980, 39). Rural-urban migration and processes of urbanization transformed Lima's socioeconomic structure, with a great increase in middle and working classes. Stein also analyzes pressures for political incorporation from those social sectors that were seeking "a shift in politics from a family-style government run by political aristocrats and based on highly limited participation to one of populism, which sought an enlarged power base in the lower sectors of society" (1980, 49). What Stein leaves aside is an analysis of the worldview, culture, and discourse characteristic of the República Aristocrática, which would necessarily be the frame of reference for explaining the populist eruptions of APRA and Sanchezcerrismo. This is precisely one of the contributions of Herbert Braun's work on Jorge Eliecer Gaitán (1985), which examines the beliefs, culture, and actions of Colombian public figures from the 1930s to the 1950s, as well as the rationality of the crowds' actions in the Bogotazo.

Braun studies the political culture and ideology of the political leaders of the Colombian Convivencia, a period initiated by the administration of Olaya Herrera in 1930 and brought to a close with the assassination of Gaitán in 1948. The political ideals of the Convivencia were based on a precapitalist ethos more moral than economic: "from a Catholic culture emerged an organic, hierarchical view of society that defined individuals by their rank and duties" (Braun 1985, 22). Those who were seen as members of the public sphere were clearly differentiated from those excluded. "Through oratory in Congress and in the public plaza, the politicians attempted to forge a sense of community by instilling moral virtues and noble thoughts in their listeners" (1985, 25). The process of governing "was perceived as the molding of the anarchic lives of followers, the encouragement of civilized comportment, and the raising of the masses above the necessities of daily life so as to ease their integration into society" (1985, 22). Political leaders referred to all those outside public life as el pueblo. This undifferentiated category was seen "more as plebs than as populace, more as laborers than as the soul of the nation" (1985, 28).

Socioeconomic processes such as dependent capitalist development, urbanization, and the growth of the state apparatus resulted in changes in the social structure, with the emergence of new groups seeking incorporation into the political community and questioning the Convivialistas' vision of politics. Braun's analysis of the cultural parameters through which elites perceived politics permits him to capture the crisis of the oligarchic social order in all its complexity: socioeconomic, political, cultural, and discursive. But the problem with his work is that he analyzes the political leaders of the time without taking into account the pressures, limitations, and opportunities posed to them by the actions of subaltern groups. Only in the final chapters of his work does Braun examine the rationality of the crowds' collective action in the Bogotazo. Prior to this, el pueblo appears in the same undifferentiated way as contemporary elites saw them.

The analysis of past populist experiences should not lead us to commit the all too common error of assuming that populism itself is a necessary phenomenon of the past linked to the transition from an oligarchical to a modern society. Chapter 4 will review the debates on populism and neopopulism sparked by the electoral successes of Alberto Fujimori, Carlos Menem, Fernando Collor de Mello, and Abdalá Bucaram. Populism is more than a phase in the history of Latin America or of nationalist and redistributive state policies, or a form of political discourse. I explore the relationship between leaders and followers and the specific forms of political incorporation in contemporary Latin America. This perspective analyzes the contradictory and ambiguous experiences of popular participation in politics.

To illustrate my approach to populism, I focus on the Ecuadorian case. I analyze the transition from the politics of notables to mass politics, studying how the different mediations between state and society were constructed. As will be illustrated in chapter 2, populist politics in Ecuador originated in the 1940s under the leadership of José María Velasco Ibarra. Ecuador was not at this time experiencing a process of import substitution industrialization. Even so, the oligarchical order was in crisis, as in other Latin American cases. Social actors such as the middle class—which had grown as a consequence of urbanization and state expansion—artisans, and a small proletariat were demanding political inclusion.

Velasco Ibarra took politics out of the salons and cafes of the elites and into the public plazas. He toured most of the country delivering his message of political incorporation through honest elections. Velasco Ibarra's followers responded to his appeals by occupying plazas, demonstrating for their leader, intimidating opponents, and—when they felt that their will at the polls had been mocked—staging insurrections and rebellions. Velasco Ibarra did not always respect democratic institutions. He assumed temporary dictatorial powers on several occasions, abolishing the constitutions of 1935, 1946, and 1970 with the assertion that they limited the general will of the people that he claimed to embody.

Velasquismo expanded the Ecuadorian electorate from 3.1 percent of the total population in 1933 to 16.83 percent in 1968, but most citizens remained excluded through the use of literacy requirements. Despite such a restricted franchise, Velasquismo cannot be reduced to a mere electoral phenomenon. It was a broader social and political movement, which included both voters and nonvoters (Maiguashca and North 1991). The novelty of Velasquismo was to inaugurate a political style wherein mass meetings, crowd actions, and self-recognition in a moralistic, Manichaean political rhetoric became more important than narrowly restricted representative political institutions.

These two distinct forms of political participation—mass mobilization of el pueblo and limited citizen participation in democratic institutions—illustrate how different mediations between the state and society have historically been constructed. Citizenship, in Charles Tilly's definition, comprises the "rights and mutual obligations binding state agents to a category of persons defined exclusively by their legal attachment to the same state" (1995, 369). The struggle for and the establishment of citizenship rights goes hand in hand with the rule of law and hence with the building and strengthening of liberal democratic institutions. As in other Latin American countries, citizenship in Ecuador has tended to be restricted and to place priority on political and social rights over civil rights; hence populism has become the principal link between state and civil society.

The continuing inability of liberal democratic institutions to provide a sense of participation and belonging to the political community have contrasted with political participation through populist, non-parliamentary politics. The main legacy of populism then has been to create a style of political mobilization and a rhetoric that link the state and civil society through mechanisms that do not correspond to the rule of law or respect for liberal democratic procedures.

Populist Seduction

Analytically, it is important to differentiate populism as regimes in power (where the analysis of state policies is central) from populism as wider social and political movements seeking power.[1] To understand the appeal of populist leaders and the expectations of their followers, the following variables must be studied: personalistic charismatic leadership, Manichaean discourse, political clientelism and patronage, and the social history of populism.

POPULIST LEADERSHIP

This section discusses those elements of the concept of charismatic leadership that describe populist experiences. Following Weber (1968), charisma is understood as a double-sided interactive social process that allows us to understand how populist leaders are created by their followers and how they have constructed themselves into leaders. The populist leader is identified with the people—el pueblo—understood as the plebs in its struggle against the oligarchy (Taguieff 1995, 38–39). The leader, due to his or her "honesty and strength of will guarantees the fulfillment of popular aspirations and wishes" (Torres Ballesteros 1987, 171). Such leaders represent "the symbolic projection of an ideal. . . . Through social rites of veneration, qualities they do not possess are often attributed to them" (Martín Arranz 1987, 84). In the process, the leader and followers are mystically linked.

Performing what is perceived as an extraordinary deed is one of the elements of charismatic leadership (Willner 1984). Examples of such deeds are Haya de la Torre's championing of Peruvian workers in the struggle for an eight-hour workday in 1919, his efforts for the creation of the Popular University, and his leadership in the fight against the dictatorship of Leguía in 1923 (Stein 1980). Obstacles to success, a leader's personal sacrifice and disinterest, risk taking, and the importance of the leader's actions for the followers are all elements underlying the emergence of such a relationship. Other examples are the role of Sánchez Cerro in putting an end to Leguía's rule and Gaitán's defense of the United Fruit banana workers massacred in 1929.

According to Willner, perceptions of the personal attributes of the leader are the second element of charismatic leadership. In racist societies in which elites treasured their whiteness, the dark complexions—and mestizo origins—of Gaitán and Sánchez Cerro in themselves represented a challenge to traditional social caste relations. Thus APRA's insults about Sánchez Cerro's mestizo features in the electoral campaign of 1930–31 backfired because the triumph of someone who physically resembled them was very important for common people. Herbert Braun (1985) argues that Gaitán presented his physical appearance as a challenge to the political norms of the Convivencia. His teeth were symbols of animal aggression, his dark skin represented the feared *malicia indígena* (Indian wickedness). In sum, the image of *"el negro* Gaitán" as a threat to "decent society" pervaded the press, electoral posters, and caricatures. In addition, in contrast to the cleanliness and serenity of his opponents, during his speeches Gaitán sweated, shouted, and growled, promoting an atmosphere of intimacy with his followers.

Charismatic leaders invoke myths. Through metaphors they are assimilated into icons of their cultures (Willner 1984). The examples of Evita as the Mater Dolorosa and Velasco Ibarra and Haya de la Torre as Christ figures show the preeminence of religion in Latin

America. Marysa Navarro characterizes the myth of Eva Perón in the
following terms:

> Blond, pale, and beautiful, Evita was the incarnation of the Mediator,
> a Virgin-like figure who despite her origins, shared the perfection of
> the Father because of her closeness to him. Her mission was to love
> infinitely, give herself to others and 'burn her life' for others, a point
> made painfully literal when she fell sick with cancer and refused to in-
> terrupt her activities. She was the Blessed Mother, chosen by God to
> be near 'the leader of the new world: Perón.' She was the childless
> mother who became the Mother of all the *descamisados,* the Mater
> Dolorosa who 'sacrificed' her life so that the poor, the old, and the
> downtrodden could find some happiness. (1982, 62)

What Navarro does not analyze is how such myths were generated. To understand the process of mythic construction of figures like
Evita, it is essential to examine popular perceptions of them. Such
images, interpretations, and meanings are contradictory—on the one
hand liberating, on the other based on an uncritical acceptance of the
leaders. Moreover, the visions and interpretations of subaltern groups
are influenced by official discourses. For this reason, when studying
populist myths one must take into account the fact that their meanings are multiple, and that official memory constitutes a reference
point from which popular sectors interpret their experiences (Popular Memory Group 1982).

MANICHAEAN DISCOURSE:
EL PUEBLO VERSUS LA OLIGARQUÍA

The publication of *Politics and Ideology in Marxist Theory* (Laclau
1977) constituted a breakthrough in the study of Latin American
populism. Discourse analysis was presented as an alternative to objectivist interpretations and a tool to understand the ambiguity of
populism for the actors involved. Through an analysis of speeches

and other written documents by political leaders, Ernesto Laclau examines the crisis of liberal discourse in Argentina and Perón's ability to transform a series of criticisms of liberalism into a discourse in which the people confront the oligarchy. To explain the rhetorical appeal to the people, Laclau demonstrates how this category is linked to the discursive elaboration of a fundamental contradiction in the social formation: "the people versus the power bloc." The particularity of populism is to be a discourse that articulates popular-democratic interpellations as antagonistic to the dominant ideology. These contradictions that cannot be processed within the system imply the possibility of a populist break. That is why Peronism, Maoism, and fascism are examples of populist ruptures.

Laclau's innovative work on populist discourse was partial. Although he shows the importance of studying the shared semantic field within which people struggle to impose their interpretations of a given moment, the analysis remains incomplete. The most common criticism of Laclau has been that he examines the conditions of only the production of discourses. One cannot assume that a politician's discourse easily or automatically generates political identities. Given that not all discourses are accepted and that there are always competing discourses, it is necessary to take into account the conditions of production, circulation, and reception of political discourses (De Ípola 1979, 1983).

Moreover, Laclau does not differentiate the analysis of political discourse from more general discourse analysis. Emilio De Ípola (1979, 949) suggests the following characteristics of political discourse: (1) its thematic is focused explicitly on the problem of the control of state power; (2) its objective is to refute and disqualify the opposing discourse; and (3) it includes a certain calculation or evaluation of its immediate political and ideological results. There are various kinds of political discourses: electoral speeches, government reports, speeches of representatives in congress, resolutions of party assemblies, and so on. To be successful, these discourses must be received as conforming to reality. Thus it is necessary to take into account the context within which such discourses are given. To understand the success or failure of political discourses, they must therefore be analyzed as events in which the expectations and actions of the audience are as important as the oration, gestures, and rituals of the speaker. Through a discussion of the discourses of Luis Sánchez Cerro, Victor Raúl Haya de la Torre, Jorge Eliecer Gaitán, Evita Perón, and Juan Domingo Perón, I shall analyze the characteristics of populist discourse as a special category of political discourse.

Scholars of populism have demonstrated that political discourses differ from scientific discourses. Because the goal of political speeches is to motivate people to act, well-reasoned arguments are less useful than emotional appeals (Álvarez Junco 1990, 234). As José Álvarez Junco notes, political discourse "does not inform or explain, but persuades and shapes attitudes. . . . It responds to areas of disquiet and problems, it offers reassurance" (1987, 220). Similarly, Braun suggests that "to search for a clear line of argumentation in Gaitán's more political speeches is to misunderstand them. The orations were designed for dramatic effect, not intellectual consistency" (1985, 100). Even Victor Raúl Haya de la Torre, whose political discourses had more substance, "urged those who did not understand the doctrine to 'feel' it" (Stein 1980, 164). More recently, when evaluating his electoral defeat in 1990 to Alberto Fujimori, Mario Vargas Llosa reached similar conclusions.

> The politician goes up onto the platform to charm, to seduce, to lull, to bill and coo. His musical phrasing is more important than his ideas, his gestures more important than his concepts. Form is everything: it can either make or destroy the content of what he says. The good orator may say absolutely nothing, but he says it with style. What matters to his audience is for him to sound good and look good. The logic, the rational order, the consistency, the critical acumen of what he is saying generally get in the way of his achieving that effect, which is attained above all through impressionistic images and

14

metaphors, ham acting, fancy turn of phrase, and defiant remarks. The good Latin American political orator bears a much closer resemblance to a bullfighter or a rock singer than to a lecturer or a professor: his communication with the audience is achieved by way of instinct, emotion, sentiment, rather than by way of intelligence. (1995, 169)

Populist discourse and rhetoric divide society into two ethically antagonistic fields: el pueblo and la oligarquía. These terms do not refer to precise social categories but rather to a series of social relations; thus it is essential to examine who is included and excluded by these terms in each specific case of populism. El pueblo is positively defined as all that is not oligarquía. Given their suffering, el pueblo is the incarnation of the authentic, the good, the just, and the moral. It confronts the *antipueblo,* or oligarquía, representing the unauthentic, the foreign, the evil, the unjust, and the immoral. The political becomes moral, even religious. For this reason, the political confrontation is total, without the possibility of compromise or dialogue.[2] The electoral campaigns of APRA and Sánchez Cerro in 1930 and 1931 illustrate the moralism, religiosity, and intransigence that characterize populist discourses.

Aprismo was presented as a moral-religious crusade for the regeneration of the Peruvian. *Aprista* political meetings always included the party hymn, the *Marsellesa Aprista:*

> Peruvians embrace the new religion
> The Popular Alliance
> will conquer our longed-for redemption!
>
> (Stein 1980, 175)

APRA was not only identified as a religious movement during political meetings, but, in addition, whenever two party members met they greeted each other with the messianic phrase, "Only Aprismo will save Peru"—a slogan also printed on electoral posters. Given his sacrifices and persecution, the figure of Haya de la Torre took on an aura

of martyrdom and sainthood. The religiosity of APRA was also reinforced in his speeches through the use of biblical language: he identified his political action with a call to the priesthood. According to
Haya de la Torre, political success absolutely required the ability to
communicate a mystical sentiment. Such was the mysticism generated by APRA that a campaign song compared the Apristas' suffering
and persecution with that of the early Christians:

> Men who suffer
> a cruel pain
> let us make
> APRA a legion.
> March! March!
> brothers in pain!
> Fight! Fight!
> with the banner of love
> with faith and unity . . .
>
> (Stein 1980, 178)

Sánchez Cerro in turn presented his program as the moral and
economic regeneration of Peru. When a foreign journalist asked him
to elaborate on his plans, Sánchez Cerro responded that only he
knew them. The mysticism inspired by this movement was reflected
in this popular song:

> When Sánchez Cerro is in power
> We won't work
> 'cause every little thing's going
> to rain on us like the manna from heaven.
>
> (Stein 1980, 105)

Like their political rivals, the *Sanchezcerristas* also made use of religious symbols and language, for instance in the *Credo Cerrista:*

I believe in *"cerrismo,"* all powerful, creator of all the liberties and all
the claims of the popular masses; in Luis M. Sánchez Cerro, our hero
and undefeated paladin, conceived by the grace of the spirit of patriotism. Like a true Peruvian he was born in Holy Democracy and in the

nationalist ideal; he suffered under the abject power of the *"oncenio"*; he was persecuted, threatened, and exiled, and because he gave us liberty he shed his blood in the sacrifice of his being; he descended triumphant from the peaks of the *Misti* (Arequipa) to give us liberty and teach us by his patriotism, rising thusly to Power, glorious and triumphant. (Stein 1980, 108–9)

The intransigence of both Apristas and Sanchezcerristas was expressed through personal insults and identifying the rival with the oligarchy, source of all evil. For instance, the Sanchezcerristas accused Apristas of being anti-Catholic, antimilitary, antinationalist, and therefore against Peruvian values—values that Sánchez Cerro was of course seen to embody. For their part, Apristas used racist arguments to degrade their rival. In doing so, they were illustrating the ambiguous relationship of populist politicians to the popular sectors, who sometimes are praised as the real essence of the nation and at other times are considered to be the embodiment of backwardness. They referred to Sánchez Cerro as "uncultured, illiterate, vain, smelly, dirty . . . a ridiculous, perverse, latent homosexual, mentally retarded and physically an epileptic, a fetid, Black-Indian half-caste whose primitive behavior and simian-like poses and attitudes suggested that a search for his origins would be like following the biological trail of a gorilla" (Stein 1980, 165–66).

Through discourse, populist leaders give new meanings to "key words" (Williams 1976) in their political cultures. Gaitán, for instance, offered his followers the dignity of human beings when he transformed the feared *chusma* (mob) into the *chusma heroica* and the despised *gleba* (servants) into the *gleba gloriosa*. Perón radically changed the significance of the meaning of words used to denigrate subaltern groups—such as the descamisados ("the shirtless"; the dispossessed)—into the essence of true Argentine identity (James 1988b). Perón also expanded the significance of key words of his epoch, such as *democracy, industrialism,* and *working class*. "Perón explicitly challenged the legitimacy of a notion of democracy which limited itself to participation in formal political rights and he extended it to include participation in the social and economic life of the nation" (James 1988b, 16). The meaning of industrialism was articulated anew within social and political parameters, and the individual workers became instead the "working class." Words like *people* and *oligarchy* acquired concrete meanings with Perón, as opposed to their purely rhetorical use. El pueblo became *el pueblo trabajador*. In addition, the nationalism implicit in the notion of pueblo as Argentine was manifested in concrete acts. For example, the slogan of the first Peronist electoral campaign was "Braden or Perón."[3]

Some populist leaders incorporate into their discourses colloquialisms and other elements of popular culture. Perón, for example, incorporated *lunfardo*, verses of Martín Fierro, and the tragic-sentimental structure of tango. Evita used the language of soap operas and transformed the political into dramas dominated by love. "Her scenarios never changed and her characters were stereotyped by the same adjectives: Perón was always 'glorious,' the people 'marvelous,' the oligarchy *egoísta y vende patria* [selfish and corrupt], and she was a 'humble' or 'weak' woman, 'burning her life for them' so that social justice could be achieved, *cueste lo que cueste y caiga quien caiga* [at whatever cost and regardless of consequences]" (Navarro 1982, 59). Gaitán, through his strong oratorical style, with shouts of *"Pueebloo aa laa caargaa,"* broke with the calm, melodic rhetorical style of his opponents (Braun 1985). Populist leaders often also make creative use of mass media such as radio. Incorporating popular music—*el porro*—Gaitán succeeded in entering the homes of his followers through his radio spots and transmitted speeches.

Discursive populist events are characterized by repetition of a series of rituals. Gaitán finished his speeches with a ritual dialogue with his audience. He shouted "pueblo" and the crowds responded "a la carga."

Pueblo.
Por la reestructuración moral y democrática de la república.
Pueblo.

A la victoria.
Pueblo.
Contra la oligarquía. (Braun 1985, 103)

Durkheimian sociology has interpreted massive political acts as rituals that evoke a sense of belonging. During populist political meetings, elements of the participants' and the leader's identities are activated and reorganized. The audience recognizes themselves in the leader and projects onto him the solution of their demands and aspirations; in addition, they identify with each other. In these populist mass meetings, where the popular sectors feel themselves participants in the political process, the script has already been written. Most of the time, common people are reduced to follow the lines of a drama that has assigned them a central though subordinate role. They are expected to delegate power to a politician who claims to be the embodiment of their redemption.

Braun's description (1985, 93–99) of one of the most important *Gaitanista* meetings illustrates many of these points. On 23 September 1945, forty to fifty thousand Gaitanistas met in Bogota's Circo de Santamaría, awaiting their leader. The caudillo arrived impeccably dressed, accompanied by his wife and father. The audience saw in their leader one of themselves, el negro Gaitán, who started at the bottom and was now running for president of the republic. The serene tone of Gaitán at this meeting contrasted with the euphoria of the spectators and with most of his previous mass political appearances. In a calm dialogue with the audience, he explained the basic points of his political vision: society's organic nature, the moral basis of the social, the necessity of regenerating national values, and the importance of meritocracy. Gaitán referred to the struggle of el pueblo that embodied the just and the good with the oligarquía. He placed el pueblo at the center of history, transcending political parties. And he, Gaitán, was the person able to understand their feelings. The impact of the discourse was manifested in the chants of the crowd as they left the event: *"En el Circo de Santamaría, murió la oligarquía"* (in the

Circo de Santamaría, the oligarchy has died) and *"Guste o no le guste, cuadre o no le cuadre, Gaitán será su padre"* (like it or not, agree or not, Gaitán shall be your father).

MECHANISMS OF CLIENTELISM AND PATRONAGE

Approaches that privilege the concept of charisma tend to ignore the concrete mechanisms of electoral articulation, assigning all explanatory weight to the figure and discourse of the leader. As several authors point out (Menéndez-Carrión 1986; Quintero 1980), this interpretation is only possible if the popular bases are understood as anomic and irrational masses. Studies that employ the concept of political clientelism have discarded the presuppositions of the irrationality of marginal sectors, demonstrating on the contrary their instrumental rationality and the importance of political organizations in the conquest of the vote (Menéndez-Carrión 1986). The usefulness of this perspective is illustrated for the Ecuadorian case in the debate between Martz (1989) and Menéndez-Carrión (1986) about the first phase of Concentración de Fuerzas Populares (CFP) in Guayaquil between 1948 and 1960.

John Martz privileges the concept of charismatic leadership, showing Carlos Guevara Moreno's success in building the CFP. But what Martz cannot explain is why Guevara Moreno lost the leadership of his party. However, Menéndez-Carrión is able to explain both the success and failure of Guevara Moreno, using the concept of political clientelism. According to Menéndez-Carrión, the exchange of votes for goods and services accounts for electoral success. Leadership within the party and therefore control over the political machinery also depend on what particular politicians can deliver. Thus the political actions of popular sectors are in fact rational responses to the precarious conditions—poverty and an unreceptive political system —in which they live.

Although the concept of political clientelism is more useful than charisma in explaining the conquest of votes, it should not become the only frame of reference within which populist appeal is explained, as in Menéndez-Carrión's work (1986). In its emphasis on formal rationality, political clientelism cannot help us to understand the generation of collective identities in populist movements. As many case studies have shown, participation in a political machine does more than merely assure the delivery of goods and services. In addition, the sense of belonging to a movement is instilled. That is why it is important to study not only the material features of the clientelist exchanges (what is given), but also the symbolic dimensions of exchanges (how it is given) (Auyero 1998).

Populist leaders such as Gaitán, Haya de la Torre, and Velasco Ibarra appealed to both voters and people excluded from the franchise. Through their meetings, slogans, and posters their message transcended the restricted electorate. Thus rather than having to choose between political clientelism and charisma as the central explanatory variable in populism, this suggests that both phenomena must be studied, in particular through an analysis of the concrete political processes in which they are joined. The leader articulates values and challenges and creates new political idioms. Political organizations, in turn, articulate strategies for electoral success, as well as creating mechanisms through which solidarities and collective identities are generated. The ways that these processes complement each other in specific cases must be examined.

SOCIAL HISTORY OF POPULISM

A major preoccupation of students of populism has been to understand the actions of the followers of populist leaders. Some authors, like Germani (1971, 1978), have based their arguments on theories of mass society; others have challenged this interpretation with structural arguments that highlight the instrumental rationality of followers (Spalding 1977; Murmis and Portantiero 1971; Weffort 1998; Ianni 1973, 1975). Recent analyses have gone further by also taking into account the values, ideologies, culture, and actions of subaltern groups (French 1989; James 1988a, 1988b; Wolfe 1994).

Gino Germani's studies of populism (1971, 1978) reflect the impressions made on him by "mass" movements such as Italian fascism, Nazism, and Peronism. Through the lenses of mass-society theories, he interpreted the collective action of Peronist followers as irrational and anomic. Rapid socioeconomic changes such as urbanization and industrialization produced anomic and available masses—mostly recent immigrants—who were easy prey for the demagogic and manipulative powers of Perón, becoming the social base for his movement. This perspective arbitrarily divides collective action and political behavior into normal and abnormal, such that whatever deviates from the theoretically prescribed path of development is denigrated. Hence, populist followers are considered irrational masses deceived by demagogic, overpowerful, charismatic leaders. This conservative understanding of crowds as "masses" does not permit the study of the specific meaning of their politics.

An alternative explanation of working-class support for Perón stresses the formal rationality of the actions of the subaltern (Murmis and Portantiero 1971; Spalding 1977). Unlike previous governments, which had not addressed workers' demands for social security and labor legislation, Perón, as the head of the National Labor Department (1943–45), met labor demands. Moreover, due to his power in the military government, Perón was able to co-opt and repress the labor movement in accordance with his interests. In the 1946 elections and through his first two presidential periods, Perón counted on the support of most of the working class, which acted rationally in supporting a leader favorable to their short-term interests.

In spite of the efforts of writers influenced by dependency theory to understand the rationality of the working class and other subaltern groups in populism, their interpretations remain trapped in the same paradoxes of their modernization colleagues. Although dependency studies tried to break with false normative assumptions of what constitutes true and autonomous working-class actions, they are still influenced by orthodox Marxist models of class formation. Because an arbitrary rationalism and transparency is imputed to the actions of the supposedly mature and fully formed working class, these authors can not take into account the values, ideologies, and rituals of working classes or other popular sectors in populism. And even when the thrust of the argument is to understand the specificity of working classes in dependent societies, they can not break with a normative prescriptive model of a what a mature working class should be. It is precisely in the study of who the popular sectors are, what they think, how they feel, and how they interpret their actions that the tools of social history are useful (French 1989; James 1988a, 1988b; Wolfe 1994). As an example, consider Daniel James's work on Peronism.

James studies the social history of the Argentine working class between 1946 and 1976, showing how Peronism arose and how the workers contributed its development. Although James recognizes the explanatory power of approaches emphasizing the instrumental rationality of workers, he questions the validity of the economistic vision of history common to such perspectives. Peronism may have responded to the material needs of the working class previously ignored, but that does not explain why this response occurred within Peronism rather than in other political movements that also addressed the workers. "What we need to understand is Peronism's success, its distinctiveness, why its political appeal was more credible for workers—which areas it touched that others did not. To do this we need to take Perón's political and ideological appeal seriously and examine the nature of Peronism's rhetoric and compare it with that of its rivals for working-class allegiance" (James 1988b, 14).

Although working-class militancy was still present, the *década infame* (1930–43) "was experienced by many workers as a time of profound collective and individual frustration and humiliation" (James 1988b, 25). This was a time of severe discipline in the factory, where workers were haunted by the threat of unemployment. Tango lyrics from this period express the humiliation and cynicism of the workers. James points out that although traditional tango themes—romantic betrayal, nostalgia for the past, and the glorification of male courage—persisted, they were expressed in a new social context. Lyrics recommended the adoption of the dominant values of the time: egotism and immorality. They go so far as to propose that instead of being resigned to the injustice of the social order, the alternative is *la mala vida*—prostitution and crime. James also analyzes how workers' degradation was expressed through silence. He explains Perón's political success in his ability to give public expression to workers' private experiences, in his capacity to affirm the value of workers' consciousness and lifestyles.

James (1988a, 1988b) analyzes the popular mobilizations from 17 October 1945 through Perón's victory in February 1946 to understand the contradictory meanings of Peronism. On 9 October 1945, General Perón resigned from his positions as vice president and secretary of labor. He was arrested on the 13th. On 17 and 18 October, the workers in the capital and provincial cities staged enormous demonstrations demanding his release. The festive and carnivalesque[4] spirit of these events contrasted sharply with the behavior typical of the 1 May demonstrations organized by the Socialists and Communists. Instead of a solemn, ordered march, on 17 and 18 October the workers sang popular songs, played huge drums, danced in the streets, costumed themselves in traditional gaucho gear, and wrote Perón's name in chalk on city walls. The surprise of the leftist press was such that they did not recognize the demonstrators as workers, but perceived them as marginal and lumpen. For example, the Communist press characterized them as "'*clanes con aspecto de murgas*' [clans with the appearance of carnival] led by elements of the '*hampa*' [underworld] and typified by the figure of the *compadrito*" (James 1988a, 451).

The workers attacked institutions that symbolized and transmitted their social subordination. Their principal targets were the cafes, bars, and clubs of the elites. They also threw stones at anti-Peronist newspaper offices and burned copies of such papers. Students were a favorite target. With the cry *"alpargatas si, libros no"* (shoes, not books) many students, especially the sons of the well-heeled (*jóvenes engominados*), were the object of the jokes and at times the violence of the workers. Shouting *"menos cultura y más trabajo"* (less high culture and more work), they threw stones at the universities. "The central column of demonstrators in Rosario was headed by an ass on which had been placed a placard with the slogan 'offensive to university professors and a certain evening paper.' . . . In La Plata during the disturbances of the 18th a group of demonstrators entered a funeral parlor and demanded a coffin which they then paraded through the fashionable area in the center of the city shouting slogans 'hostile to the students and newspapers'" (1988a, 452). Young men made obscene gestures and dropped their pants in front of upper-class ladies. Monuments to national heroes, considered sacred by the elite, were covered with Peronist slogans.

James shows that these actions, which appeared to both elites and the left as acts of barbarism committed by the lumpen and recent migrants to the cities, had a rationality. The workers attacked the symbols marking their exclusion from the public sphere: universities and students, social clubs, and the press. Moreover, their actions constituted a kind of countertheater through which they mocked and abused the symbols of elite pretensions and authority, as well as affirming their own pride in being workers.

The workers marched from the outlying areas to the central plazas. Their presence was seen by elites and middle classes as the eruption of barbarism, of the *cabecitas negras* (the dark-skinned) in places reserved for the high society (*gente bien*). By invading the public plazas—spaces where citizens gather and political power resides—the workers from outlying areas challenged the spatial hierarchy, affirming their right to belong to the public sphere.

The Paradoxes of Populism and Liberal Democracy

I have stressed the importance of studying the complex and ambiguous meanings of populism. Particular emphasis has been placed on the social historical analysis of collective action, as well as on discursive political events. This approach to the study of populism takes into account both the actions and discourses of the leaders and the autonomous actions of the followers. It requires examining the concrete mechanisms of electoral articulation in the context of particular political cultures.

Perhaps the principal effect of populism has been the entrance of the masses into politics. That is why Carlos Vilas interprets populism as a "fundamental democratizing force" (1995b, 98). Populist movements not only expanded the number of voters, they also gave large social groups within exclusionary and racist societies access to a symbolic dignity. Alberto Adrianzén (1998) has argued that the fundamental quality of Peruvian populism has been its antiaristocratic and proplebeian traits. Similarly, the chusma of Gaitán and Velasco Ibarra and the descamisados of the Peróns were transformed into the bearers of the "true" nation in their struggle against the "aristocratic" oligarchical antination. This search for support and legitimation from the people, placing at political center stage sectors previously regarded as undeserving, is to a certain extent irreversible. As shown by the most recent experiences of dictatorship and democratization in the Southern Cone, once the people become activated they cannot be permanently ignored.

The political emergence of previously excluded groups through populism has ambiguous if not contradictory effects for Latin American democracies. On the one hand, in the incorporation of people through the expansion of the vote and their presence in the public plazas, populism is democratizing. On the other hand, this popular activation occurs through movements that acritically identify with charismatic leaders, who in many cases are authoritarian. Moreover, the Manichaean populist discourse that divides society into two antagonistic fields does not permit the recognition of the opposition. This latter point suggests one of the great difficulties of consolidating democracy in the region. Instead of recognizing the adversary, accepting diversity, and proposing dialogue—implying conflict but not the destruction of rivals—populists through their discourse seek the destruction of opponents and impose their authoritarian vision of the 'true' national community.[5]

Chapter 2

Velasquista Seduction

BY COMBINING AN analysis of the social creation of the populist leader José María Velasco Ibarra in La Revolución Gloriosa (the May Revolution) with a study of his discourse, this chapter explains why Velasco Ibarra became the central political figure in Ecuador in the mid-1940s. La Gloriosa, an insurrection in the name of the exiled former President José María Velasco Ibarra in May 1944, is a critical site for analyzing the complexities of the social creation of a populist leader.[1] La Gloriosa was a revolt against an elected civilian Liberal regime. It occurred in the name of democracy and an exiled politician who had acquired the aura of the Great Absentee, and indeed did not himself participate in the insurrection. The uprisings that together make up La Gloriosa took place in Guayaquil and other Ecuadorian cities on 28 and 29 May 1944. In these uprisings, common citizens fought together with conscripts and junior officers of the armed forces in the name of Velasco Ibarra against the Liberal regime and its elite police corps, the *carabineros*. Popular collective violence targeted the institutions and supporters of the Liberal regime, especially the carabineros, while respecting the property of wealthy non-Liberals. As a result of this insurrection, former president Velasco Ibarra came to power for his second administration, which lasted from June 1944 to August 1947.

In July 1943, in preparation for the elections planned for June 1944, most political parties and associations of civil society had joined forces to form the Alianza Democrática Ecuatoriana (ADE; Ecuadorian Democratic Alliance). They promoted the candidacy of José María Velasco Ibarra for the upcoming presidential elections, which, however, did not take place because of the insurrection in support of Velasco on 28 and 29 May. How could Conservatives, Catholics, Socialists, and Communists unite in a common program of democratization and under the name of a politician, who came to represent the salvation of the nation? How was Velasco transformed in 1944 into the embodiment of the solution to all of Ecuador's problems? What were Velasco's actions and words that made him the country's redeemer and the personification of the democratic ideal?

By the time of the Gloriosa, José María Velasco Ibarra was far from an unknown public personality. A son of a mathematician of Colombian origin and a lady from "high society," Velasco was born in 1893. He studied with the Jesuits and became a lawyer. In 1930, in recognition of his journalistic and academic work, he was appointed a member of the most important elite literary institution, the Real Academia Ecuatoriana de la Lengua [The Ecuadorian Royal Academy of Language]. He was elected to Congress in 1931 while he was living in Paris and with no affiliation with any political party. Velasco's political career from this point on was meteoric. In 1932 and 1933 he became president of Congress and later in that year he was elected president of the republic itself. Of a total of 64,682 votes, Velasco obtained 51,848 or 80.2 percent (Quintero 1980, 282). On 1 September 1934, Velasco assumed the presidency of Ecuador. He was overthrown by a coup d'état a year later, on 20 August 1935. Velasco's first presidency was short and full of strife. He had an autocratic style: he dismissed public employees, closed newspapers and Quito's university, exiled or jailed some of his opponents, and relied on the support of thugs in his conflicts with a Congress that did not behave as a loyal oppositional force. After being overthrown, Velasco lived in exile in Colombia, Chile, and Argentina until he returned to the country for the 1940 elections. After losing the elections and staging a failed insurrection, he went again into exile until 1944 when he returned as the Great Absentee.

The political movement named after José María Velasco Ibarra, Velasquismo, was the most important political phenomenon in Ecuador from the 1930s to the early 1970s. With very few exceptions, most politicians who were Velasco's contemporaries, regardless of their ideology or party affiliation, were Velasquistas at some point in their careers. Velasco's populist movement attracted more than political elites. More important, this was the political movement that introduced mass politics in Ecuador, partially incorporating previously excluded people into the political community.

Velasquismo did not only appeal to some of Velasco's contemporaries, it has also captured the attention of social scientists, who have passionately debated its meanings and origins. Indeed, the analysis of Velasquismo has been one of the main avenues through which Ecuadorian political sociology has been constructed.[2] This chapter analyzes the dual process that produced Velasquismo. It examines how Velasco Ibarra was socially created and how he constructed himself into such a leader. Here I study a particular phase of Velasquismo: La Gloriosa. Given Velasquismo's forty-year span, it would be an error to draw general conclusions about it from the study of the 1940s. That era was particularly important, however, because it marked the beginning of mass politics in Ecuador and because, as in other Latin American nations, it was a period of failed democratization (Bethell and Roxborough 1988; Rock 1994).

Existing Approaches to the Study of Velasquismo

Velasquismo has been researched by historians and social scientists since at least 1951, with the publication of George Blanksten's *Ecuador: Constitutions and Caudillos.* Three approaches to its study, which reflect more general trends in the analysis of Latin American populism, can be differentiated: mass-society theories, Marxism, and discourse analysis. Osvaldo Hurtado (1988), following the insights of mass-society theory, used two key sociological categories—anomie and charisma—to analyze Velasquismo. The principal consequence of modernization is the destruction of previously existing communities and the formation of anonymous, isolated, and alienated "masses." The individuals within these groups, whose normative framework has been shattered, and who have not yet been integrated into a new normative framework, become "available masses." Hence, they are easy prey for "demagogic" leaders who can use them for their personalistic interests. The charismatic leader, like the great man in traditional historiography, becomes the key to analyze populist movements.

The main flaws of the mass-society theory lie in the vision of history as the history of great personalities and the consequent conservative interpretation of followers as deceived "masses." By overemphasizing the role of the political leader, authors who follow this theory cannot account for the actions of followers. As a reaction to the study of politics through great personalities, Marxists have deemphasized the role of the leader, studying instead the social conditions that produce populist movements.[3] They focus on the analysis of socioeconomic processes and class formation, in particular the history of the formation of the working class, the revolutionary subject.

Ecuadorian orthodox Marxist analyses, which originated as a legitimate reaction against the vision of history as made by "great men" and as an attempt to study the autonomous actions of subaltern groups, have not, however, fulfilled their promise. Ironically, they

31

share mass-society theorists' view of common folk as "masses." Due to their objectivist and dogmatic Marxism, the history of subaltern groups, particularly of the proletariat, is theoretically predetermined. Only when the proletariat acts on behalf of its "true interests," which of course are known by the theorist, do they act as a class; otherwise they are misled or irrational "masses." Although Ecuadorian Marxists tend to minimize the role of political leaders, at some point they have to face the inevitable and account for the importance of Velasco's authority. To do so, they use the category of Bonapartism, which refers to exceptional moments in which the executive, under the rule of an individual, achieves dictatorial powers over all parts of the state and civil society. These moments occur at conjunctures when the ruling classes are divided and the proletariat is strong enough to challenge bourgeois domination but too weak to replace it. The problem with the Bonapartist hypothesis is that most of Ecuadorian history could be characterized by these extraordinary moments, turning what is supposed to be the exception into the rule.

Marxists have fervently debated the origins and meanings of Velasquismo, especially whether it was populism. For Agustín Cueva (1988), Velasquismo represented a new mechanism of political domination or manipulation that he interchangeably describes as *caudillismo* or populism. Cueva understands the socioeconomic crisis of the 1930s as the end of three previous forms of political domination: liberalism, representing the interests of the agro-exporting bourgeoisie of the coast; conservatism, representing the interests of the highland *hacendados;* and the military, petit bourgeois reformism of the Revolución Juliana (9 July 1925). This crisis also marks the entrance of new political actors: the subproletariat. Cueva interprets this group, whose political behavior could have been a challenge to elite rule, as, in fact, deceived and manipulated by the rhetoric of the caudillo, converting them into the electoral and social base of Velasco's populism. For this reason, Velasquismo is explained as a sociopolitical movement serving the interests of the ruling classes, and

Velasco as a mediator of the interests of the coastal agro-exporting bourgeoisie and the highland landowners. But, for Cueva, Velasquismo was also a new sociopolitical phenomenon that articulated subproletarian demands for incorporation into the political community.

Revealing the empirical inconsistencies and lack of theoretical rigor in Cueva's work, Rafael Quintero (1980) challenges his interpretation and accuses him of introducing a series of myths about Ecuadorian populism. From an orthodox Marxist perspective and through an analysis of the 1931 and 1933 presidential elections, Quintero shows that due to the small size of Ecuadorian cities (Guayaquil had 126,717 inhabitants in 1933; Quito had 107,192) and of the electorate (3.1 percent of the population), it is absurd to emphasize the role of the subproletariat in explaining the origins of Velasquismo. For Quintero, the so-called Velasquismo was not a new political phenomenon. On the contrary, the first election of Velasco marked the triumph of the Partido Conservador, and the consolidation of the Junker path of authoritarian capitalist development from above. Moreover, Quintero denies any explanatory value to the concept of populism, proposing instead the analysis of class relations and alliances in each of Velasco's elections and administrations.

Cueva is right in analyzing Velasquismo as a new sociopolitical phenomenon. Quintero arbitrarily projects the results of Velasco's first electoral victory over the entire forty-year period of Velasquismo. Given that he does not analyze voting patterns at the local level, he cannot argue convincingly that any particular group (such as the subproletariat) did or did not vote for Velasco (Menéndez-Carrión 1986). Moreover, Quintero does not differentiate Velasquismo as an electoral movement from Velasquismo as a broader sociopolitical phenomenon.

Going beyond Cueva and Quintero and applying E. P. Thompson's concept of the moral economy of the crowd, Juan Maiguashca and Liisa North (1991), in contrast, interpret Velasco's populism as a political and ideological phenomenon that challenges the country's capitalist modernization from a moral perspective. Unfortunately, their suggestive argument is incomplete because they do not carry through with the Thompsonian analysis they promise. Nevertheless, it is important to point out the limitations of this popular category in anthropological and historical writings. The category of moral economy refers to the way in which subaltern groups interpret and challenge the dislocations of capitalist modernization via their perceptions of the past. But, as William Roseberry (1989) points out, many authors who use this category tend to present the precapitalist past as homogeneous and undifferentiated. They fail to consider power relations within "traditional" communities, such that they cannot capture the multiple and contradictory images and values that different actors have of the past. Thus, the historical movement from heterogeneous precapitalist pasts to heterogeneous capitalist presents is often oversimplified through the use of this category.

Existing works on Velasco's discourse, such as Cárdenas Reyes (1991) and Ojeda (1971), do not study the broader discursive field from which it emerged, hence they cannot show why it was successful over rival discourses. Moreover, these studies do not differentiate the analysis of discourse in general from political discourse, whose specificity is the struggle over and about state power.

Given the theoretical and methodological problems inherent in existing studies of Velasquismo and Latin American populism in general, a new account is needed to explain the success of political leaders. This chapter applies a multidisciplinary approach to study Velasco Ibarra's leadership as a dual process. To understand how Velasco Ibarra was produced socially, I employ the tools of social historians to study the meanings of politics through an analysis of collective violence in the May Revolution. Discourse analysis is used to map how the shared (if contested) frame of discourse in Ecuador in the 1940s transformed Velasco Ibarra into the savior of the country. To see how Velasco Ibarra produced himself as the key leader in this conjuncture, I thoroughly analyze his speech in Guayaquil on 4 June after returning to the country as the Great Absentee. Finally, I study his oratory strategies to explain the success of his discourse over rival alternatives.

La Gloriosa: The Social Production of Velasco Ibarra

Contemporary newspaper reports and memoirs of participants in La Gloriosa propose the following causes for the May Revolution: a rejection of Liberal electoral fraud; Ecuador's military defeat by Peru in 1941; the animosity between the government's elite police force (the carabineros) and the regular army and broad sectors of the population; and the Liberal government's economic policies, which resulted in an almost unbearable increase in the cost of living (Arízaga Vega 1990; Girón 1945; Muñoz Vicuña 1984; Naranjo 1945; Pérez Castro 1990).

Broad sectors of the population perceived that the Liberals had remained in power by electoral fraud. Eloy Alfaro, leader of the 1895 Liberal Revolution, was rumored to have said, "What we won with bullets we will not lose by ballots," and this became an ongoing Liberal strategy. More recently, the 1940 presidential election, won by the Liberal Carlos Arroyo del Río against José María Velasco Ibarra and the Conservative Jacinto Jijón y Caamaño, was seen as no exception. The perception that the 1940 election was dishonest—despite the fact that it was approved by Congress—had motivated defeated candidate Velasco Ibarra to lead a failed insurrection in Guayaquil in January 1940, which resulted in his political exile.

The significance of the 1940 election was to show the Liberal elites that their strategy of electoral fraud could not longer work because of the beginning of a new electoral style. Velasco Ibarra, unlike the other presidential candidates, campaigned by touring most of the country and delivered his message of honest election to voters and nonvoters. In Quito he proclaimed, "the streets and plazas are for citizens to express their aspirations and yearnings, and not for slaves to rattle their chains" (de la Torre 1993, 160). Velasco democratized public spaces by bringing politics from the salons of the elites to the streets. His followers, who were for the first time addressed in the public plazas, asserted their right to occupy public sites. They cheered Velasco Ibarra, booed his opponents, and, when they felt that the elections were dishonest, revolted in the name of their leader. The 1940 elections, thus, showed that the costs of electoral fraud were too high. That election also marked the beginning of a new electoral strategy—from then on, to win an election, a presidential candidate had to visit most of the country.

The political incorporation in the 1940s, however, was more symbolic than real. The franchise excluded most of the population because it was restricted to literate voters, excluding de facto most poor mestizos and Indians—literacy rates were 20 percent in 1939 and 22 percent in 1944 (Cremieux 1946, 77). Electoral laws further discouraged poor people and immigrants from voting because voters had to reregister and pay a fee for each election and return to the district where they had first registered to cast their ballots (Maiguashca and North 1991, 133). The small proportion of voters, which had nonetheless increased from 3.1 percent in 1933 to 8.8 percent in 1948 did not mean political apathy. Starting with the 1939–40 presidential campaign, Velasco Ibarra's followers felt they were participants in the political struggle and asserted their rights by symbolically occupying public spaces and demonstrating for their leader. This occupation of public spaces was in itself an act of self-recognition and affirmation of the political rights of people excluded by the lack of honesty at the polls and a restricted franchise from the political decision-making apparatus.

Four years later, the country prepared to elect a new president in the elections of early June 1944. After a series of discussions, debates, and maneuvers, two candidates emerged: the Liberal Miguel Albornoz, supported by President Arroyo del Río, and José María Velasco

Ibarra, whose candidacy was promoted by the broad-based Alianza Democrática Ecuatoriana (ADE). All the principal political parties except the Partido Liberal-Radical had joined forces to form ADE in July 1943 (Partido Conservador [Conservative Party], Partido Comunista [Communist Party], Partido Socialista [Socialist Party], Vanguardia Socialista Revolucionaria [Revolutionary Socialist Vanguard], Partido Liberal Independiente [Independent Liberal Party], and Frente Democrático [Democratic Front]), and sponsor Velasco Ibarra as their candidate for the upcoming elections. This coalition also included organizations of civil society, such as workers' unions, student federations, electoral committees, artisan associations, and truck and bus drivers' organizations. The Liberal government prevented Velasco from returning to the country to direct his own presidential campaign. This arbitrary executive order, the repression of Velasquistas, and the memories of previous electoral frauds led the opposition to conclude that the Liberals were preparing yet another fraud for June 1944.

The second cause for the revolt was Ecuador's military defeat by Peru in 1941, which resulted in the loss of half of the national territory located in the Amazonian tropical rain forest. For many people, especially young army officers, the cause of the defeat was the ineptitude and corruption of the Liberal regime. The anonymous anti-Arroyo del Río flyer "Death to the Traitor," circulated in 1941, concluded: "Ecuadorian soldiers, Why don't you take up the weapons of the homeland, to punish the Traitor and trafficker who has sold the national soil! How much longer will you tolerate the infamy of obeying the orders of such a monster?" (Biblioteca Aurelio Espinosa Pólit, Cotocollao [hereafter BAEP], Hojas volantes [flyers] 1939–45, no. 100). Nationalistic feelings were reinforced in late May 1944, when the government agreed to the establishment of a new frontier with Peru, which validated the loss of half of the national territory.

The third cause for the revolt was the rivalry between the regular army and the carabineros. Established in 1938, this repressive elite police force was not only autonomous from the army, it was also a parallel repressive institution with superior attributes of authority. Logically, the relationship between the carabineros and the army was one of rivalry. For example, Major Luis A. Nuñez, director of the May Revolution in the central highland city of Riobamba, related the following incidents between carabineros and the army: "The mockeries and insults of the carabineros continually fed animosity to them . . . they used to come to the barracks of the battalion Córdova with rude and defiant attitudes to try to scare people and to look for trouble, saying things such as: 'We don't think of you as men, and when the fight comes we'll punish you as lads'" (Girón 1945, 307). The carabineros were hated by young army officers, who suspected that their institution was going to be replaced by this elite police force. Velasquistas and other opponents of the regime also detested them, leading officials of the carabineros to say in a press interview that the shout "Viva Velasco Ibarra" had become an "insult to our institution and they should not be surprised that we defend the decency of our corps" (*El telégrafo*, 15 May 1944). In this context, Albert Franklin, an American who lived in Ecuador in the 1930s and 1940s, wrote, "The shout 'Viva Velasco Ibarra!' which for nine years had only been an insult to authority, started to be heard with more frequency and with a new meaning. Velasco's absence, instead of diminishing had increased his legend. In Quito, to the V for Victory was added another V, and nobody doubted the meaning of the two Vs formed with both hands: 'Viva Velasco!' These words became a crime, and jails started to be filled with offenders" (1984, 350–51).

In Guayaquil on 19 May 1944, carabineros assassinated a university student, Héctor Hugo Paute. On 21 May in Quito, they killed a fifteen-year-old girl, María del Carmen Espinosa. The funerals of these victims turned into mass demonstrations against the government. Both funerals also transformed the victims of police brutality into martyrs. As suggested by José Álvarez Junco in his study of Spanish populist leader Alejandro Lerroux in Catholic cultures, "the strength of martyrdom ... does not only demand posthumous honors, but also produces guilt and commands revenge; it does not calm but stirs up passions. It is precisely what is convenient for mobilizing movements" (1990, 255).

The fourth cause of La Gloriosa was popular discontent with the high cost of living. As a consequence of the export boom of war-related products such as balsa wood, rubber, and chinchona bark, the country experienced an inflationary spiral. The price of basic foods increased by 400 percent from 1938 to 1944, while real monthly wages decreased from an average of 164.44 sucres in 1941 to 133.31 sucres in 1943 (INIESEC 1984, 46–47). These inflationary processes were felt most strongly in the cities, in the context of important socioeconomic changes produced by the collapse of cacao exports and the emergence of new export products. The 1930s and 1940s were decades of important economic and social change that resulted in a relative crisis of paternalistic authority in the countryside, in dramatic processes of urbanization, and, most important, in the growth of popular organizations.

The conventional view depicts the 1930s and 1940s as a time of overall stagnation and transition from cacao to banana production. Recent scholarship, however, points to the diversity of experiences in different regions of the country (Maiguashca 1991; Maiguashca and North 1991). This historical period was not only characterized by the crash of the first cycle of agro-export-led cacao development,[4] but also by the growth of other export crops and products such as coffee, panama hats, ivory nuts *(tagua),* rice, oil, gold, and, during the Second World War era, rubber and balsa. This economic period, characterized by the decline of cacao and the growth and diversification of other export products, resulted in a crisis and reconstitution of paternalistic authority that was experienced differently in the three regions of Ecuador.

The cacao crisis changed the agricultural and social landscape of the coast. Unlike the highlands, the patriarchal hacienda system had not had time to develop here. Rice production and sugar refining took the place left by cacao. Big cacao hacienda owners, who were more an exporting than an agricultural elite, shifted the emphasis of their operations, whereas medium and small cacao hacienda owners were eventually wiped out by the crisis (Marchán 1987, 276). Some cacao haciendas disappeared, others became fragmented, and a new elite of banana and sugar interests eventually replaced the cacao elite. For many agricultural workers, the first effect of the crisis was unemployment. Some of the former cacao plantation laborers became sharecroppers, others went to work in sugar plantations, still others stayed in the cacao haciendas, and others migrated to Guayaquil.

In the northern and central highlands, at least from the beginning of the century, a process of differentiation between modernizing and traditional haciendas had taken place (Arcos 1984; Arcos and Marchán 1978; Marchán 1987). Some hacendados responded to increasing market opportunities by specializing in dairy production, modernizing production techniques, and abolishing precapitalist labor systems and introducing wage labor relations. These modernization efforts, which took place in selected areas, did not result in the transformation of most traditional haciendas or in the overall establishment of capitalist relations of production. The traditional hacienda system and the *latifundia-minifundia* polarity continued to characterize the highlands and the country's agrarian scene in general until the 1970s.

Information about the southern highlands is somewhat scattered. What we know, however, is that the misnamed panama hat industry, previously centered in the coastal province of Manabí, developed in this region in the 1930s and 1940s to become a major export product. Most panama hat production was located in the rural areas. The development of this cottage industry presented an alternative to work on the haciendas and created a middle class that challenged traditional agrarian elites (Maiguashca 1991, 84–85).

During the 1930s and 1940s, Ecuador had seen dramatic urbanization processes. Guayaquil's population grew from 58,000 in 1896 to

100,000 in 1920 and doubled again by 1944, when the city had 200,000 residents (Rojas and Villavicencio 1988). Although less impressively than in Guayaquil, Quito's population also grew in this period. It went from 51,858 in 1906 to 120,000 in 1933 and to 138,906 in 1942 (Dirección Nacional de Estadísticas 1944). The increase in urban population, however, did not mean proletarianization. In spite of very modest processes of import substitution industrialization, in both cities there were fewer blue-collar workers than artisans, and most people were marginally employed as servants, day laborers, and street vendors. These modernization processes and the growth of the state meant that white-collar workers represented 14 to 25 percent of the employed population.[5]

The changes in the social relations of production that resulted in a crisis of paternalistic authority in some parts of the countryside (Maiguashca 1991), and the increasing urbanization of the country coincided with the growth of popular organizations in civil society. Although only 42 organizations were established between 1925 and 1930, 191 were founded between 1931 and 1940, and 682 in the 1940s (Maiguashca and North 1991, 106). By the 1940s, the labor movement had been transformed by the establishment of two national federations: the Catholic Confederación Ecuatoriana de Obreros Católicos (CEDOC) in 1938 and, in 1944, the Communist and Socialist Confederación de Trabajadores del Ecuador (CTE). The middle classes also became organized. Whereas before 1930 only two office employees' associations existed, twenty-one were formed between 1931 and 1940, and sixty-eight between 1941 and 1950 (Maiguashca and North 1991, 106).

All the above issues—the belief that the government was going to commit electoral fraud, the defeat by Peru, the carabineros' arrogance and brutality, and the government's failure to stop inflation—were expressed in messianic terms of the immediate need to save the nation.

"Ecuador is experiencing the most serious moments of its history, in these days of civil hurricanes, only cowards will stay in their beds."

(José V. Ordeñana, Secretary of Unión Democrática Universitaria of Guayaquil)

"We are living at the crucial moment of our history." (Partido Comunista del Ecuador, 24 July 1943)

"Our nationality has been threatened with death." (Comité Nacional de los Trabajadores del Ecuador)

"This is the definitive time for our homeland." (Comité Femenino de Chimborazo pro Velasco Ibarra, Riobamba, 12 May 1944)

"If we do not save ourselves at this crucial moment of our history, we will disappear." (Alianza Democrática Ecuatoriana, Guayas, 26 December 1943)

"These are dreadful times of misery, uncertainty, and agony." (*La voz del pueblo,* 20 February 1944)

"We are in the moment of to be or not to be." *(estamos en el instante de ser o no ser)* (Velasco Ibarra, 7 March 1944)

La Gloriosa in Guayaquil

According to participants, in the context of all of the above, young army officers and civilians had agreed to stage an uprising in Guayaquil. The contacts between ADE politicians and young officers had begun in Guayaquil in April 1944. By 17 May they had agreed that they would revolt in response to any of the following events: "(1) massacre against the people; (2) imprisonment of an involved officer; or (3) electoral fraud" (Naranjo 1945, 13). The military high commanders suspected that a revolt was being planned and arrested junior military officers. The government also jailed some of ADE's civilians involved with the plot. Thus, the conspirators had to move up the insurrection to the night of Sunday, 28 May—Mother's Day.

On the night of 28 May civilians and draftees under the command of the "known Communist leader Lara Cruz" attacked the telegraph office, interrupting communications with Quito. At 11:15 P.M. conscripts and civilians assaulted the security office and proceeded to destroy furniture and liberate prisoners. Meanwhile, civilians marched through the city shouting, "Viva Velasco Ibarra." Liberal meeting places, such as the dance salons El Pigal and El Dixie belonging to the Echeverría brothers, were destroyed, as well as the bar-restaurant Miraflores of Enrique Zamora and the food and liquor store of Tarquiño Alaña. The transit police headquarters and the provincial alcohol tax office were also ravaged. Crowds burned the car of the governor of Guayas province and the house of the police chief, Manuel Carbo Paredes.

Meanwhile, young military officers, with the support of organized civilian militia, were preparing for the main military objective: the attack on the carabineros' barracks. In front of the military garrison, there were "lots of people . . . offering their services and asking for weapons; the cries of 'Viva la Revolución,' 'Viva Velasco Ibarra,' 'Viva el Ejército,' 'Abajo Arroyo,' could be heard" (Naranjo 1945, 23). The bloody attack on the carabineros' barracks lasted through the night.

On the morning of the 29th, around 7:30 A.M., civilian and military combatants, along with other bystanders, entered the defeated carabineros' barracks. They proceeded to "throw to the crowds all the weaponry they found . . . , and a few moments later the doors . . . were opened so all the people could come inside" (Girón 1945, 211). Finally the crowds burned the barracks. "After inquiring why the building was burned, the conclusion was that a group of angry people with intense hatred did not want the quarters of the Carabinero Battalion of Guayaquil to exist any more" (Naranjo 1945, 32).

After securing the military triumph and knowing that Arroyo del Río had resigned from the presidency, the fiesta started in Guayaquil's streets. Some participants inverted and mocked the symbols of power of the deposed regime. For example, "it was striking how a group of citizens mounting the horses of the sword squadron of the carabineros rode around the city championing Dr. Velasco Ibarra and the army" (Girón 1945, 222). These iconoclastic actions destroyed accepted and sometimes feared symbols like the sword, which had been used to punish those who dared to shout the subversive words "Viva Velasco." In Bruce Lincoln's words, "It is their intent to demonstrate dramatically and in public the *powerlessness* of the image and thereby to inflict a double disgrace on its champions, first by exposing the bankruptcy of their vaunted symbols and, second, their impotence in the face of the attack" (1989, 120; emphasis in original). That is why the assailants of the carabineros' barracks kept "as mementos the former swords of the carabineros, which they displayed insistently to the cheering public" (Girón 1945, 222).

It is difficult to know the exact number of dead and wounded in Guayaquil on 28 and 29 May. Some newspapers reported more than 200 wounded and 20 dead; others described 55 funerals and from 15 to 63 unidentified corpses. However, from the newspaper accounts, which sometimes gave the names of the victims, their ages, and professions, a partial analysis of participants in the revolt can be reconstructed. Most of the 32 identified corpses were carabineros. Of the approximately 200 wounded, 119 were identified. Most of them (76) were civilians from different occupational categories: one student, one writer, and a cross-section of occupations of common people (de la Torre 1993, 239–40).

The crowds carefully chose their targets. They destroyed the symbols, institutions, and properties of the hated Liberal regime, while leaving intact the properties of wealthy people who did not support Albornoz and Arroyo. The rationale was to mete out justice to the representatives of a fraudulently elected regime that was also repressive. Beyond this, the aim was to burn the symbols of the "Arroyista tyranny." But how were the Liberals and their henchmen, the carabineros, transformed into devils who had to be eradicated for the well-being and the reconstruction of the nation, while Velasco Ibarra was transformed into the nation's savior? Before answering this question, the events in Quito, Cuenca, and Riobamba will be analyzed.

The events in other cities of the country were less dramatic. In Quito, the carabineros did not resist the insurrection. After being informed of Arroyo's resignation in the early evening of the 29th, crowds from the different neighborhoods of Quito gathered down-town in the Plaza de la Independencia. Cheering "Guayaquil, Guay-aquil," carrying portraits of Velasco and national flags, and the V for victory with their hands, "by 10 P.M. half of Quito's population was celebrating in the streets" (*El comercio,* 30 May 1944). Celebrations continued the next day when the city was adorned with flags. *El comercio* also reports that the cheer "Viva Velasco Ibarra" was the gener-alized greeting among citizens.

In Cuenca, in Ecuador's southern highlands, the celebrations of Arroyo's fall were countered by police repression. When demonstra-tors shouting "'Viva Velasco, Down with the Tyrannous Regime, Viva la Revolución' passed in front of the alcohol tax building, they were shot at by the carabineros" (*El telégrafo,* 3 June 1944). Three people died and ten were wounded. The cabinetmaker Luis Mon-cayo was quoted as saying as he died, "Viva Velasco, *compañeros,* keep on struggling until the homeland is saved. Don't look at my blood, look at how the homeland bleeds to death and is crushed" (*El comercio,* 31 May 1944).

The next day, as Rafael Arízaga Vega narrates in his memoirs, "An enormous crowd marched around the streets of Cuenca, and while passing in front of the house of one of the most fanatical Arroyistas, we were provoked in a cowardly way, which resulted in an assault on that house. Angry people threw the furniture and a big piano from the window, later to burn them. . . . However when they found money they didn't touch even a cent, because the aim of the assault was not to steal but to punish the four years of insolence of the owners of the house" (1990, 163–64). To have taken that money would have been an immoral act, and the rationale of the revolt was precisely to restore public morality.

In the central highland city of Riobamba on 29 May, several lead-ers of ADE were jailed. When the university student V. Haro was beaten and stabbed by the carabineros for shouting to a group of people, "Viva Velasco Ibarra, continue your struggle against oppression," popular anger exploded (*El comercio,* 5 June 1944). Sergio Enrique Girón recounts the events.

> Suddenly a rumor was spread that [carabinero] commander Carbo Paredes was staying at the Hotel Ecuador; but the lack of leaders to direct the movement was . . . evident, because all hesitated. Then [a] railroad worker walked toward the hotel, followed by some other people; with his fist he broke the window of Carbo Paredes's room. They found two women, who denied that any one else was in the room. . . . Meanwhile, the housebreakers saw two men under the bed, who were forced to come out. The railroad worker kicked the shorter one, and while questioning him, forced him out of the hotel; the same was being done to his companion, a heavily built, sinister-looking black. Because some of the people said he was not Carbo Paredes, they were going to let him go, until a young man named Meneses said, he is the executioner Carbo Paredes.
>
> The railroad worker disarmed Carbo Paredes. Then he tried to take off his pants, but could only get them down to the knees. Meanwhile, the people started to stone Carbo Paredes and drag him to the San Nicolás garrison, and he died in the way we have just mentioned; but when he arrived, the corpse was totally naked and his only clothing was a tie.
>
> While Carbo Paredes was dying, the people were also attacking his companion and bodyguard, the black Quiñónez; in their indignation some railroad workers went looking for fuel to burn him alive, but they could not find any. Then they went somewhere else to look for fuel, but several people who had not lost their minds convinced them that such an act would dishonor Riobamba, so the [would-be] incinerators changed their mind and instead killed Quiñónez with stones and shots, as we have already mentioned. (Girón 1945, 314–16).

These acts of popular justice are remembered as even more savage episodes. People say, for instance, that soccer was played with Carbo Paredes's head. In fact, these acts were not quite that brutal, and, indeed, the burning of Quiñónez, which might have been motivated by racial prejudice against blacks, was stopped because it would "dishonor Riobamba." Nonetheless, how can we explain people's joy in dragging, stoning, and killing Carbo Paredes and Quiñónez?

Natalie Davis, in her study of rituals of religious collective violence, explains that such acts of torture and violence are produced in "guilt free massacres." The victims have to be transformed into devils, harmful beings who must be eradicated. "The crucial fact that the killers must forget is that their victims are human beings. These harmful people in the community have already been transformed for the crowd into 'vermin' or 'devils.' The rites of . . . violence complete the process of dehumanization" (Davis 1975, 181).

What remains to be explained is the discursive process by which the carabineros and the Liberals were dehumanized and the simultaneous transformation of Velasco Ibarra into the solution to all the country's problems.

Viva Velasco Ibarra!

To understand why the Liberals and the carabineros were the only targets of popular collective violence and why this revolt was made in the name of the Great Absentee, we must analyze the transformation of politics into an all-out fight between the people and their Liberal oppressors. The key is the simultaneous transformation of Liberals and carabineros into devils and Velasco Ibarra into the savior of the nation. I will examine contemporary analyses of democracy by political parties and sectors of civil society, their images of the Liberals and Velasco Ibarra, and the challenges of the political conjuncture of 1944. After looking at these key issues of Ecuadorian political discourse in the 1940s, I examine the irreconcilable struggle between two camps: the Liberal oligarquía and the Velasquista pueblo.

For Conservative politicians, journalists, and pamphleteers, the roots of the country's social problems lay in the lack of morality. In a radio speech, Conservative leader Camilo Ponce Enríquez, accused the Liberals of provoking the country's problems by "turning away from the moral order." This caused "religious anarchy [which] prepared the way for social and political anarchy, and for the relaxation of private and public morals" (*La patria,* 1 May 1944). For his part, the archbishop of Quito, Carlos María de la Torre, in April 1944 said, "Ecuador is at the point of perishing because immorality, as a pernicious cancer, has invaded all social organs . . . because God has been banished" (de la Torre 1944, 12–13). In this view, the solution had to come from Catholic morality and respect for Catholic education. The archbishop of Quito, in a letter to president Velasco, said, "If immorality like a repugnant leprosy has polluted all the social organs, to cure it it is necessary to inoculate in the veins of the national organism great doses of morality, but of the only true one, which was carved by God's hand when he created the human heart, and was ratified, confirmed, and again promulgated by his Incarnated Son, Our Lord Jesus" (*El diario del sur,* 18 June 1944).

The Liberals, however, had not only caused the country's miseries, they also represented sin. Liberals were equated with freemasons and, according to Pope Pius IX, freemasonry "is *Satan's Synagogue* and their [the freemasons'] purpose is nothing else but to destroy the religious and civil organizations born with Christianity" (Carlos María de la Torre 1954, 235; emphasis in original). These images of freemasons were widely shared. In 1930, a British diplomat reported, "A Freemason is considered by the majority of people here as a person closely associated with the Devil, and not long ago ladies of the society of Quito were induced by their confessors to sign a pledge that they would not shake hands or have any social intercourse with a Freemason" (Mr. Kohan to Mr. A. Henderson, British Foreign Office, General Correspondence, Political [FO 371/14224 A 2502/2502/54], Archivo Histórico del Banco Central del Ecuador, Quito).

Freemasons were interested not only in destroying religion; their diabolic plans were wider. They were said to be involved in politics and business with the aim of dominating the world. Thus, when the Liberal Party nominated Miguel Angel Albornoz for the 1944 presidential election, Conservatives reproduced a photograph of the Freemasonic Board [Consejo Masónico], among whose members was Albornoz. To the photograph they affixed the question, "What Catholic would vote for Albornoz? . . . servant of the anti-Ecuadorian Freemasonry, which obeys the directions of the Peruvian Lodge, which caused our international crisis" (BAEP, Hojas volantes, 1943–45). Conservative chauvinism also linked freemasons with Jews and Marxists. Jews were referred to as a "disgusting race," a "caste" who had in common with freemasons and Marxists that they followed international dictates and were different and foreign to what was perceived as the nation's social fabric (*La voz del pueblo*, 12 March 1944). An editorial in the same newspaper stated that, "It is not possible to be a Christian worker and acknowledge the doctrines of hatred, or belong to societies that are moved by the drunken passions of the Jew Carlos Marx" (4 July 1944).

Conservatives, therefore, perceived the political conjuncture in the following way. Liberals had destroyed the moral fabric by undermining religious education. Moreover, Liberals were the antination who followed the orders of a closed international sect, the freemasonic ring *(argolla)*, who sought to remain in power by illegal and immoral means—electoral fraud. Also, the Liberals' antinationalism was manifested in their responsibility for losing half the national territory to Peru. The solution to this moral crisis would come from electoral honesty and the rule of a person willing to respect and promote Catholic religion and morality—namely, Velasco Ibarra.

Some organized groups of civil society shared this language of moral reform. For example, for the electoral committees of the San Marcos parish of Quito, the Comités Femeninos Patria y Libertad and Reivindicación Nacional, the cause of the country's problems were the Liberals, who were referred to as "dominant gangs," "professional politicians, traffickers, and merchants of the homeland's honor." The Liberals had left "a homeland broken into a thousand pieces; a hungry people craving liberty; a bankrupt economy; an industry chained by foreign competition; a rich land without irrigation and crops; an undernourished working class prey to illness, without bread or work; a public employee deceived of his aspirations; a public administration without responsibilities; a national budget without technical or hedonistic planning . . . ." The solution would be a government of "national unity," carrying to power "the most honest, and austere of Ecuador's children whose merits embellished the figure of el señor doctor don José María Velasco Ibarra" (BAEP, Hojas volantes, 1943–45, no. 39).

For the bus and truck drivers of Pichincha, what was needed was the "redemption of Ecuador, to bring about the right of the majorities to govern themselves. . . . The men of the steering wheel, strong to fight against nature, committed to follow a route, energetic to defeat obstacles and distances, will use all our abilities to facilitate the triumph of Dr. Velasco Ibarra, the symbol of the Ecuadorian redemption" (*El día*, 1 May 1944).

Through their newspaper *Surcos,* university students articulated a different language to interpret the country's problems: class analysis. Like other leftist organizations and political parties, they saw the cause of Ecuador's problems in the country's feudal agrarian structure, and the resulting strictures on democracy. The solution would be found in a series of structural reforms such as industrialization, the elimination of feudalism, but especially in honest elections (*Surcos,* 4 October 1944). Of course, ultimately they agreed with other leftists who saw bourgeois democracy as but a phase on the path to true, or Socialist, democracy (21 March 1944).

The coming elections were interpreted by university students as a contest between the Liberal government and the pueblo. The Liberal government was the oligarquía, defined as: "a small group of capitalists, large landowners, workers without class consciousness, and workers who for a few cents betray their common cause." Although, "the word *pueblo* lacks a precise social content, . . . it generally denotes economically poor classes." Thus el pueblo was: "The majority of the nation, as well as certain circles of capitalists and landowners, intellectuals who have not sold their ideas, but above all el pueblo, the working masses, the thousands of workers" (*Surcos*, Quito, 19 October 1944).

In that critical moment, the struggle was perceived to be between Velasco Ibarra as the representative of democracy and the Liberal candidate as the negation of the democratic ideal. According to *Surcos*, the Manichaean struggle between Velasco and the official candidate Albornoz, had the following characteristics.

> The front of democracy and the front of antidemocracy; the front that represents progress and the front that represents Ecuador's abyss; the front that represents the unity of all Ecuadorians for the reconstruction of the nationality, and the front that gathers the most terrifying seeds of total disintegration; the front that represents the popular well-being, and the one that represents the horrible phantom of misery that today menaces most of the population; the front that represents a true democracy and the one that threatens persecution, exile, and jail; the front that promises a vigorous international personality for our country supported and dignified by the joint alliance of the army and the people, and the front of speculation and glut that unconditionally surrenders our richness, that humiliates our army, that endangers it with other forces, and that conspires with external forces that constantly threaten our territorial disintegration; the front that represents the most decided and consequent cooperation with the United Nations for the triumph of democracy in the world, and the front that represents Nazi interests. These are the two forces that face each other in our country, through a tumultuous history and in a singularly dramatic environment. One is represented by the candidate of National Unity, Dr. José María Velasco Ibarra; the other, by the official candidate. (*Surcos*, 18 September 1943)

In forming Alianza Democrática Ecuatoriana (ADE), the directors of the different political parties were able to agree on a minimum program of national unity and democratic reconstruction. This common program integrated the different languages of moral reform and class, presenting at the same time a common new language of political inclusion and personalism. The concrete proposals of ADE's program of national unity were making elections free, developing national industries and mechanizing agricultural production, increasing the moral and economic status of the working classes through minimum wages, setting upper price limits for basic necessities, incorporating Indians into national life, raising the culture and hygiene of the popular sectors, increasing national sovereignty through the strengthening of the armed forces, enhancing the international image and presence of the country, and supporting the democratic nations in their struggle against Nazism and fascism (*Surcos,* 18 September 1943).

Even though this was a broad and ambiguous program, and various components of the Alianza emphasized different points of it, most members of ADE could agree on the decisive nature of electoral honesty and freedom.

> It can be affirmed that Ecuadorian history is in essence the struggle between the popular masses against different oligarchies who have always undemocratically taken power. . . .
>
> For a long time, Ecuadorian politics has been fixed behind the backs of the people, with clever dealings in lawyers' offices, in army cafes, in elegant salons. . . . Nobody could think that democracy can work behind the backs of the people. . . . It is urgent to publicly debate each one of the national problems. And, most urgent is freedom and honesty of election, to debate who will govern, how and for whom. . . . It is obvious that when talking about freedom of election we are also implying freedom of expression and of the organization of political parties, so they can disseminate their programs and political lines, so they can become structured and developed. (ADE, Sección Provincial del Guayas, 26 December 1943, in Alianza Democrática Ecuatoriana 1981, 14–18)

In conclusion, a broad political spectrum agreed to struggle for electoral freedom as a first and fundamental step to democratize the country. The political decision-making process was seen as the first step to further reforms, which, for the left, also included the social question. But the struggle for political inclusion was not carried out in abstract terms. Rather, politics was personalized. Whereas the Liberals, in particular Arroyo del Río, Albornoz, and the carabineros, became the incarnation of sin, the exiled former president Velasco Ibarra became the Great Absentee (El Gran Ausente) and represented the solution to all the problems.

Velasco's image did not only unify the opposition against Arroyo del Río's Liberal regime. He was considered the embodiment of all values betrayed by Liberal governments: honesty, sincerity, respect for the decisions of the electorate, the guarantee for the unity of all Ecuadorians at this critical turning point, and, for some, Catholicism.

Velasco Ibarra is the man of destiny, who appears as a beneficent heavenly body, victorious and shining. Yet the candidate of National Redemption enjoys the fame of all his virtues . . . , of his capacity as a statesman, of his unquestionable honesty, of his organizing genius, and, above all, the love of the Ecuadorian people. *[Es Velasco Ibarra, el hombre del destino que aparece, como un astro bienhechor, victorioso y resplandesciente. Pero el candidato de la Redención Nacional goza de la fama de sus virtudes y de sus luces, de su capacidad de hombre de estado, de su honradez acrisolada, de su genio organizador y, sobre todo, del amor del pueblo ecuatoriano.]* (Marcos B. Espinel, "Ya viene el ídolo del pueblo ecuatoriano," BAEP, Hojas volantes, 1943–45, no. 38)

In their edition immediately after the May insurrection, *El diario del sur* of Cuenca had carried the following caption below a photo of Velasco Ibarra: "President elected by the popular Ecuadorian vote drowned in the blood of the martyrs of 12 January 1940, and resurrected in the blood of the martyrs of 29 May 1944." This same publication refers to Velasco as "a man of rock who has destroyed the infested swamp of fifty years," and to Velasquismo as "an immense sacrifice well-nourished in hope and irrigated by innocent blood.

The glory of Velasquismo lies in the fecund miracle that blood has never been spilled without a reason."

The electoral slogans for Velasco in his 1944 campaign summarized people's expectations of his ability to solve all the problems of the country, and even the world.

"With Velasco, *churrasco.*"[6]
"With Velasco, sugar."
"Everything with Velasco." (*El universo,* 10 May 1944)

In the small town of Sibambe, Chimborazo province:

"If Velasco Ibarra comes, there will be sugar."
"With Velasco Ibarra, Hitler will ask for peace."
"Velasco Ibarra is coming." (*El día,* 4 May 1944)

In sum, the discourse of broad sectors of civil society and the main political parties of the country can be characterized by the coexistence of languages of moral reform and class, which coincided in their emphasis on personalism and political inclusion. This shared, if contested, frame of discourse also divided the social field into two antagonistic political camps, represented by Velasco and the Liberals. This division can be characterized, following Bruce Lincoln, as a schism: "the formal separation of two (or more) irreconcilable parties that had earlier been contending segments within one encompassing society" (1989, 98). These antagonistic camps can be summarized by the contrasts illustrated in tables 1 and 2.

The political segmentation of the country, represented in table 1, was complemented by a social segmentation (see table 2) between two camps: the pueblo and the oligarquía. The inherent ambiguity of these two terms is manifested in the imprecision of the social categories discursively assigned to each of the camps. What is clear, regardless of the ideologies of the members of the opposition to the Liberal regime, is that the term *oligarquía* referred to closed, impermeable groups, such as the Liberal ring (argolla) which had dominated the country through electoral fraud for the previous fifty years.

The total antagonism between the Liberals and Velasco, as shown in table 3, was further personalized in a series of attributes that transformed each party into the embodiment of sin or virtue.

Of course, not all sectors of civil society or political parties supported Velasco Ibarra. The anarchist Gran Asamblea Popular Obrera formed by "manual workers and Guayaquil's popular classes" on 1 May 1944, expressed their rejection of the Great Absentee's candidacy with the following arguments: "The vindications of the working

Table 1

Political Segmentation in Ecuador in the 1940s

Velasco Ibarra	Liberal Government
-ADE*	-Partido Liberal Radical
-Organizations of civil society: students; workers	-Carabineros
-Electoral committees	-Electoral committees
-Young army officers	-High command armed forces

*The Alianza Democrática Ecuatoriana included: the Partido Conservador; Partido Comunista; Partido Socialista; Vanguardia Socialista Revolucionaria; Partido Liberal Independiente; Frente Democrático.

Table 2

Social Segmentation in Ecuador in the 1940s, according to the Opposition to the Liberal Government

Pueblo	Oligarquía
-majorities	-minorities, rings (argollas) or sects
-popular masses	-Free Masons; Partido Liberal Radical; Nazis; professional politicians;
-manual workers; intellectuals; national bourgeoisie; artisans; some capitalists; professionals; small merchants; bureaucrats	-feudal lords; some capitalists; and workers without class consciousness

Table 3
Portrayal of the Political Candidates for the 1944 Elections,
According to the Opposition to the Liberal Government

Velasco Ibarra	Liberals: Arroyo del Río and Albornoz
-open	-closed; rings (argollas)
-free suffrage	-electoral fraud
-antifascist	-Nazi supporters
-democrat	-antidemocrat
-national integration	-national disintegration
-hope	-despair
-salvation	-downfall
-progress	-abyss
-popular well-being	-misery
-true democracy	-persecution, exile, jail
-unity between pueblo and army	-army humiliation
-patriot	-antipatriot
-nation	-antination
-honest; poor; austere	-immoral; vices; arrogant
-Catholic morality*	-anti-Catholic sect*
-secret antinational sect (Freemasons)**	

*Only in the Catholic-Conservative publications
**In Catholic and in some non-Catholic publications about the Liberals.

classes and the proletariat should not be attached to the ideas of political parties, or, what is the same, to pseudo-redemptive charlatan caudillos who surprise naive mobs with their demagogy and false promises of redemption and freedom" (BAEP, Hojas volantes, 1943–45, no. 33).

The themes of Velasco as demagogue and manipulator of the feelings of naive crowds, his lack of ideological coherence, and his caudillismo were articulated in the following Liberal manifesto.

These times are not made for idols. They cannot be because providential times have passed away. The true statesman has replaced the demagogue and the caudillo. The new leader incarnates principles, personifies collective aspirations, and synthesizes ideals. The same organization of political parties, as orienting forces into the political life of the nations, implies the extinction of old absolutely personalistic forms of government. . . .

Doctor Velasco Ibarra does not have any program. To his capricious character, which has made him cover the entire political spectrum and cloak himself in all political creeds, has been added the new condition that any personal definition will destroy the capricious block that has been integrated as a counterfeit of the famous French Popular Front. . . . As soon as a government of Velasco Ibarra is inaugurated, it will destroy the apparent harmony between the antagonistic groups who have formed ADE. ("Alrededor de un hombre o alrededor de principios?" signed by Liberales, in *El telégrafo*, 19 May 1944)

For these Liberal politicians, the times also reflected the struggle between democracy and the lack of it, traditional politics and modern political parties, but, above all, between a political party and a demagogue. Table 4 summarizes the images of Velasco's adversaries on the Great Absentee and on democracy.

The political crisis of May 1944 was experienced by participants as a struggle for democracy. This emphasis on democracy was not just a local reproduction of world events, of the struggle between the democratic nations against fascism and Nazism, but a struggle for

Table 4
Velasco and Democracy, According to His Opponents

Velasco	Democracy
-demagogy, no ideologies	-doctrinaire definition
-no political program	-concrete program
-exploitation of feelings	
-sensationalist words	
-personalism, caudillismo	-political party with program
-unwary mobs	-thinking pueblo

what was considered to be the answer to the country's problems. For Liberals, Velasco's demagogy, lack of clear ideology, instability of character, and caudillismo were a danger to the country's political stability in a world situation that they characterized as the competition and rule of ideologically motivated political parties.

For the opponents of the Liberals, the main obstacle to reestablishing democracy was Liberal rule through electoral fraud. This shared vision of democracy as a fundamental right defined above all by honesty at the polls was, however, fragmented into diverse concrete proposals by the right and left. The former proposed free elections and the remoralization of the country through Catholic morality and education. Leftists, for their part, saw the struggle for electoral freedom and the establishment of the rights of the individual as part of a broader struggle for socialist democracy and the eventual abolition of both private property and the same institutions of bourgeois democracy that they were struggling for in this period.

As for the image of Velasco Ibarra, for some he was the person capable of welding different political parties and groups of civil society in their fight against the Liberals. For others, Velasco and his supporters, the Velasquistas, were the essence of the Ecuadorian nationality, existing above and beyond any political party.

This populist shared, if contested, frame of discourse, articulated by political parties and associations of civil society of the right and the left in the different regions of Ecuador in the early 1940s, transformed politics into a moral and Manichaean fight between a sinful Liberal oligarchy and a virtuous people embodied in Velasco Ibarra. That this type of political discourse was so widespread has strong implications for the study of populism.

Most studies have analyzed political leaders' Manichaean speeches without studying the existing frames of discourse within which they articulate their orations. Therefore they have emphasized the role of the leader in creating a populist political discourse. The analysis of the already existing frame of discourse makes the success of any type of political discourse contingent on whether a political leader can articulate existing demands and aspirations in a form that can be recognized as valid for his audiences. In Ecuador in the 1940s, this was a political discourse of a moral and religious fight between the virtuous people and the sinful Liberal oligarchy. The fact, however, that certain politicians are able to articulate existing frames of discourse does not make them mere social products. Populist leaders are also innovators, but the success of their discourse depends on their ability to articulate and give form to existing grievances and aspirations.

The Success of Velasco Ibarra's Leadership

This section explores the actions and words of Velasco Ibarra that transformed him into the Great Absentee. The analysis begins with his speech in Guayaquil on 4 June, after his triumphal return to the country on 31 May.

The fourth of June 1944 in Guayaquil began as a day of fiesta. Flags, banners, and flowers were arranged to celebrate victory and welcome José María Velasco Ibarra. Eighty thousand people in a city of around 200,000 inhabitants gathered to receive President Velasco, who arrived by plane from Quito at 2:15 P.M. A parade took him to El Palacio de la Zona, where he was received by a speech by Francisco Arízaga Luque, director of ADE in Guayas province.

Velasco starts his oration by referring to the audience as the "heroic, heroic pueblo of Guayaquil."[7] He elaborates a moral and political definition of *pueblo*.

> All of you, in this solemn moment of the nation's history, are showing the world that the material is only a transitory aspect of the life of man; that which is eternal is the striving for moral greatness, for progress, and for liberty; that which is eternal in men is the hatred of hypocrisy and tyranny, and you, *Guayaquileños,* who have written another glorious episode in your history by the emotion through which

you distinguish yourselves among all the peoples of Ecuador, have broken forever the most ignoble of tyrannies and have established forever in our homeland the great principles of liberation, democracy, and equal justice for all men.

Velasco Ibarra has emotional links to the people of Guayaquil, whose latest heroic act is comparable to their other patriotic feats.

Heroic pueblo, whom I love and with whom I feel connected, after bearing *four years of the most ignoble of tyrannies, confusion, and fright in the national soul,* you destroyed *the secret police,* which allows us to speak now, you achieved *power for all citizens,* wresting from the police the absolute power that they maintained through the person of a *despot* who promoted the *arbitrary disposition of the national territory and of her revenues, the squandering of public funds, the corruption of local government, of judicial Power, and of all the nation.*

He then refers to the political leaders of ADE, and especially to the soldiers.

Oh, soldiers of Villamil [regiment]! You showed the carabineros and the *tyrants of the homeland* (applause) that the force of ideals is greater than the force of imbeciles; and that savage force, however great it seems, is *helpless and must be imprisoned and burned and destroyed when it meets the fire of the guayaquileño bullets and the army that was affected by the guayaquileños' emotion* (loud applause and *vivas* for the army).

He then changes his tone of voice and message. In the remainder of his oration, Velasco uses two discursive appeals: the presentation of the crisis as part of a movement from oppression and unhappiness to redemption, and the personification of the political event. Velasco recounts to his audience that their suffering has finally achieved democratic redemption. Velasco tells them that although they have shed their blood, they have given Quito the power to govern the country, and that is an act of selflessness and generosity. These acts show the purity of the people of Guayaquil. This long-suffering pueblo has

finally achieved redemption. These two traits of the people of Guayaquil—purity and suffering—have established them, in Álvarez Junco's
words, as the "liberating subject" (1987, 252–53).

Now that you have suffered and waited so long and are now gathered
here, allow me [to speak or to talk]. . . . Guayaquileños, this is a complete revolution; but it is a transcendental revolution, a profound revolution; it is a true and purposeful revolution because it is a total
revolution; you have here a magnificent synthesis of the political parties; the Communists . . . the Conservatives . . . and the Liberals . . .
and all the parties are congregated here today. And why? Precisely because the current revolution is synthesized in something that is like
the whole of honorable people and that can only be rejected by slaves
and the vile: the regime of popular autonomy, of suffrage of the people, of the government of the people by their own collective will (applause, "Viva el Ecuador," "Viva el doctor Velasco Ibarra").

In such a moment of national purification, the perpetrators of
crimes against the nation will not be forgiven. Suffering and purity
give to the people of Guayaquil the right to revenge. "Will we forgive
the perverse? Will we be *indulgent and tolerant? No! No! the perverse
will be punished"* (applause). They will punish *"the thieves and ex-
ploiters"* (thunderous applause). But punishment will be conducted
with discipline, serenity, and the proper respect for international
norms. *"It pains my soul to respect them. I wish we could crush the
traitor who threw away half of the national territory"* (loud applause
and "Death to Arroyo" and "Viva Velasco Ibarra").

After pointing to Arroyo de Río and the carabineros as personify-
ing evil, Velasco proceeds to present himself as the opposite—the embodiment of the betrayed values and qualities that are nothing else
but the qualities of the people of Guayaquil. "Believe, señores, believe in me. I do not belong to the school of men who make politics a
question of cleverness. For me politics is part of morality."

Velasco argues that although he might not be prepared to assume
the responsibility of being president of the country, he does not have
any other choice but to set aside his own personal interests and come

to serve all of his pueblo. The end result of what started as an unpretentious presentation of Velasco's uncertainty is the transformation of the humble man into the deserving leader of all the Ecuadorians, who embodies the opposite of the past sufferings under Arroyo del Río's regime.

> To this modest citizen you have entrusted executive power. Believe me, friends, believe me; this responsibility *fills me with terror,* fills me with fear. Perhaps I will not succeed. If I fail I will not be able to hold up my head. The country will remain in diapers before progress and all the Americas, perhaps my life itself, will be, rightly, in danger. Would I betray this revolution? Believe me. I am a man of conscience. I am terrified by the position that I occupy. But I am also aware that Ecuador trusts me because I have never stolen, because I have never led you astray (great applause and "Viva Ecuador" and "Viva Velasco Ibarra"). Because I have never attempted to use national power as a pedestal to elevate my own self-importance. . . . No, citizens, what I have always tried to do is to serve you, to express to you some modest idea of mine that might serve in your collective orientation, and I prefer a single minute of command—if that minute of command is translated into a sense of direction—to twenty days of command, to twenty years of command, if those twenty years produce rejection by the pueblo, the tyranny of individuals, and the international discredit of the country (applause and *vivas*).

After paying lip service to ADE's program of government, Velasco puts himself above and beyond any political party or doctrine. He, the leader, is the one called to interpret the needs of the country in such a difficult and uncertain moment. He is the deserving leader because he is like the people: he has suffered and he is pure.

> Do not oblige me to develop a Socialist, Communist, Liberal, or Conservative program. Don't force it on me; I am not for that.
> The current moment is a difficult moment. It is an essentially vital moment. It is a moment in which the Communist stands side by side with the Catholic. It is a moment in which the basis of the homeland

must be demonstrated. I will not serve any specific ideology. I will not serve any specific party, I will be the leader of all the nation, I will be the servant of the pueblo, I will be the servant of Ecuador in search of its nationality, of morality, of a tolerant government, of liberalism, of national concentration, of hygiene, of social reform, so that others, younger, stronger, with fewer gray hairs than I, who have suffered less, can develop to the maximum their respective programs of social reform, liberal or conservative or whatever. . . .

Demand from me then that I govern in accordance with the moment. Demand sincerity from me. Recognize that the falseness of the government of Arroyo del Río is the most repugnant thing on earth.

The content of Velasco Ibarra's oration is summarized in table 5. He personalizes politics and presents the political as part of a struggle for higher moral and transcendental ideals. As in most of his speeches, he does not elaborate a political program. Rather, he speaks of the struggle as a fight between himself as the personification of redemption against Arroyo and the carabineros as the embodiment of suffering. This transformation of politics into something else, into a fight

Table 5

Velasco Ibarra and Arroyo del Río as Embodiments of Virtues

Arroyo	Velasco
-tyranny, confusion, fright	-democracy
-carabinero, tyrant	-heroic pueblo, soldiers
-the material	-the spiritual, the moral
-savage force	-emotion
-tutelage	-institutions, suffrage
-slaves, vile men	-honorable people
-vain and traitorous leader	-modest citizen
-falseness	-sincerity
-immorality	-morality
-suffering of pueblo	-revolution that is transcendental, profound, truthful

for higher moral values, is presented as a confrontation between the spiritual and the material.

We do not know much about what was going on while Velasco Ibarra was talking. Press reports tell us only about applause and cheers. But, from the transcription of his speech, it can be determined that the leader was engaging in a dialogue with the audience. For example, he asks rhetorically,

"Will we forgive the perverse?"
"Will we be indulgent and tolerant?"

He answers the obvious and no doubt gives the response that people were shouting to his questions:

"No!"
"No!"

This transcription also tells us that Velasco Ibarra consciously divided his speech into two parts that might have been given with different tones of voice. First, he talks about the moment, the past, and the glorious acts of the people and the soldiers. In the second part, he personalizes the struggle and presents himself as the embodiment of redemption above any political ideology.

The first striking element of this event is that, as when he campaigned in 1939 and 1940, Velasco Ibarra dramatized his returns from exile as those of the redeemer who has come to save the country.[8] His arrivals were festive occasions. Followers adorned their cities with banners and flags. Large crowds, made up of both supporters and the curious, went to receive him at airports, train stations, and at the outskirts of cities and towns. Parades were organized in his honor with decorated cars, bands, and marching groups. The large crowds that he had begun to attract during his political campaign in 1939 and 1940 cheered him as the national savior in many places that had never before been visited by a campaigning politician.

For his part, he cultivated the image of the Great Absentee. He never stayed in the country after being in office nor after he unsuccessfully tried to orchestrate an insurrection when he lost the 1940 elections. From outside the country, the seduction of nostalgia worked. "By contrasting the present with the past . . . all that was disagreeable, negative and unbearable is discarded, we tend to retain the agreeable, positive, remunerative aspects" (Moscovici 1985, 374–75). His supporters always kept alive his memory and blamed the failures of the exiled politician on bad advisors and people who took advantage of his sincere good will.

These dramatizations of Velasco Ibarra's arrivals from exile evoked religious sentiments. He, like Christ, had been banished, persecuted, and misunderstood. By suffering poverty, longing for his fatherland, and being separated from relatives and friends in exile he had learned to understand even more the sufferings of his people. He was like them insofar as he suffered and was poor, but he was also different from them. In his exiles he taught in universities, published books, studied to understand further the roots that caused these pains. That is why the poor, honest, and banished politician returns as a messiah. This time, as he repeatedly suggested, regardless of his personal discomfort, he would rescue the people from their misfortunes. For this he was willing to sacrifice even his own life.

As is evident in the speech analyzed above, Velasco Ibarra made use of three discursive strategies: Manichaean presentation of reality, subjectivization, and transmutation. The most obvious strategy in Velasco's political speeches are their Manichaean presentation of reality as a struggle between two antagonistic camps, el pueblo and la oligarquía. These terms do not refer to precise social categories but rather to a series of social relations; thus it is essential to examine who was included and excluded in the Ecuadorian case during the 1940s.

The analysis of the broad semantic field in the 1940s showed that most of the political parties and associations of civil society defined the terms *pueblo* and *oligarquía* in a political way as exclusion from or inclusion in the polity. More specifically, *oligarquía* was defined as those who retain political power by electoral fraud. They were the leadership of the Liberal Party. *Pueblo* was also defined politically as all those who had been mocked at the polls. This political definition excluded from the pueblo indigenous peoples, the poor, and illiterate. Given these broadly shared definitions of who were el pueblo and la oligarquía, the success of Velasco's speeches comes as no surprise. Velasco did not only reproduce these cleavages in his discourse, he accomplished something more. He personalized the image, the incarnation of the democratic ideal understood as respect for people's will at the polls.

Velasco's ability to personalize political problems constitutes his second discursive strategy. Following José Álvarez Junco, subjectivization or personalization of politics is understood as the "rhetorical function of the leader as the object or principal content of the discourse, in place of programs and doctrines" (1990, 243). For broad sections of Ecuadorian society, the political field was personalized as a struggle between Velasco, as the embodiment of honest elections, and the Liberals, as representatives of fraud. Velasco for his part assumed the role of the Great Absentee, presenting his personal figure as the only hope to solve all the country's miseries. That is why, for example, in Guayaquil on 4 June 1944, instead of presenting a concrete plan of government, he asked the people to believe in him. He told audiences that faith in the leader was enough to carry through the promises of the revolution.

Velasco spoke as a prophet. He thought of himself as the embodiment of the people. He felt above political ideologies, parties, and programs of government. His lack of respect and faith in any political party or ideology and his faith in "the people" as the only political organization (that of course he himself embodied) provoked, even from his first appearances, fissures in the alliance that brought him to power in May 1944.

Velasco Ibarra, like other populist leaders, transformed political struggles into fights for higher moral values (Álvarez Junco 1990, 252). This transmutation of politics into ethics or even into eschatological redemption, constitutes Velasco's third discursive strategy. The struggle of the people and Velasco as their incarnation against the Liberal-oligarchic regime is Manichaean. It is a fight between good and evil, spirit and matter, honesty and dishonesty, sincerity and insincerity, morality and immorality. Thus the political confrontation is total, without the possibility of compromise or dialogue.

If the struggle between Velasco and his enemies is ethical, the terms of reference of who represents evil will change with the political circumstances and also with the whims of the leader. Thus during his 1944–47 administration, Velasco Ibarra, acting in the name of the people, first attacked the supporters of the Liberal regime, later turned against his leftist supporters, and then also antagonized the right. He became politically isolated and was finally forced out of the country yet again in 1947 by a military coup. This also explains Velasco Ibarra's ambivalent attitudes toward democratic institutions. As he argued in his academic works, in extraordinary times the leader stands above common folk to interpret how to obey higher moral values. And he, the leader, the national embodiment, was certainly above "bad" constitutions, "corrupt" politicians, and "ignorant or misled" citizens whose antagonistic opinions had to be silenced.

Velasco Ibarra transmuted politics into ethics not just by the power of his words, but also, and maybe of more importance, by the whole ceremony of his public appearances. Agustín Cueva recalls Velasco's public appearance in May 1944 with the following words. "Lean and ascetic, the caudillo lifted his arms, as if trying to reach the height of the bells extolling him. At the climax of the ceremony, his face, his eyes, even his voice, were pointed toward heaven. His bodily tension had something of crucifixion, and the whole rite evoked a passion in which both the words and the mise-en-scène pointed to a dramatic if not tragic sense of existence" (1988, 152).

From National Unity to the Isolation of the Leader

After the political avalanche that brought Velasco Ibarra back to the country and into the presidential palace in May 1944, the different political and economic interests that had come together in ADE had an inevitable collision. Velasco's praised alliance of "the friar and the Communist" became a war between irreconcilable enemies. In the process, Velasco's government shifted political alliances to the right, becoming increasingly isolated until "the prophet" was left alone and had to go into exile yet again in August 1947. This second Velasquista administration lasted slightly more than three years, from 31 May 1944 to 23 August 1947.

After the euphoria with which he had been received, Velasco attempted to hold together the coalition that brought him to power by forming a government of "national unity" in which Conservatives, Socialists, Communists, and independent Liberals participated. But, as Velasco made clear on 11 June in front of a predominantly leftist audience in Quito's bullfight ring (Plaza Arenas), his goal was to stand above all political parties and associations of civil society. "I will be above all the political parties I will follow the teachings of the homeland. . . . I will try to listen to all suggestions. I will listen to ADE, and I will listen to the youth. But in governing, these actions will be mine, absolutely mine. Listen well to me. I will be the only one responsible" (Velasco Ibarra 1946, 85).

The new president tried to keep everybody happy by satisfying the left and the right. On 30 June he presided over the inauguration of the Second Congress of the Ecuadorian Confederation of Catholic Workers (CEDOC), and a few days later, on 4 July, he was the honorary guest at the founding Congress of the Socialist and Communist Confederación de Trabajadores del Ecuador (CTE). However, the honeymoon could not last. Elections for Congress were to be held on 23 July 1944. The government, in accord with its interpretation of the meaning of the May Revolution, was determined to have honest elections, and indeed the July elections fulfilled that goal. But the atmosphere before the elections pointed to the internal differences in the coalition that had brought Velasco back as the Great Absentee.

ADE divided into two groups: on the one hand, the Independent Liberal Party, the Socialist Party, the Communist Party, and Vanguardia Socialista Revolucionaria (who kept the original name of the coalition, Alianza Democrática Ecuatoriana), and on the other, the Conservative Party and Frente Democrático Nacional, which had been transformed into the Frente Electoral Velasquista (FEV). The principal topics of the struggle prior to the July elections were religion and anticommunism. Quito's Archbishop, Carlos María de la Torre, in a pastoral letter stated: "The Catholic cannot favor with his vote those who will not do good to religion and to the nation" (3 July 1944). The archbishop's intervention into politics was echoed by some priests who threatened Catholics who supported ADE. Anticommunism was articulated by Pedro Velasco Ibarra, brother of the president and leader of the Catholic workers' organization, CEDOC. In a flier entitled, "Is Communism Menacing Us?" he differentiated the rational and peaceful aspirations of the working class from the values of the "true Communists": hatred, revenge, and the desire to kill (BAEP, Hojas volantes, 1943–45, no. 56).

Despite the attacks from the right, ADE triumphed in the July 1944 congressional elections. Of a total of 58 democratically elected representatives, 37 belonged to ADE, 20 to the FEV, and 1 was an independent. The total number of representatives—who included delegates from agriculture, industry, commerce, the armed forces, teachers, the universities, the federation of university students, the press, lay workers, and Catholic workers—improved ADE's majority. Of a total of 92 representatives, 67 were members of ADE's political parties, 23 belonged to the FEV, and 2 were independents (Vega Ugalde 1987, 112–13, 185–88).

Reflecting ADE's electoral triumph, Francisco Arízaga Luque, leader of the Independent Liberal Party, was elected president of

Congress, and the general secretary of the Socialist Party, Manuel Agustín Aguirre, was elected vice president. The first act of Congress was to unanimously appoint José María Velasco Ibarra as president of Ecuador until 1948. For the first time in the country's history, parliamentary sessions were broadcast (Arízaga Vega 1990, 199). Representatives debated issues such as sanctions to the members of the deposed Liberal government, the appropriateness of including God's name in the Constitution, and substantive clauses of the Constitution.

By January 1945, the internal fissures in ADE came violently to the fore. On 16 January, a demonstration in support of President Velasco Ibarra against charges brought by former president Arroyo del Río from his exile in Colombia was held in Quito. The two opposing groups clashed. The left argued that the demonstration was on behalf of the president and the Constitutional Assembly. The Central de Trabajadores del Ecuador, for example, issued an invitation to the demonstration in the following terms: "Let us save the ideals of the May Revolution! Let us support the work of Velasco Ibarra and Congress!" (BAEP, Hojas volantes, 1943–45, no. 193). Rightist and independent Velasquistas supported the president but were against Congress. In several leaflets, they demanded that Congress finish its activities as soon as possible. They were also opposed to congressional initiatives to establish diplomatic relationships with the Soviet Union (BAEP, Hojas volantes, 1943–45, nos. 194, 195). The shouts of each group—"Viva Velasco Ibarra!" "Abajo la Asamblea!" "Viva Velasco Ibarra!" "Viva la Asamblea!"—were followed by a fight with stones and sticks. A leftist attacked a priest, and right-wing demonstrators attacked Communist representatives.

In January 1945 President Velasco accepted the resignations (which had not in fact been presented) of the Socialist minister of social welfare, Alfonso Calderón, and of the Communist minister of education, Alfredo Vera (Aguirre 1946, 20). After this provocation, as expected, the Socialist and Communist parties resolved to abstain from participating in the government. "As Communists and Socialists proceeded to resign in large numbers from government posts, the president asserted with some defiance that 'bureaucrats who do not agree with the administration can continue resigning'" (Blanksten 1951, 52).

Despite Velasco's opposition, a new constitution was approved on March 1945. For the Left it was a progressive charter. "Together with the rights of the individual, for the first time in our constitutional history important social rights such as family, education, culture, economy, work, and social welfare were included" (Aguirre 1946, 48). For others, including the president, it was an unacceptable document.

Like many another Constitution of Ecuador, the 1945 Charter was divorced from reality. The short-lived instrument imposed a number of severe checks on the executive, rendering the cabinet partially responsible to Congress, establishing a court of constitutional guarantees and a permanent legislative commission to serve as watchdogs against the president, and radically curtailing his veto power. The Constitution stated that the 'three political tendencies' of the republic—the right, the left, and the center—were to be equally represented as such in the permanent legislative commission and the independent superior electoral tribunal. September 1, 1948, was set as the date on which President Velasco Ibarra's term would expire although full and ample powers to depose him before then were conferred upon Congress in the event that sufficient impeachment charges were brought by the court of constitutional guarantees, the permanent commission, or both. This Constitution was promulgated on March 6, 1945. President Velasco Ibarra refused to take a ceremonial oath to support the document, although he "signed it against my personal convictions and only to save the country from evil times." (Blanksten 1951, 51–52)

Economic policies aimed to satisfy popular aspirations, in particular to improve wages, but inflation could not be controlled. It remained the worst economic problem during Velasco's second presidency. "The cost of living that in 1944 had an index of 207 (base year: 1937), rose to 268 in 1945, 310 in 1946, and 355 in 1947" (Cueva

1988, 64). The inflationary process was caused, in part, by the government's ambitious road-building program, which had been financed by printing more money. To solve the government's fiscal crisis, Velasco's administration toyed with the idea of renting military bases in the Galapagos Islands to the United States. The left, increasingly alienated from Velasco, protested against this "attempt to surrender the country's sovereignty," and stopped the government's plan.

The climate of political instability, the reluctant acceptance of the 1945 constitution, the conflict between the executive and Congress, and the declining influence of the left led the government to jail and exile some of its opponents and abolish the 1945 Charter. The reason given by Velasco's government was a supposed conspiracy to topple the government. Though Velasco's actions were supported by demonstrations in Quito and Guayaquil (Arízaga Vega 1990, 215) and by fliers that stated "Viva Velasco Ibarra's dictatorship! Down with the Socialist dogs. Velasquistas until death" (BAEP, Hojas volantes, 1946–50, no. 43), most public reactions were antagonistic to the government. Leftist political parties and associations of civil society, such as the CTE and university students, rejected Velasco's dictatorship.

After repressing the opposition, the government called for elections for a new constitutional assembly. Alleging a lack of constitutional guarantees and a climate of repression, the Independent Liberal and the leftist political parties declined to participate. The rightist and independent Velasquistas supported the call to write a new constitution. Given that voting had been made compulsory, participation was no lower than in previous elections. However, the base of support for the new government had been reduced to conservative politicians. "The 1946 constituent assembly, convening in August, confirmed Velasco Ibarra until September 1, 1948, and turned to the task of giving the republic its fifteenth constitution. Promulgated 'in the name of God,' on December 31, the Constitution of 1946 was a moderate instrument. . . . the president was freed from such encumbrances as the court of constitutional guarantees and the permanent legislative commission. Of cardinal significance for the immediate future was the resurrection of the office of vice president" (Blanksten 1951, 54).

Arguing that the country was in economic and political chaos (it had had twenty-eight different cabinet ministers in a little more than three years), Colonel Carlos Mancheno, minister of defense, deposed Velasco Ibarra on 23 August 1947. At first, President Velasco Ibarra, hoping for a popular insurrection to "save democracy," was reluctant to resign. According to *El comercio,* "the night of the coup . . . the public did not react and 'his pueblo,' as Velasco called them in his inflammatory speeches, was not present to offer any opinion" (2 January 1948). Later that night, when he realized that he was left alone, Velasco signed his resignation letter. Velasco's departure to his third political exile did not mean that his political career was over. He was to become president on three further occasions (1952–56, 1960–61, and 1968–72).

A few days later, Colonel Mancheno explained his action with the following words: "All the country was against the personalist regime of Doctor Velasco Ibarra. It is enough to read the Ecuadorian press, both from the left and the right, to convince oneself that for two years people, for a series of reasons, waited for Velasco's fall from power: the economic crisis and the absolute incapacity of the government to solve it; the personalist and antidemocratic character of the regime; Velasco respected laws and the Constitution only when it seemed convenient; he stepped on the laws and the Constitution when he felt like doing so" (*El telégrafo,* 20 September 1947, quoted in Arroyo del Río 1948, 139).

Democracy and La Gloriosa

Throughout Latin America the years immediately following the Second World War brought democratization and political opening. By

1946, with the exception of Paraguay "and a handful of smaller republics in Central America and the Caribbean—El Salvador, Honduras, Nicaragua, and the Dominican Republic—all the Latin American States could claim to be in some sense democratic. At least they were not dictatorships" (Bethell and Roxborough 1988, 170–71). Labor made gains especially by organizing centralized national organizations. And democracy became "a central symbol with almost universal resonance" (176). By 1948, with different timing in each country, the trend was revoked, "the democratic advance was for the most part contained, and in some cases reversed" (168).

Ecuador seems to fit the pattern described by Bethell and Roxborough. The first year of Velasco's second administration was a period of democratic opening. A progressive constitution was written in 1945, and labor—both Catholic and secular—founded and strengthened their central organizations. Also, as in the other republics studied by Bethell and Roxborough, starting in 1945 and 1946, a trend to the right is observed. The left was persecuted, Velasco assumed temporary dictatorial powers, the progressive constitution was replaced by a more conservative charter, and finally in 1947 Velasco himself was toppled by a military coup. If analyzed more profoundly, however, the Ecuadorian case does not fit the pattern. To begin with, the insurrection of 1944 was against a elected civilian regime. Moreover, after the unstable years of Velasco's second term in office, from 1948 until 1961, Ecuador experienced a phase of elected civilian governments. This democratic wave of the 1950s, which has not been deeply researched, cannot be explained by the defeat of the left and other progressive forces and the taming of organized labor, which is the hypothesis of Bethell and Roxborough.

The relationship between La Gloriosa and democracy are therefore worth exploring. The May Revolution, like most historical events, did not end with the fall of Velasco Ibarra in 1947. It is no surprise that the series of events captured under the heading La Gloriosa have been used differently by friends and foes of Velasco. In particular, the

74

left has interpreted it as a missed opportunity to make the revolution, or at least to carry out fundamental democratic reforms. An analysis of these somewhat contradictory interpretations of this event will illuminate the different understandings the participants had of the term *democracy*. In what follows, the interpretations of Arroyo del Río, the official Velasquista account, and leftist politicians are analyzed.

For Velasco's archenemy, Carlos Arroyo del Río, La Gloriosa was yet another coup d'état against a democratically elected regime. In his extensive writings in the mid and late 1940s, Arroyo del Río (1946, 1948) tried to show how ADE was far from an electoral coalition. For him it was a group of conspirators who, motivated by hatred, revolted against the country's constitutional government. The resulting regime was characterized by instability, chaos, and an arbitrary disrespect for civil rights. Granted the excesses of Arroyo's self-defense, the former Liberal president was right in stressing that it was an undemocratic event within an understanding of democracy as the respect for procedures. His election had been approved by the 1940 Congress, and ADE had made plans to carry out an insurrection even before knowing whether fraud would be committed in June 1944. Moreover, Velasco's regime disregarded the civil rights of various opponents and did not respect the Constitution. Yet, Arroyo del Río's government also repressed and hindered the expression of the civil and constitutional rights of his opponents. Thus, there was a lack of respect for fundamental democratic rights and procedures by both Arroyo del Río and Velasco Ibarra, who professed liberalism in their writings. Indeed, this lack of respect for civil rights, including those of the opposition, and of basic human rights and democratic procedures has been a constant in the political scene of the country up to present.

The official Velasquista interpretation characterized La Gloriosa as a democratic reaction against a series of Liberal regimes that had been fraudulently elected, causing the moral degeneration of the nation (Velasco Ibarra 1946; Guevara Moreno 1946). The main accomplishment of La Gloriosa had to be honesty at the polls as the first

and basic step in the moral regeneration of the nation, which also included social justice. Velasquista understanding of democracy as the
respect of procedures—honest elections and basic freedoms such as
freedom of association, expression, and enterprise—was complemented by a belief in plebiscitary democracy. Velasco constantly celebrated crowd action on his behalf, claiming that it was democratic.
These contradictory views of democracy, which could not be reconciled, were not fully implemented. For Velasco and broad political
sectors, the principal cause of the country's problems was the lack of
honest elections. That is why most politicians supported Velasco in
implementing this basic democratic procedure. But, as shown above,
most of the population was excluded from the vote. Also, the 1946
elections for Congress were not free and honest. Velasco's opponents
refused to participate due to repression and the lack of guarantees.
Plebiscitary democracy was not given institutional channels, hence it
was reduced to the noncritical acclamation of the leader in his changing definition of who his allies and his foes were.

Most Marxist politicians and intellectuals had agreed on the need
to unite with bourgeois forces to end the corrupt Liberal-oligarchic
government (Benites Vinueza 1986; Vera 1948). They had a contradictory view of democracy. Although they were fighting to implement
bourgeois democratic rights and struggling at the same time to expand these rights to the social question, they were not theoretically or
normatively committed to preserve these achievements in the future
Socialist society for which they were struggling. Even their support
for Velasco was inconsistent and in some cases opportunistic. Naively
or with good faith, some saw in Velasco the opportunity to get rid
of the Liberals and start a democratization process that included
state support to establish a national lay federation of workers. For
others, Velasco was the opportunity to generate "a mass movement"
(Maldonado Tamayo 1947, 37). After their isolation from the regime
and later repression by Velasco, they claimed that they had been
deceived.

What emerges clearly from the analysis of the term democracy by participants in La Gloriosa is their lack of respect for democratic institutions, which were repeatedly praised in their speeches and published works. In sum, nearly everyone agreed that democracy, as a notion, meant respect for free elections and basic democratic rights, but this principle was only partially honored in practice. Despite their praise for democracy, political actors in the 1940s used the concept strategically for their personal or collective political advantage.

Conclusions

This chapter has argued that the success of Velasco Ibarra's leadership was due to his ability to articulate existing societal grievances and, in so doing, embody the simultaneous desire for electoral democracy and morality that characterized Ecuadorian politics during the 1940s. I have also developed a model to analyze the social construction of populist leaders in movements seeking political power. The socioeconomic conditions of a country at a particular time, the shared if contested frames of discourse, and the patterns of collective violence all have to be studied in their interrelationships to understand the social production of a populist leader. But to research Velasquismo or any populist movement, it is not enough to study its social and discursive production; the role of the political leader also has to be explained. My analysis of the success of Velasco's oratory shows the need, first of all, to know the discursive field in which he articulated his discourse. Velasco's discourse was not the only alternative present in the 1940s, yet it was successful. He not only articulated existing demands, aspirations, and critiques, but he gave them a new form that appeared valid and credible for broad sectors of the population.

Velasco's moralistic transformation of politics into a personalistic and Manichaean struggle between one camp that embodies virtue and another that symbolizes wickedness had profound implications for democracy in the 1940s. Populist movements—and Velasquismo is no exception—incorporated previously excluded people into the political arena. They marked the transition, in Max Weber's terms, from the politics of notables to mass politics. In Ecuador, that transition occurred during the 1939–40 presidential elections, when Velasco Ibarra toured most of the country overland attracting large crowds that included both voters and nonvoters. However, this was a restricted political inclusion because most people were excluded from voting. Moreover, Velasco's followers, who symbolically asserted their citizenship rights between 1939 and 1940 by occupying public spaces, from which they were previously excluded, at the same time negated the right of their adversaries to speak in these newly democratized sites by disrupting political meetings held by other parties. In democratic politics, in contrast, adversary political groups or factions are given a space to exist. They are understood as rivals who have the right to agree or disagree. Populist moralism, however, negates the right of the opposition to exist. The other, their rivals, are transformed into devils whose existence jeopardizes the purity of the nation. The possibility of dissent is denied, and an authoritarian morality is imposed.

Populist Manichaeism not only negates the right of dissent, it also transforms a single individual into the source of all virtue. Therefore it is no surprise that such leaders act as if they are the embodiments of the national will: they *are* the people. Because they embody the people, they are not accountable to any political platform, they instinctively know what is the common good, and whoever is against their plans or policies is an enemy of not only the political leader but the entire nation.

Populist politics tends not to respect democratic procedures or legality. The leaders of ADE decided to carry out a military revolt against a civilian regime that they claimed had come to power through fraud although the honesty of its election had been certified by Congress even before it knew whether the upcoming elections would be fraud-ulent. And, once in power, Velasco Ibarra abolished the constitution of 1945 when he could not impose his definition of the national inter-est within legal constraints. However, in Ecuador in the 1940s, Ve-lasco and his followers were not the only ones who disregarded democratic procedures. As stated above, their Liberal rivals, in spite of assertions to the contrary, were notorious for coming to and staying in power through electoral fraud.

Chapter 3

Leader of the Poor or Repugnant Other?
Abdalá Bucaram's Populismis

FIFTY-THREE YEARS AFTER La Gloriosa, the biggest demonstrations in Ecuador's history took place. On 5 February 1997, two million people took to the streets to peacefully demand that populist President Abdalá Bucaram step down (*¡Que se vaya Bucaram!*). By a simple majority, Congress dismissed Bucaram from office on the grounds of "mental incapacity" the next day. They had no medical proof of the president's insanity and invoked arguments of doubtful legal validity. Congress designated its own president, Fabián Alarcón, as president of the republic. Vice President Rosalía Arteaga proclaimed herself president of Ecuador, and Bucaram himself refused to step down. The military withdrew support from Bucaram, and Congress, the vice president, and the military agreed that a few hours after Arteaga had taken over the presidency she would turn it over to Alarcón until new elections in 1998. This is how the short government of the "leader of the poor" ended. An elected president who had obtained 54 percent of the vote was dismissed after being in office for less than six months, but unlike the past, the military did not take over. Rather, the ex-president of Congress was proclaimed the new "protector" of democracy.

Contrary to the wishes of modernizing politicians and the predictions of many social scientists, populism did not disappear with the death of Velasco Ibarra in 1979. Defying the intentions of a newly legislated system of political domination designed to prevent the cycle of populism and military coup, populist politicians have continued to be important contestants in local and national elections. In the runoff election of July 1996, Abdalá Bucaram was elected with 2,230,841 votes. He drew on popular culture to personify the dignity of common people and present the established elites—the "oligarchy," in his words—as the cause of all evils. His populist movement was an alliance of the very poor with a marginal elite of Lebanese descent, who had acquired economic success but not social status. This coalition included middle-class professionals and some formerly Marxist intellectuals displaced from positions of power and authority. Bucaram was elected to office in a fragmented political system. Since the transition to elected civilian regimes in 1978, more than six candidates have competed for office in each election, and the two finalists, who have obtained less than a third of the total vote, have faced each other in runoffs. The July 1996 elections were no different. Jaime Nebot of the right-wing Partido Social Cristiano (Social Christian Party), who had captured 26.3 percent of the vote, confronted Bucaram, who had obtained 27.2 percent. In this runoff, many electors were not just voting for the populist politician, they were demonstrating their rejection of Nebot's party.

During his short term in office, Bucaram tried to implement a drastic neoliberal economic plan based on convertibility and to apply antipoverty programs to strengthen his base of support. The combination of a populist political style and rhetoric with neoliberal economic policies made Bucaram a neopopulist leader similar to Menem, Fujimori, Salinas de Gortari, and Collor de Mello (Knight 1998; Roberts 1995; Roberts and Arce 1998; Weyland 1996). His economic plan was rejected by the elites who, paradoxically, were going to be the beneficiaries of his reforms. They argued that, due to extensive corruption, they could not trust Bucaram. The cost of living dramatically increased before antipoverty programs had time to work, provoking the poor—Bucaram's electoral base—to demonstrate against the government. In the end, a broad alliance of elites, politicians, the middle class, and popular sectors took to the streets to demand his resignation. What do the election and the semilegal removal of Bucaram from the presidency tell us about the uneasy coexistence of democracy with populism? Why did Bucaram fail to implement a combination of neopopulist and neoliberal policies in the style of the "successful" plans of Menem and Fujimori (Roberts 1995; Roberts and Arce 1998; Weyland 1996)?

This chapter examines Abdalá Bucaram's populist style through the study of two moments of "collective effervescence": the electoral rituals of 1996 that brought him to power and the political mobilization that overthrew his government in February 1997. I analyze the interrelation between politics and daily life to determine how political culture is produced and reproduced in Ecuador. Bucaram has been portrayed as the embodiment of barbarism and unruly rabble. He is seen as a danger not only to democracy, but to civility tout court. This construction of the populist leader and his followers as the embodiment of antireason allows elites to legitimate themselves as the bearers of modernity, reason, and civilization.

Civilization and Barbarism

Abdalá Bucaram is the latest expression of Ecuadorian populism.[1] He has had a convoluted political career that coincides with the last phase of elected civilian regimes. Bucaram was named head of Guayaquil's police by his brother-in-law, President Jaime Roldós.[2] In 1983 Bucaram founded his own party, the Partido Roldosista Ecuatoriano (PRE—Ecuadorian Roldosista Party, named for the deceased president Jaime Roldós). In 1984 Abdalá Bucaram was elected mayor of Guayaquil. Despite a series of political scandals, charges of embezzlement, and a brief incarceration for alleged drug trafficking in Panama, his political career was not destroyed. He received 17.6 percent of the votes in the January 1988 presidential election and 46 percent in the May 1988 runoff, when he was defeated by Rodrigo Borja, a Social Democrat. In the 1992 election, he captured 22 percent of the votes, not enough to go to the runoff. He became president in July 1996 with 54 percent of the total vote in a runoff election against Nebot.

Abdalá's strong presence on the political scene has allowed modernizing intellectuals and politicians to define their own identity by constructing images of what modern political subjects should be. The elite of technocrats, politicians, and intellectuals formed around the growth of the state apparatus in the 1960s and 1970s devised a plan of antioligarchic capitalist modernization. They envisioned a different Ecuador where, in former president Osvaldo Hurtado's words (1988, 337), the socially and politically dominant hacienda system would be replaced by an urban-capitalist society. The hacienda system had excluded most of the rural population from politics through literacy requirements to vote and, most fundamentally, through the power of the hacendados to control rural cultivators. This new society would require a different system of political domination, one based on strong political party competition (Hurtado 1988, 330). Ecuador's recent transition to elected civilian regimes has provided these elites with an opportunity to design what they consider a modern political system.

Ecuador's "transition to democracy" (1976–79) was envisioned not simply as a return to elected civilian governments, but rather as the political complement of the economic and social modernization achieved by Ecuador during the military regimes of the 1970s.[3] Ecuador was transformed from a banana- and cacao-exporting country into an oil-producing nation. This predominantly rural society, where hacendados controlled rural cultivators, saw the erosion of the power of the hacienda system, high levels of urbanization, the growth

of the state, and the expansion of the urban informal sector as well as
the working-class and middle-class sectors. Until approximately the
1960s, traditional haciendas were the dominant institutions. The first
agrarian census showed that in the 1950s, when most of the highland
population (73.8 percent) was rural, "large haciendas monopolized
more than three quarters of the total area" (Zamosc 1994, 43). The hacienda was also a system of "political and ideological domination that
allowed landowners, directly or via the mediation of *mestizo* priests
and village authorities, to monopolize power at local levels" (53). The
agrarian reform laws of the 1960s and 1970s eroded the social and political power of the traditional haciendas. By 1985, 36.2 percent of the
land belonged to large farms, 30.3 percent to medium-sized units,
and 33.5 percent to small units (43). These agrarian transformations
did not finish with the latifundio-minifundio system, and the peas-
ants' "third of the agricultural land is physically insufficient to sustain
the majority of the rural population and invariably includes the highest, driest, and least fertile tracts" (43). Due to insufficient land, "reproduction of the rural household is achieved through complex
combination of agricultural production (for household consumption
and for the market), rural employment, and urban-based labor" (Waters 1997, 55–56). Agrarian transformations nonetheless created a
power vacuum in the countryside that allowed for the eruption of autonomous Indian organizations and the increasing presence of political parties.

Ecuador is currently an urban country. In 1988 urban voters accounted for 75 percent of registered voters (Conaghan 1995, 452). As
in other Latin American nations, capitalist development has not resulted in full proletarianization (Oxhorn 1998; Pérez Sáinz 1986, 76).
Moreover, the crises of the 1980s have diminished the number of
workers employed in manufacturing by 10 percent "from 113,000 in
1980 to 102,00 in 1986" (Zamosc 1994, 52). Industrial workers rely on
various strategies to make up for the lack of adequate family wages
(Pérez Sáinz 1985). Neoliberal adjustment policies have resulted in a

"drastic decline of real wages, which decreased by almost 30 percent between 1980 and 1985 and even further at an annual rate of 8 percent between 1986 and 1990" (Zamosc 1994, 52). Most workers survive in a wide range of informal activities such as street vending, domestic service, and self-employment in microenterprises. Official estimations of the informal sector vary from 41 to 50 percent of the economically active population (Waters 1997, 54).

The social transformations that resulted from urbanization and the transformation of the traditional hacienda system were seen as the precondition for a novel political system. To design new political institutions and create a "modern" political system based on party competition, the military government appointed three commissions composed of representatives of political parties, employers' associations, labor unions, and other organized groups. The commissions enabled modernizing, antioligarchical technocrats and politicians to design a new political system. Their goal was to rationalize the party system to avoid the cycle of populism and military coup that had characterized the country's history since the emergence of Velasquismo. The franchise was expanded from two million to more than four million voters between 1979 and 1988 due to, population growth, voter registration drives, and the elimination of literacy requirements to vote (Conaghan 1995, 450).

The plan to create an electoral political system has been somewhat successful. Ecuador is experiencing its longest phase of elected civilian regimes to date. From 1979 to the present, presidents of different ideological persuasions have succeeded one another in office.[4] Even so, a party-based political system has not been successfully installed. Political parties continue to be weak and numerous. Personalism, clientelism, and populism still characterize political struggles. Political parties, politicians, and politics in general appear discredited in public opinion surveys (Conaghan 1995; Isaacs 1991). The semilegal demise of Bucaram in February 1997 revealed that democracy, even in its more restricted definition as the respect for procedures by political elites, has not become the norm. In light of the persisting importance of clientelism for establishing and maintaining political support (Conaghan 1995, 451; Menéndez-Carrión 1986), it is not surprising that political elites still view "the state as an entity set off against society to be either captured, in whole or in part, and/or to be defended against" (Malloy 1987, 243). The Ecuadorian state is seen as booty, and political elites are more interested in capturing state resources to be able to build and maintain clientelist networks and increase the pool of patronage resources than in respecting democratic procedures once in power (Conaghan 1987). Civilian regimes, ruling in an economic crisis, have applied neoliberal policies, which have further increased social inequalities and political instability. Thus far, the military has abstained from carrying out a coup d'état. Its respect for civilian regimes, however, cannot be explained by a new democratic conversion. More likely, as Anita Isaacs (1993) has argued, the military has been deterred by economic crisis, by the dangers intervention would present to professional unity, and especially by a new international conjuncture. The military has not been subordinated to civilian rule but maintains a series of privileges and veto powers, which, in Brian Loveman's apt characterization, make Ecuador at best a "protected democracy" (1994).

The sobering reality of Ecuador's political system is that common citizens and political elites typically do not behave according to the expectations of the modernizing intellectuals and politicians, who designed the new political institutions. Instead of reflecting on the failure to fully realize this (restricted) conception of democracy, these intellectuals and politicians have defined their own identity by constructing images of who they have considered to be the nonmodern or antimodern populist "other." They have used the actions and words of Abdalá Bucaram to differentiate what they perceive as their own "positive, modern, and rational" politics from "negative irrational" populist politics. Populist leaders and their followers have been constructed as outsiders to the rule of reason and democracy.

86

Populist followers are told that instead of shouting in public plazas in response to demagogues, they should "rationally" consider how to vote in the solitude of their homes. A quixotic task indeed, but one that nonetheless allows "modernizing" elites to prescribe how politics should be conducted and reinforces their self-designation as the moral guides of "modern" Ecuador. Reflecting global changes in political discourse, neoliberalism has become the new dogma and panacea since the 1992 elections, replacing the modernizing social democratic plan of the 1980s.

Today, as in the past, populist politics continues to challenge the restricted character of Ecuadorian democracy. Contrary to the interpretations of many politicians and academics, populism is a specifically modern phenomenon. It is a form of political incorporation and a rhetoric that has been present in Ecuador since the eruption of mass politics sparked by Velasquismo in the late 1930s and early 1940s. Given the ways in which existing conceptions of democracy and citizenship silence and exclude the popular sectors, populist followers continue to seek empowerment by staging mass dramas and occupying public spaces in the name of their leader. The continuing relevance of the rhetoric and mobilization style that appeals to *lo popular* has not been matched by a strengthening of citizenship rights. As in the past, citizenship has been reduced to political rights, even if citizenship is broader nowadays. Civil rights are not respected, and neoliberal economic policies have further reduced limited entitlements to social rights.

Plans for democratization, which appeal to supposedly universalist conceptions of rationality, tend to silence and exclude large segments of the population. "It is important to remember that subjects are constituted through exclusions, that is, through the creation of a domain of deauthorized subjects, presubjects, figures of abjection, populations erased from view" (Butler 1995, 47). Yet, despite elite wishes that the excluded "other" will adapt and conform to proper notions of modern and rational politics, these subjects have not accepted such impositions even if defiance has been articulated through the delegation of power to authoritarian leaders. Populist politics presents an important example of how the marginal "other" does not conform to elitist "democratic" politics.

The Leader of the Poor

Presidential campaigns are rituals that legitimize the liberal-democratic system. Their mass meetings, slogans, marches, flags, songs, and propaganda also serve to mark differences between groups. Moreover, presidential campaigns "orchestrate a national theater of democracy in which candidates seek to display mass support and their followers seek to position themselves favorably within the changing configuration of clientelistic ties" (Coronil and Skurski 1991, 294).

Six presidential campaigns have been successfully completed in Ecuador during the last phase of elected civilian governments (1979 to the present), an impressive record in a country with a history of cycles of civilian and military regimes. Because of the fragmented nature of the Ecuadorian political system, nine candidates competed in the 1996 presidential election, and the two runoff candidates displayed different political styles and programs. Nebot, the candidate of the right-wing Social Christian Party and the protegé of León Febres Cordero (mayor of Guayaquil and former president of Ecuador [1984–88]), obtained 26.3 percent of the vote in May 1996. He presented an image of a responsible statesman with a clear neoliberal plan. Despite his efforts to show independence from Febres Cordero, his candidacy was closely associated with Febres Cordero's regime, remembered by some for its human rights violations and probusiness policies; and by others as a time of law and order. Nebot's candidacy evoked strong feelings of rejection in many who preferred any other candidate to the right-wing neoliberal plan. Abdalá Bucaram, who had 27.2 percent of the vote, presented himself as a rejection of the

88

elites rather than a clear plan. Through humor, music, and mockery, he transformed mass political rallies into spectacles of transgression in which he challenged the elite's power and privileges. Bucaram's transgression, analyzed below, was ambiguous. On the one hand, he questioned the social order when, for instance, he referred to ladies of high society as "a bunch of lazy old women that have never cooked or ironed." On the other hand, he also accepted and strengthened the structural bases of domination. He believed in neoliberalism, professing that it would benefit the poor. Moreover, Bucaram's authoritarian appropriation of the people's will, which he claimed to embody, posed fundamental dangers to the institutionalization of democracy.

Abdalá Bucaram's electoral strategy was based on the performance of political spectacles staged all over the country. These political spectacles combined the show of *el loco* (the crazy one), who sings and dances with the emotion of attending a concert to sing familiar melodies. Through the repetition of ballads by the Uruguayan pop group Los Iracundos, Bucaram created feelings of brotherhood and sisterhood in the plazas. People sang along with him and watched him dance on the platform with Rosalía Arteaga, the vice presidential candidate.

What was the meaning of Bucaram's dance with the vice presidential candidate? The response of the media and the opposition was simple: Bucaram gives the people what they like—bread and circuses. For instance, the well-respected journalist Francisco Febres Cordero wrote: "The singer [Bucaram] gathered all the filth from the most pestilent sewers to throw them at the face of his audience with no other intention than to perform a spectacle" (*Hoy*, 4 July 1996). Sociologically, the image of a politician singing and dancing has deeper meanings. Bucaram explained his performances by comparing himself to President Menem, who sings tangos, and to President Clinton, who plays the saxophone. He also asked his critics: "What man has not charmed a woman by singing a serenade?" Now, using Los Iracundos, the pop group with which he captivated his wife, Bucaram was seducing the Ecuadorian people.

Abdalá Bucaram was not only serenading the people to get their votes, he was also inviting them to see him dance with the future vice president. He always introduced her as a "doctor, a scientist, a journalist, a sociologist, a great teacher, and foremost, a very beautiful woman." Bucaram, a common man, was seducing an attractive woman of a higher social class personified by Rosalía Arteaga. She dressed elegantly, paid great attention to her makeup and hair, and danced like a lady, with poise and serenity. Bucaram dressed casually in jeans and guayaberas. By dancing with a lady from a higher social class, Bucaram was acting out a male sexual fantasy: to dance with and seduce a "lady."

In patriarchal societies, men construct their masculinity in competition with other men. Because men are never sure of their virility, they must prove it constantly to themselves and, above all, to other men by looking for their approval. This is usually accomplished by "conquering" women desired by other men. "Women become a kind of currency that men use to improve their ranking on the masculine social scale" (Kimmel 1994, 129). The preferred women come from a higher social class and fit colonial-racist standards of beauty. Bucaram not only represented the male sexual fantasy of the popular sectors; but instead of referring to his testicles or the quality of his semen (as he did in his 1988 presidential campaign), he showed true manhood by dancing with a lady.

Doris Sommer (1990, 75) argues that several Latin American novels written by novelist-politicians symbolically united the nation by reconciling people of different races, classes, and regions. Bucaram and Arteaga's dance can be read similarly. Latin American gender stereotypes assign women the strength of moral superiority, and their role is to domesticate men's uncontrolled masculinity. Rosalía Arteaga's even temper was harmonized with Bucaram's primitive passion. Rosalía, the educator, was civilizing Bucaram. Their performance was not only a symbol of gender and class reconciliation. It also united in one big Ecuadorian family the main regions of the country—Arteaga's highlands with Bucaram's coast. This was a successful strategy given the history of profound regional differences and animosities. Since the turn of the century different export crops were produced in the coast, and Guayaquil has remained as the center of financial and commercial activity. The highlands specialized in agricultural production for the internal market, with Quito as the center of bureaucractic power. Guayaquil and the other provinces have charged that the capital parasitically appropriates resources. Elites from Guayaquil think of themselves as liberal entrepreneurs free from the tutelage and conservatism of the Catholic Church. Middle- and upper-class highlanders, for their part, think of themselves as more educated and cultured than the rest of their countrymen.

Like other populist politicians, Bucaram personalized politics. Ideologies or concrete electoral proposals were not important; what mattered was the role of personalities as the embodiment of different social classes and lifestyles. Bucaram presented himself as a person from a humble background who not only understood the people, but belonged to el pueblo. Because he was the son of Lebanese immigrants, he was discriminated against by the elites, who considered him a parvenu with poor taste and bad habits.[5] Bucaram's claim to be part of el pueblo is also illustrated by his way of speaking; his penchant for guayaberas and jeans; his passion for playing soccer; his way of eating with a spoon like the poor, rather than a fork and a knife like the rich; and by his love for popular Ecuadorian cooking. Like other populist leaders, Abdalá sought to make clear that even though he was of the pueblo, he was much more than pueblo. In public speeches, interviews, and his books *Las verdades de Abdalá* (1990) and *Golpe de estado* (1998), he narrated in detail how his humble social origins had not prevented him from becoming a successful lawyer, politician, and businessman.

Because Bucaram came from humble origins, he shared the purity of the poor. In Michelet's words, "El pueblo is the new Christ because it embodies two treasures: first is the virtue of sacrifice, and second are instinctual ways of life that are more precious than all the sophisticated knowledge of the so-called cultured men" (Álvarez Junco 1987, 251). That is why Bucaram did not use the cultured language of economists and lawyers. Unlike Nebot's complex economic analysis, Bucaram resorted to commonplaces and generalities. Because problems such as poverty, inadequate housing, and deficient healthcare and education are self-evident, they do not need to be explained with obscure language. To address these problems, he argued, what one needs is a political leader with honesty, virility, and good will.

Abdalá Bucaram is el pueblo because he, too, has suffered. He has been sued, and the people know the class bias of the justice system. The laws and the jails are not for the rich. Thanks to his superior character and great manhood, Bucaram has sacrificed himself for the poor; and like many of them, he has become a martyr. "I paid my political dues, I was exiled, imprisoned, and sued."[6] His purity and dedication to the needs of the people have transformed him into the leader of the poor. These two qualities—his sacrifices for the poor and his simultaneous membership in el pueblo, but also his superiority to most common people—transform a man of humble social origins into a person who deserves to become the president of Ecuador. That is why he said, "I have the right to the presidency of the republic."

Bucaram inverted the meanings of the accusations that he was "crazy" and unfit for the presidency, transforming himself into the beloved *loquito* (the diminutive of loco) Abdalá. He argued that geniuses and leaders with exceptional qualities are often stigmatized as crazy: "They call anyone crazy who lets his mind and imagination run free." The denigrating connotation of Bucaram's epithet *el loco,* unqualified to govern, was transformed into its opposite: the genius who could save the country. Also, he was perceived as an innocent martyr who was jailed on false charges of drug trafficking in Panama. His purity and suffering transformed him into the liberating subject, the new messiah who would save the Ecuadorian people.

Following the Ecuadorian populist tradition, Abdalá Bucaram used religious symbols. Velasco Ibarra had transformed his political speeches into religious representations that evoked Christ's Passion. Unlike Velasco Ibarra, who followed austere Catholic rituals, Bucaram imitated the televangelist style of praising the Lord with music, songs, and the participation of the people. His style also simulated the charismatic Pentecostal leaders who go into trances while adoring God. This is why he jumped off the platform after each speech and walked through the masses. The audience tried to touch their leader, who, like Christ and the Saints, touched the people to heal and redeem them.

Bucaram destroyed the electoral strategy of the Social Christian Party and their motto *primero la gente* (the people first), with the counterslogan *primero los pobres* (the poor come first). Bucaram's slogan articulated an important experience in the quotidian life of common Ecuadorians, the distinction between good people *(la gente)* and the poor. In Ecuador, as in other Latin American countries, there are two different ways in which people interact with each other (Matta 1991, 137–98). On the one hand, there exists a state of law in which all citizens are considered individuals with rights and duties. There is a tradition that believes that the enactment of new laws will guarantee the transformation of society. Laws are created with the intention of solving all economic, social, and political problems. This legalistic tradition coexists with practices designed to escape from following laws. However, as everyone knows, when the law puts its foot down, it does so on the backs of the poor and the helpless. The powerful, in addition to being individuals with rights and duties under a state of law, also become important persons with recognized positions of authority in the community, when it is on their interests. In Bucaram's vocabulary, they become *gente.* They are Colonel X, Doctor Y, or a person with recognized connections with powerful people. Laws will probably not apply to them, or will apply only if it is in their best interest. They can always escape from or shape the law depending on their self-interest.

Like other populist leaders, Bucaram promised to create a family where class, ethnic, and regional divisions would be reconciled under his patriarchal protection. "The family unit became a metaphor for the unification of the fatherland under a central authority which could defend it" (Skurski 1994, 614). Because Bucaram loved the poor, he would protect them by becoming their father. The poor "are both subordinated and subsumed into the figure of the leader" (Rowe and Schelling 1991, 171). The leader claims to know their true interests and sees the poor as children who need his patriarchal protection, and not as citizens with rights and duties.

Bucaram's discourse restored the dignity of those who were constantly treated with disrespect in their everyday lives. In one of several mass public appearances, he engaged in the following dialogue with a middle-aged man attending the rally:

> Let's see, sir, let's talk straight—no bull. I'll show you that you're not Nebot's equal. Sir, with all due respect, if your eighteen-year-old son fell in love with Nebot's daughter, would he let him enter their house? (the public responds "no, no, no, no"). He would throw him out, right? But if Nebot's son impregnated your daughter, what would Nebot say? (With an effeminate voice) "It's just boyish mischief." Is it true or not? ("yes, yes, yes, yes," says the public through applause and screams). Would he give the child his last name? ("no, no, no"). He would force her to have an abortion, take her to prison, or leave her with a bastard child like they have left our homeland.

It is telling that Bucaram chose sexuality to demonstrate how power relations work between unequal groups. His example builds on the daily experiences of poor women, who are the potential targets of harassment, sexual assaults, and dishonor by men from superordinate groups, and also on the humiliation of poor men, who are deprived of their masculinity. This anecdote also shows how the relations between different social groups are marked by unequal access to space. The poor cannot enter the homes of the rich as equals: they are either servants or they are received in the kitchen, not in the dining or living room. These taboos that mark and reproduce inequalities in everyday activities are deeply resented by subordinate groups because the rich have access to their intimate spaces, not only to their homes, but also to "their" women.

Bucaram always spoke about love: he loved el pueblo, he loved the poor, he loved Ecuador. The only ones he did not love were the oligarchy, who were excluded from the "real" Ecuador, personified by Abdalá Bucaram. His Manichaean discourse underscored his authoritarianism. Because he did not clearly define what the oligarchy was, this immoral being, now embodied by the Social Christian Party, could become any of his future rivals. Given that oligarchy is "a state of the soul," it could become anyone who disagreed with how he wanted to interpret the popular will.[7] The ethical construction of the profoundly ambiguous term *el pueblo* allowed him to include in this category wealthy business people who supported him.

Like other populist movements, Bucaram was supported by a multiclass coalition. These groups included an emergent elite of Lebanese descent, popular groups, and "professionals not able to participate in the labor market because of its limitations and their lack of qualifications" (Villavicencio 1988, 24). His political movement was financed by an emergent marginal political and economic elite. Unlike the members of the Syrian and Lebanese community who became integrated into the traditional elite, Bucaram himself, his closest friends and collaborators (Alfredo Adum, who invested two to three million dollars in the campaign; Eduardo Azar; the Salem brothers) are descendants of Lebanese immigrants who have made a lot of money but are excluded from the traditional elite. Some, like Alfredo Adum, are seen by the elites as millionaires who made money from contraband (Diana Jean Schemo, "Populist Victory in Ecuador Worries the Elite," *New York Times,* 22 July 1996, p. A5).

Bucaram's mass political meetings, performed in all regions of the country, in poor neighborhoods and forgotten cities, showed much organization and little political irrationality, contradicting the elitist view of populist followers as disorganized and anomic masses. Many local power brokers took their clients to the plazas. Civic associations like unions, peasant groups, women's organizations, and professional groups were also present. Moreover, many supporters were skeptical of him. Bucaram was not regarded as the messiah he claimed to be. Compared to the Social Christian candidate, he was seen as the lesser of two evils. In his study of Brazilian workers during the presidency of Getulio Vargas (1994), Joel Wolfe shows that workers viewed Vargas differently from the images he projected of himself. Instead of considering Vargas as the father of the poor, workers used the political openings of his regime and his discourse on behalf of the poor to advance their autonomous class interests. Interviews with Bucaram's followers during my ethnographic study of his political rallies in different towns and cities of the coast and the highlands during his 1996 presidential campaign confirmed Wolfe's hypothesis.[8]

In Santa Elena, Guayas province, for example, a peasant leader, after telling the story of the process of expropriation of communal land by landowners linked to the Social Christian Party of Nebot, argued that at least with Bucaram there was the opportunity to struggle against forced land appropriations. He was not optimistic, but knew that with the Social Christians the battle was already over. In the Plaza of San Francisco in Quito, we had a similar conversation with militants of the Socialist Party. They opposed the Social Christian neoliberal plan and had vivid memories of Febres Cordero's (1984–88) authoritarian government. They believed that Bucaram's regime would create a nonrepressive environment that would allow them to organize workers. But they did not hold high hopes for Bucaram and expected that in about a year they would be in the opposition. A local broker from a poor neighborhood of Guayaquil supported Bucaram with everything he had. He knew that he and his clients would be ruined by the Social Christians, whereas Bucaram gave them the opportunity to have access to resources.

As these examples illustrate, Bucaram was considered as a rational alternative within a limited choice between two evils. For the members of his clientelist networks, he was the rational utilitarian choice. For others, the memories of Febres Cordero's authoritarianism and Bucaram's discourse against the oligarchy and on behalf of the poor, together with a lack of a clear economic plan, were enough to give them some hope in the leader of the poor. Bucaram's victory can not be explained solely by his populist political style and rhetoric. In a fragmented political system where electors are given two options in the runoff, for many, he was the lesser of two ills. Many even claimed that this election offered a choice between cancer and AIDS.

By stressing the rationality of Bucaram's followers, I am not privileging a utilitarian concept of rationality. The Ecuadorian electorate is quite utilitarian, and all political parties, regardless of their ideologies, work through clientelistic networks (Burgwal 1995; Conaghan 1995; Menéndez-Carrión 1986). Clientelism, thus, continues to operate as one of the main mechanisms of political control and access to resources that functions in daily life as a concrete problem-solving mechanism. For instance, to have access to education or health benefits, the poor must establish personalized relations with a broker, who belongs to a wider network that guarantees access to people with influence, who can deliver these services. In contexts of extreme poverty and lack of fundamental rights "the vote," as Carlos Vilas argues, "works as the poor's credit card" (1998, 132), which provides limited access to fundamental social services, protection from the police, and even job opportunities.

Bucaram's appeal, however, cannot be based solely on the strength of his clientelist networks. His election was also a result of his use of populist rhetoric and antioligarchical symbols of status. He presented himself as the embodiment of el pueblo. His mannerisms, tastes, and words simultaneously embodied the people and challenged the status symbols of the elites. His antioligarchical stance was nationalistic. He symbolically united the Ecuadorian nation by reconciling different social classes, ethnic groups, regions, and the left and center-left into one common opposition against the Social Christians, who appeared as the embodiment of the antinational oligarchy. His successful strategy to unite these groups was not limited only to agreements with different groups. His mass political meetings and his dance with Rosalía Arteaga also reconciled different classes and regions. His dicourse was very nationalistic. He constructed Ecuador as a country with richness that has been made poor because of the evil and immoral oligarchy. Part of his successful strategy was to avoid using foul language to insult his opposition. He said, "I have to be well-behaved." This was a good strategy against the aggressive campaign of his rivals, who concentrated on the negative aspects of Bucaram to portray Nebot as his opposite—the incarnation of the rationality and seriousness of the modern politician.

The Repugnant Other

On 5 February 1997, less than six months after Bucaram's election, two million people, approximately the same number who had voted for the Leader of the Poor, demanded that Bucaram step down (¡Que se vaya Bucaram!). How can we explain the transformation of the Leader of the Poor into "the repugnant other," who had to be removed from the presidency? What is the meaning of the hatred toward Bucaram expressed by different social classes, associations of civil society, the military, the Catholic Church, political parties, and the U.S. embassy? How can we understand the dismissal, through not very democratic procedures, of an elected president who defined himself as the embodiment of the true popular and national values, in the name of democracy and of the people?[9]

The February mobilizations had their origin in popular opposition to Bucaram's economic program. Although in his electoral campaign he had promised to govern to benefit the poor and had signed agreements with unions against neoliberalism, he never voiced his opposition to these policies.[10] His vague electoral promise was to abolish monopolies. He hoped for an Ecuador "where we can all become business people, where we can all have possibilities to sell . . . not just certain groups that hold monopolies." Bucaram did not question neoliberal policies; instead he proposed that all producers, especially small and medium-sized business would benefit from the opening of the economy. He claimed that the poor have the right to benefit from globalization, and, most important, that they have the right to learn English. In a county were many are "small entrepreneurs" in the informal sector, this strategy was successful. As Alberto Adrianzén (1998, 299) has argued, people employed in informal occupations are interested in the simultaneous expansion of the market and, in the end, of the caste privileges of the traditional elites. Bucaram was not only demanding the democratization of everyday life and the recognition of the worth of common people, his vague electoral promises also saw the market as an arena for the democratization of the assumed benefits of globalization.

Bucaram hired Menem's former minister of economy, Domingo Cavallo, to design an economic program based on convertibility. The aim was to deepen neoliberal economic reforms to attain a projected level of growth of four to five percent a year, create 6,000 new jobs, and tie inflation levels and interest rates to international rates. These policies, based on fiscal discipline, forced the government to look for "new earnings by raising taxes and the charges for public services" (Acosta 1997, 46). In early January "the charges for gas for domestic use were increased by 245 percent, electricity by 300 percent, transportation by 60 percent, and telephones by around 1,000 percent" (*El país*, 6 February 1997, p. 2).

Unions, indigenous groups, students, and other popular organizations quickly responded. On 11 January 1997, the Patriotic Front was formed. This umbrella organization included workers in the United Workers Front; students and teachers in the Popular Front; and the Coordinadora de Movimientos Sociales, which groups together the

Confederation of Indigenous Nationalities of Ecuador, women's groups, petroleum workers, and ecologists. These groups decided to hold a national work stoppage and mass demonstrations on 5 February, to demand the dismissal or resignation of the president and end neoliberal reforms. Student protests began on 10 January, and, by 2 February, indigenous groups blocked the roads.

This national stoppage is part of common people's repertoire of collective action against neoliberal economic policies. Since the recent transition to civilian regimes, more than twenty national strikes have been organized by labor unions (León and Pérez Sáinz 1986). The February mobilizations also included the indigenous organizations that had staged two national uprisings in 1990 and 1994 with demands that ranged from agrarian proposals to a reconsideration of the mestizo national identity (Zamosc 1994). Apart from linking workers with indigenous groups, the novelty of this national mobilization was that business associations joined their class antagonists to demand that the president resign.

The exponential increase in prices of basic goods and services in January 1997 was seen as a hypocritical slap in the face by someone who defined himself as Leader of the Poor in a country where, in 1995, 65 percent of the population lived in poverty (Acosta 1996, 13). Opinion polls of 11 January 1997 showed that 82 percent of poor people in Guayaquil and 87.6 percent in Quito had a negative image of the president (Informe Confidencial 1997). Bucaram's implementation of his economic reform package was poorly timed. He had alienated trade unions that supported his regime when he antagonized his minister of labor, Guadalupe León. He had also offended some leaders of the Confederation of Indigenous Nationalities by intensifying divisions between the Quichuas of the highlands and the Shuars of Amazonia, naming a Shuar as minister of the Ministerio de las Étnias (Ministry of ethnic groups). His populist programs, moreover, did not work. His subsidized milk *abdalac* was documented by the press as unfit for human consumption (Pallares and Cevallos 1997). The televised fund to buy toys for "the Christmas of the poor" was denounced as corrupt because not all the toys got to the children. Finally, he did not have time to implement his goal to build 200,000 subsidized houses for the very poor.

In mid-January, business associations, the Assembly of Quito (chaired by the mayor of the city, Jamil Mahuad, and including such different sectors as intellectuals, business associations, the church, popular organizations, and some notables) and the representatives of the opposition parties joined the national stoppage. So many participants in the event were from the middle and upper classes that a Chilean who had witnessed the anti-Allende demonstrations told a journalist "when high-society ladies join demonstrations, governments fall" (Ortiz 1997, 82).

Entrepreneurs did not trust Bucaram's currency conversion plan. They pointed out that, unlike Argentina, which in 1989 had a 5,000 percent annual inflation rate, Ecuador's moderate level of inflation—around 25 percent—did not justify this plan.[11] The vice president of the chamber of industry, for example, expressed his fear that the opening of the economy would "force many companies out of business" (Diana Jean Schemo, "Ecuador Chief, the Populist, Is Anything but Popular," *New York Times*, 11 January 1997). Businessmen argued that corruption, the intervention by Bucaram's government into private company matters, and the lack of political stability made them distrust Bucaram. Their rejection of Bucaram can also be explained by their fear that privatization would benefit only Bucaram's group of friends and supporters. These fears were based on the corrupt practices of Bucaram's government. For example, they requested a bribe of 10 to 15 percent for any firm to do business with the state.

Upper-class rejection of Bucaram had a long history that went beyond the challenges to his economic policies. Bucaram was perceived by high society as the personification of those who have no manners and are uncultured: "The notion of being cultured is applied to define the border between those who are inside the system and those who are excluded" (Touraine 1989, 154). This is why Bucaram's use of popular values and his defiant style that attracted the popular classes were rejected by the upper classes and by sectors of the middle class that identify with the values of "high society." Upper- and middle-class participants in the February demonstrations emphasized their rejection of Bucaram's vulgarity (Ibarra 1997, 30). In 1988, for example, Bucaram compared himself to President León Febres Cordero by saying, "I have bigger balls than León." While in power, he said that former president Borja was a burro and later apologized to donkeys for the unflattering comparison.

These social classes also rejected Bucaram's use of political spectacle. Following Menem, Bucaram staged his governmental actions as a televised show that represented power as the dramatization of non-political spaces of popular culture such as football and mass entertainment. Bucaram, a former athlete who had participated in the Munich Olympics, became president of Barcelona, Guayaquil's most important soccer team. He recorded a CD, *El loco que ama* (The crazy one who loves), with the pop group Los Iracundos and presented it on national television. He auctioned off his mustache for a million dollars for charity on a televised show where he danced with bleached-blonde models and told jokes. Lorena Bobbit, the Ecuadorian woman who gained notoriety by cutting off her abusive husband's penis, was his honorary guest.

By staging his triumphs in two valued realms of mass culture, Bucaram was representing common people's dreams of success and social mobility: to play soccer with well-known stars or to become a TV show personality. Bucaram's novel use of the mass media also transformed the meaning of politics. "Aesthetic antipolitics subverts the power of words through the power of images. It downgrades political deliberations and decision making to mere acts of backstage performance and as a countermove pushes theatrical forms of action to the center stage of politics. With aesthetic antipolitics the political sphere suffers from intrusion and foreign occupation by the logic of theater and drama, rock and roll, sports and entertainment, design and advertisement" (Schedler 1997, 13).

Using constant media exposure, he attempted to construct his persona as the central political event. His image as a winner in nonpolitical spheres like sports arenas and his transformation into a singer and television star were constantly broadcast into people's homes. He was acting on television for the public while simultaneously transforming the meaning of public political debates. The discussion of his personal life, his dreams, and televised performances became as important as the debates on his policies. That is why his opinions on which soccer players should be hired by Barcelona were announced simultaneously with his defense of his economic program. This constant media exposure also transformed the figure of the president. Instead of following the conventions of a rational bureaucratic ruler, he showed that even though he was the leader of the nation, he was like the common people. He did not follow the rules and protocols expected of a president. He refused to live in Quito's Presidential Palace because he claimed that it was haunted. He preferred to stay in expensive hotels during his short visits to Quito, and to rule from his private home in Guayaquil. He was thus reinforcing regionalist tensions between the highlands and the coast,[12] so that many participants in the February demonstration in Quito said that they were defending "the honor of the capital of the republic" as the center of bureaucratic power.[13]

By not following the rules of official ceremonies based on strict conventions of formality and respect, Bucaram attempted to exercise power in new ways. He staged on television a world of everyday life centered on his private dreams and accomplishments as a substitute for the serious official world of politics. Even the language he used contrasted with the words of rational bureaucratic government. In order to create an intimacy with his followers, he used commonsense expressions and the language of the street, or what Bakhtin calls "marketplace speech and gesture" (1984). By using these colloquialisms, he intended to created an atmosphere of frankness between the president and his followers and to validate the unofficial world of common people. The profanity and verbal improprieties of Bucaram, his ministers, and advisors "were and are still conceived as a break from the established norm of verbal address; they refuse to conform to convention, to etiquette, civility, respectability" (Bakhtin 1984, 187).

Bucaram's style not only explains why he was elected to office, it also partly reveals why he was overthrown. Bucaram's language, gestures, and performances limited his capacity to establish alliances with key institutional players and further antagonized the business elites, the military, politicians, the Catholic Church, and upper- and middle-class journalists, who participated in the construction of public opinion. He had been elected despite the opposition of 90 percent of newspapers editorials (Carrión 1997, 118). For the first time in the history of the country, the most prestigious newspapers and television news shows opposed an elected president. They questioned his unorthodox and flamboyant style, his authoritarian appropriation of the people's will, and the impossibility of having dialogues in which different opinions could be voiced. Bucaram forced journalists to be with him—the leader of the poor—or to be his enemies, allied with the oligarchy. In response to Bucaram's and his collaborators' violent language against reporters, the association of Ecuadorian journalists held a demonstration in Quito in early January. Journalists' democratic opposition to Bucaram and their rejection of his mass-entertainment-based antipolitics coexisted with upper-class prejudices that saw Bucaram as the incarnation of popular culture, and as an embarrassment to the country's civility. This opposition had xenophobic overtones when his detractors focused on his Lebanese origins, and regionalist overtones in the highlands when Bucaram was labeled the embodiment of Guayaquil's rabble. As a representative of a marginal economic and political elite, Bucaram could not control or neutralize the privately owned media, who reproduced upper- and middle-class prejudices. The media constructed him and continues to present him as the embodiment of all the country's ills. Several anti-Bucaram media products have appeared, including television shows, books, a CD, and even a CD-ROM.

Upper-class fears of Bucaram were also a reflection of their anxieties of how quotidian relationships of domination would be restructured after the partial process of democratization that resulted from the abolition of traditional haciendas, urbanization, and relative social mobility. Mary Jackman (1994, 76–77) argues that everyday relations between unequals are marked by a series of rules of etiquette that guarantee that each group remains in its place, thus perpetuating social domination. The subordinated groups have to demonstrate deference to their "superiors." But when the institutions and the structures that regulate their unequal everyday treatment disappear, the dominant groups feel great apprehension. They will not only be questioned about their prerogatives to status, but the possibilities for social mobility will increase. Because Bucaram symbolizes the invasion of the rabble into spaces formerly reserved for high society, his lack of manners and his masculinity threaten the respectability of decent society; his presence provokes horror in the upper class. Elite representations of Bucaram confirm Mary Douglas's argument (1966) that things that are out of order provoke images of pollution. Bucaram symbolized the social mobility and pride of people formerly seen as servants who now demand equal access to spaces formerly reserved for members of high society.

The massive protests that demanded Bucaram's dismissal counted on the support of politicians. Unlike what had happened in Peru, where Fujimori dissolved the congress, Ecuadorian politicians dismissed the elected president. Anti-Bucaram congressional representatives of different ideological tendencies began to meet on 13 January to look for a formula to remove him from the presidency. The key questions were how "to convince representatives that the method used would be effective, and how to choose the figure who would replace Bucaram" (*El comercio*, 19 February 1997). The legal formula was found in the literal application of Article 100 of the Constitution. This article stipulates that the president can be deposed for "mental incapacity" as declared by Congress (Ortiz 1997, 82). With this loophole, they could dismiss the president without a long and heated political trial. Fabián Alarcón, who was elected president of Congress with the support of Bucaram's party, decided to abandon the government in exchange for the presidency of the republic. The next problem was how to secure a majority of the eighty-two congressional votes. The answer was to buy them. Because of the fragmentation of the Ecuadorian political system, presidents who do not have a majority in Congress have exchanged patronage resources for the support of individual congressmen. Elected representatives have been willing to switch parties in exchange for monies that guarantee their capacity to build clientelist networks that will help them be reelected to office. Following conventional practice, Bucaram's government had secured a majority in Congress through vote buying. According to journalists' accounts, the opposition offered one million dollars to congressmen in exchange for their switching sides to the anti-Bucaram camp (Vaca 1997, 20). The result of these schemes secured forty-four votes, enough to dismiss the president. But, to be successful, the politicians needed the approval of the military and the U.S. embassy.

U.S. Ambassador Leslie Alexander met with representatives of the entrepreneurial associations in mid-January to discuss the high level of corruption in Bucaram's government. "This was the first time in which the possibility that Bucaram would leave before finishing his term was discussed. Alexander demanded that any change of government be constitutional" (Ortiz 1997, 76). When, on 30 January, Alexander publicly accused Bucaram's government of corruption, "a lot of people thought that Bucaram had received his last blessings" (Ortiz 1997, 76).

It is worth reflecting on why corruption became the key issue that mobilized the U.S. embassy, opposition politicians, the hierarchy of the Catholic Church, the press and the mass media against Bucaram, and why corruption continues to be remembered as one of his government's worst characteristics. Corruption is an integral component of fragmented political systems based on clientelism and patronage. Presidents who do not control the legislature allocate patronage resources to buy votes to be able to pass legislation and stop the opposition from vetoing their bills. Representatives need money to continue to build clientelist networks and are thus willing to accept resources in exchange for political support. Malloy and Gamarra argue that in these systems "the ruler must constantly expand his support networks, and, therefore, constantly expand the pool of patronage resources. Because the central state becomes the main patrimonial resource, increasingly the executive tends to view the state not as a public phenomenon but as his personal property, by which to maintain his rule" (1987, 105).

In recent years, corruption has become a political issue in Ecuador due to increasing demands from citizens for government accountability. Investigative journalists and civil associations like Manos Limpias (Clean hands) have denounced the illegal use and appropriation of public funds. For instance, Sixto Durán's vice president, Alberto Dahik, had to escape the country in early 1996 to avoid corruption charges (Cornejo 1996). President Durán, who claimed ignorance of the actions of his close associate, was able to complete his term. Unlike Sixto Durán, Bucaram could not survive the accusations of corruption. Bucaram's extensive corruption perhaps transcended "normal" levels (Pachano 1997, 252), or maybe, due to his political insulation and lack of acceptance by traditional elites and political parties, he was more vulnerable to charges of corruption. Reflecting on the overthrow of Fernando Collor de Mello, Kurt Weyland argues that "corruption in and of itself, is not sufficient to bring a politician down; it becomes politically fatal only when employed as a weapon by powerful adversaries" (1993, 3). It became lethal in Ecuador because Bucaram was insulated from key institutional players and did not have the resources to fight against the increasing number of powerful antagonists, such as business elites, opposition politicians, the press, the U.S. embassy, and an array of popular and middle-class organizations.

Civilians relied on the military to solve their own problems. Bucaram had involved the military in his government, thereby interfer-
ing with the internal unity of the armed forces. One of his first actions
was to militarize the customs office to stop corruption. The continuing corruption in customs, in which Bucaram's son was involved, led
the military to ask to be removed from this duty in December 1996.
Bucaram also involved the military in the distribution of Christmas
toys, which was denounced as corrupt. The appointment of Víctor
Manuel Bayas as minister of defense was not approved by many high-
ranking officers. Finally, General Paco Moncayo, considered a hero in
the last armed conflict with Peru in 1995, "was condemned to a kind
of exile by Bucaram's government, his destiny was to wait until February," when he would be replaced (Ortiz 1997, 79).

Bucaram's visit to Peru and his emotional declarations that the
two countries should ask (one another's) pardon in the name of peace
were used by politicians to involve the armed forces in opposition to
the president. Former presidents León Febres Cordero and Rodrigo
Borja declared that Bucaram had betrayed the country by asking for-
giveness from Peru. Lastly, the semilegal dismissal of Bucaram and
the legally suspicious proclamation of Alarcón as the new president
named the military referees of the political destiny of Ecuador.

Conclusions

Bucaram's populist movement was a multiclass alliance of the marginalized, a group not understood as the informal poor, but as those
who are excluded from power. Economic elites without social prestige looked to replace the established elites and legitimize their
fortunes of questionable origin. The poor rebelled against their
employer's candidate, and displaced professionals and intellectuals
looked for positions of authority in Bucaram's coalition. The electoral success of Abdalá Bucaram is explained by the way in which his
campaign validated elements of popular culture. He presented him-

self as a common man who had been unjustly persecuted by the oligarchy. He also claimed to be a superior man because, despite his humble origins, he was educated, had made a fortune, and could now embody the people's will. Bucaram also used religious elements of popular culture, especially of the Protestant sects, to present himself as a new Christ, the new messiah who would redeem the people from their suffering. He validated mestizo popular culture as the essence of true Ecuadorianess, in contrast to the foreign, imported values of the oligarchy. Finally, Abdalá Bucaram presented his own virility as a form of resistance to "effeminate" elites, affirming the masculinity of the poor. He also denounced the age-old humiliations that elite women inflict on servant women, presenting common women as the essence of true womanhood. He seduced poor women with his gallantry, with attacks on the privileges of the elites, and with his defense of their dignity and self-worth. But this vindication of a *machista* popular culture accepts and reproduces an authoritarian culture based on the subordination of women. Bucaram's use of his sexuality to challenge the privileges of the well-established elites was authoritarian. By staging male sexual dreams such as seducing ladies from high society or dancing with attractive models on television, he was symbolically democratizing the access by all men, especially common men, to the gender privileges of elite men. In this way, he was broadening the authoritarian male pact of domination based on the subordination of all women (Cuvi and Martínez 1997). Even his defense of poor women's sexuality was based on the notion that their men have been emasculated by elite men and that to become equals they should have the same gender privileges as elite men (i.e., access to any women and the resources to protect them from other men). However, given the importance of class-specific grievances, it is questionable that poor women interpreted his displays of masculinity through a middle-class feminist lens.

Following the populist tradition that Velasco Ibarra had inaugurated in the late 1930s and 1940s, Bucaram's performances in the plazas gave to the popular sectors the sensation of being participants in the political scene. But in these dramas, in which the domination of the oligarchy is questioned and popular culture is vindicated, the script has already been written. The poor and the humble feel like participants but do not write their own script. They delegate power to an authoritarian politician who claims to embody their will.

Illustrating what Clifford Geertz calls the paradoxes of charisma, Bucaram's flamboyant populist movement appeared "amongst people at some distance from the center, indeed . . . at a rather enormous distance, who want[ed] very much to be closer" (1985, 31). However, due to his social origin but, most important, because of his style and rhetoric, Bucaram could not become part of the center of the social order. He was not able to establish alliances with key institutional players. The upper and middle classes were repelled by his language, eating habits, and presentation of self that, in their view, constituted the eruption of the barbaric rabble. Businessmen felt excluded from the potential benefits of privatization and questioned Bucaram's economic policies, which, in principle, would have benefited some of them. Unlike the situations in Peru and Argentina when Fujimori and Menem assumed power, relatively low inflation meant that entrepreneurs were not willing to accept any means to end the crisis. Politicians were not given opportunities to enter into pacts and agreements with the government. In a perfect example of what Guillermo O'Donnell (1994) characterizes as a "delegative democracy," Bucaram trapped politicians in the short-term logic of unconditional support or total opposition. When they had the opportunity, they did not hesitate to use any means to oust him from power. Bucaram had a very bad relationship with the armed forces. He interfered with the internal unity of this institution. When the politicians knocked on their barracks, they acted with serenity, did not use violence, and became the mediators and judges of the country's destiny. Although they did not assume power, they accepted the semilegal acts of Congress.

Once in power, Abdalá Bucaram considered himself the incarnation of popular and national will, and he acted against those who had voted for him. His aggressive, arrogant style cut short possibilities of dialogue with indigenous and union leaders. Unlike Menem and Fujimori, his populist policies targeting the very poor (such as his housing program, the abdalac milk, and Christmas for the poor) failed because of corruption and poor planning. His economic package ended his honeymoon with the poor at a moment when he had not yet secured patronage and clientelist networks that would have guaranteed unconditional support.

Ecuadorian democracy was further weakened after Bucaram's presidency. Because politicians did not follow constitutional procedures to oust the president, many of his supporters accepted Bucaram's interpretation that the oligarchy had illegally overthrown him. Despite all the accusations of corruption against Bucaram and his party, the Partido Roldosista Ecuatoriano (PRE) continues to be the county's third electoral force in the Congress. The strength of Bucaram's base of support was dramatically revealed in the last presidential elections when Álvaro Noboa, the PRE's candidate and a millionaire political outsider, entered into the runoff and narrowly lost the election. Whereas the candidate of the center-right Popular Democracy, Jamil Mahuad, got 2,242,836 votes in July 1998, Noboa captured 2,140,628 votes, losing only by approximately 102,000 votes (2 percent of the total). Noboa's accusation that there had been electoral fraud was well received by many of his supporters, who staged violent acts to demand that each vote be recounted. Jamil Mahuad, the new president, started his term not only with a weak electoral mandate, but also with accusations of fraud.

The Return of Bucaram

Abdalá Bucaram returned to Ecuador on 2 April 2005, the day Pope John Paul II died.[14] He came back to Guayaquil, after eight years of self-imposed exile in Panama, due to accusations of embezzlement during his presidency. The charges included corrupt customs practices (in which his son was rumored to have made $1 million), the purchase of overpriced and defective school supplies, and misappropriation of discretionary funds (Conaghan 2008b, 251). However, the charges were dropped by the new president of the Supreme Court of Justice, Guillermo Castro, a friend of Bucaram since their childhood (258). President Lucio Gutiérrez replaced the previous supreme court, which he claimed was controlled by the Partido Social Cristiano (Social Christian Party, PSC) and by former president León Febres Cordero, with a new court staffed by militants and sympathizers of the country's populist parties, Bucaram's Partido Roldosista Ecuatoriano (Ecuadorian Roldosista Party, PRE) and Álvaro Noboa's Partido Renovador Institucional Acción Nacional (Institutional Renewal Party of National Action, PRIAN). Gutiérrez sought the support of these parties in order to stop threats of a political trial and possible destitution by congressional representatives from the Social Christian and Social Democratic parties. Running as an outsider, Lucio Gutiérrez ascended to power in 2002, despite not having the support of a strong political party. With the support of only five representatives out of one hundred, he was forced to seek alliances with other parties. Initially, he was supported by the left-leaning Pachakutik, then by the right Social Christian Party, and after his alliance with the Social Christians deteriorated, he sought the support of PRIAN and the PRE. The second of the two parties lent its support to the president in exchange for his allowing Bucaram's return (Conaghan 2008b).

Bucaram's arrival became a media event broadcast live by all the country's major television stations. It also represented one of the main reasons why middle-class people in Quito took to the streets to demonstrate against Gutiérrez later in April. Congress used these demonstrations as justification for ousting President Gutiérrez after the armed forces declared that they could not longer preserve public order. For media commentators and opinion makers, as well as for most middle- and upper-class citizens, Bucaram's return symbolized the lack of moral values of Gutiérrez's administration. Gutiérrez was portrayed as a corrupt figure who had illegally appointed a new supreme court with men of dubious ethical principles, such as Gulliermo Castro, who valued his friendship with Bucaram more than the rule of law. Citizens expressed outrage toward the media because of the decision to publicize and transmit live Bucaram's return to Guayaquil. But despite these negative feelings, for the members of Bucaram's political party as well as for his family, this was a moment of euphoria. The party wanted to rebuild itself after losing ground to other personalistic parties, such as Álvaro Noboa's PRIAN, and to Gutiérrez's Sociedad Patriótica (Patriotic Society). There was even speculation about a possible alliance between Lucio Gutiérrez and Abdalá Bucaram for the coming 2006 presidential elections.

Rather than a political celebration, many of those in attendance at Bucaram's return were enticed by a free show featuring the retro-pop Uruguayan band Los Iracundos. They also expected to see Bucaram in the flesh, and to experience firsthand how "the *loco*" would criticize Guayaquil's oligarchy, poke fun at the rich, and possibly perform spectacular tricks, such as arriving in a helicopter or jumping into the crowd in rock star fashion.

"CRAZY ENOUGH TO SMASH THE SOUL OF THE ECUADORIAN OLIGARCHY"

Organizers had only two days to put together his homecoming reception. From early in the morning on April 2, Bucaram's party began to distribute banners, T-shirts, and stickers with messianic messages. The slogans contained phrases such as "Only God knows how much we had suffered during your absence"; "Abdalá my passion"; "Save your people"; and "Tremble with fear because I came back." Buses carrying people from many provinces and rural areas started to arrive in Guayaquil in the afternoon. Many of these travelers came because they were urged by caciques and local politicians. Others went out of curiosity to see the loco. Party militants and loyal followers came to welcome their leader. Couples wore their Sunday best; families, neighborhood associations, and peasant organizations all went to see free music and a political event. Many youngsters acted as if they were going to a concert—not a political rally—and drank the alcoholic beverages provided by the organizers. However, order was maintained and people remained peaceful. Older women and men controlled the crowd, reminding them that there were many children there and that they needed to stay calm. The weather was very hot, and informal vendors made a good profit selling water, soda, and beer. The Iracundos played and people sang along to tunes that continue to be popular, especially around Saint Valentine's Day. Bucaram's loyalists remembered the tunes he had used in his 1996 presidential campaign and during his presidency and prompted the crowd to sing along to these as well.

When the crowd saw the helicopter transporting Abdalá, an eruption of euphoria ensued. Bucaram landed on top of a building in Guayaquil's most important commercial street, Ninth of October Avenue. Bucaram and his eldest son, Jacobo, stood in the bed of a pickup truck that slowly moved toward the platform assembled for the event. Waiting atop the stage were the Iracundos, Abdalá's wife, their younger sons and daughter with their girlfriends and boyfriend, other relatives, and top PRE officials. A group of strongmen walked in front of the pickup, and the crowd tried its best to allow it to pass. When Bucaram passed in front of us smiling, agitating his fist, and jumping euphorically, the crowd responded by laughing and yelling, "Loco son of a bitch." After the truck went by, a group of coastal cowboys rode past on horseback, miraculously injuring no one in the crowd. When Bucaram reached the stage he and Jacobo, who is overweight, were helped onto the platform by their bodyguards.

Bucaram's public appearance and speech evoked jubilation because people felt close to their leader. These feelings helped promote the hierarchical order inscribed by the performance. Bucaram and his family positioned themselves on the high stage, looking down upon his people in the street. The people were thus close and yet far away from their leader. Many men tried to climb the platform to touch Bucaram but were stopped by his private security personnel. From the stage Bucaram promised to redeem the people, but it appeared as if he did not respect them because he had made them wait for hours under the equatorial sun. Nor did he appear concerned for their safety, as his truck or the horses could have easily run over one of his supporters in the packed street.

Because the wait was so long, speeches were kept short. As during his campaign in 1996, Bucaram employed a melancholic tone of voice to refer to his sufferings and those of his family that are not other than the suffering of his people. His tone became virile while he hurled accusations with fury against the oligarchy. Bucaram asserted that he had grown older and perhaps had become "crazy enough to smash the soul of the Ecuadorian oligarchy." He made fun of Social Christian politicians, portraying them as weak and effeminate. Abdalá did not miss the opportunity to insult his archrival, former president León Febres Cordero, calling him an "old marijuana smoker." The main topics of his oration were his family and his people.

BUCARAM'S EXTENDED FAMILY

Bucaram's return was undoubtedly a family event. Abdalá began his discourse by thanking Omar Quintana (president of Congress and his close friend) and his own family, using the nicknames that he probably uses in his home. He talked about intimate family problems. For instance, he disclosed that his eldest son has weight problems that started "when he was seven years old [because] Febres Cordero kicked him in Panama, when they took me to jail accusing me of international drug trafficking. Jacobito, my son, I have come back to Ecuador."

He invited the crowd to become part of his family. He presented himself as the father of his party, whose top leadership is crowded with his relatives and close friends. He also argued that he is the father of his poor, and of his blacks of the Province of Esmeraldas. The lines separating the public from the private became blurred. His party, the nation, and his poor belong to the Roldosista "family" and will be redeemed by him, the family patriarch. Oligarchs are excluded from his love and from his nation. His people share his interests and identities. They belong to the same moral community incarnated in his new fatherly figure. The blurring of the private and the public also explains why there was so much corruption during his tenure as president; because there is an identity between his state, his nation, and his people why should he have to be accountable to anyone? A populist leader claims to embody the virtues of the nation and of his people. By usurping the will of the people, he also locates himself beyond the norms and procedures of accountability of a liberal democracy. The redeemer, who knows the needs of his people, is embarked on a struggle for moral and transcendental values. His task is to "lead the revolution of the poor, the revolution of the hungry." Thus, since his mission is divine, he asserted that the pope "did not want to die until the leader of the homeland had returned home." Then, Bucaram requested a minute of silence in memory of the Holy Father.

THE PEOPLE

Bucaram addressed the crowd as the "poor of my homeland." Every time he used the phrase *the poor,* the crowd responded with an ovation. Abdalá contrasted his welcoming ceremony to the White March, organized by Jaime Nebot, major of Guayaquil, and by the Social Christian Party in January 2005. He asserted that, unlike the march against insecurity and against Gutiérrez' government, where mostly white middle-class people participated, "Here there are not only the whites, the blondes, the white butts, the blue eyes. Here are the blacks, the *cholos,* the Indians, the workers; the poor of my homeland."

One of the objectives of the organizers was to present a different picture of the poor than that represented in the views held by the rich and by the media. Many speakers commented that the crowd was organized, educated, well behaved, and well mannered. The people responded by not following the stereotypes about the rabble that the media continuously reproduces. No fights broke out, nor did the crowd pillage or steal from luxury stores. Moreover, the people patiently endured many hours under the sun and survived the imprudence of organizers who put horses in an overcrowded avenue. Many went to see an event with a predictable script. They were not disappointed. Bucaram arrived in a helicopter; he was close to yet distant from the crowd; he used foul language to mock the oligarchy; he even doused himself with a glass of water.

Many people who went to see Bucaram told me that they did not believe he was the answer to all their problems, such as poverty or unemployment. They acknowledged that Bucaram is corrupt but noted that he is not the only corrupt politician, yet he is the most persecuted, not because of his corruption but because of his struggle against the oligarchy. A few said that, unlike other politicians, Bucaram gives them "hope and good vibes." The hope, that he might redeem them from the humiliations that they have to endure daily at the hands of the powerful. The good vibes he generated with his jokes and insults at the expense of the rich and powerful permeated the crowd. A few were not interested in listening to the words of the "leader of the poor." They went to enjoy a free trip from the countryside to Guayaquil, a free concert, and the food and beverages distributed by their caciques. Many left the event before the speeches had begun. But most probably went to enjoy the insults to the oligarchs and to listen to Bucaram's glorification of the people.

This event was organized to be watched on television. Not even the death of the charismatic pope prevented the media in this predominantly Catholic nation from broadcasting live Bucaram's return. And its status as a media event was highlighted by the choice of site, Ninth of October Avenue, which has become one of the symbols of urban renewal under the Social Christian Party. This street was also recently filled by supporters of Social Christian mayor Jaime Nebot during a massive demonstration against Gutiérrez called the White March. A goal of the organizers was to show the nation that Bucaram's party, the PRE, still has the power to organize a mass rally. Another goal was to symbolically take away this symbol of urban renewal from the PSC. For the first time since I have been studying Abdalá Bucaram, organizers set up television screens in the streets so people could watch the event without crowding the stage. Also, they could watch the same images as other television viewers but with the advantage of being at the center of this media event, being close to their leader, his party, and the family of the Roldosista Party.

The meaning of Bucaram's return was to an extent determined by people's social class and politics. For some this was a nightmare for democracy. It showed the lack of accountability, the unrule of law, and the free reign of corruption. For others, Bucaram's welcoming ceremony was the incarnation of vulgarity. Seeing Abdalá on TV, sweaty and overweight, with his shirt unbuttoned and showing his gold chains and glitter, climbing on a horse to leave the stage as a cowboy, reminded them of the vulgarity of Bucaram's presidency. Fresh memories of media images of former president Bucaram eating with a spoon, gulping Pepsi directly from the bottle, or dancing with bleach blond models came back to their minds. Many organizers spent money on this event in the hope of getting a return for their investment in a future government of the leader of the poor. To the majority of spectators, the poor, Bucaram again offered material and spiritual redemption. "Give me your vote I will give you a school," he promised. Above all, he offered "empathy" and "dignified Ecuadorian soil where you can live with your head up."

Chapter 4

The Continuing Populist Temptation

THE ELECTORAL SUCCESS of political mavericks such as Fujimori in Peru, Silvio Berlusconi in Italy, Menem in Argentina, Ross Perot in the United States, Jean-Marie Le Pen of France's National Front, Collor in Brazil, Bucaram in Ecuador, and an array of local right-wing politicians in Western Europe (Betz 1994) is explained in the literature as a result of a widespread sense of economic, political, and ideological crises. The argument is that the profound socioeconomic transformations that have resulted from increasing globalization and the restructuring of the state have produced a sense of insecurity and distrust in traditional mechanisms of political representation. Political parties that once mediated between the state and civil society have entered into a profound crisis (Offe 1984; Novaro 1996). New forms of political representation that include but are not reduced to the emergence of self-designed national saviors have appeared and are replacing political parties.

Most authors see an affinity between the words and the images presented by these new politicians and the feelings of the electorate. These politicians have used their success in nonpolitical areas such

as the business world (Perot, Berlusconi) or sports (Collor, Berlusconi) to represent themselves as political outsiders. These new political figures have given voice to the perceptions that these crises are
politicians' fault, and that only political outsiders like themselves have
the capacity to solve these problems pragmatically and nonideologi-
cally. Social scientists have used the categories "neopopulism" (Mayorga 1998; Novaro 1994, 1996; Roberts 1995; Weyland 1996) or "the
politics of antipolitics" (Panfichi 1997; Schedler 1996, 1997) to explain why these "new" leaders emerge and to discuss their impact on
democratic politics.

The fundamental social and economic transformations associated
in Latin America with the crises of import substitution industrialization, the end of nationalist and distributive state policies, the increasing levels of poverty and of people precariously employed in the
informal sector, and the quandaries of class-based politics and ideologies explain the ascent of these "electoral caudillos of postmodernity"
(Vilas 1995a). By focusing on the structural transformations of the
economy and class structure, researchers can thus explain the differences between movements usually labeled as classically populist and
these new experiences. The base of support for neopopulism, for example, includes alliances between emergent elites with the very poor,
excluding the industrial bourgeoisie and the organized working and
middle classes, which were the advocates of classical populism. Neopopulist leaders have also pursued economic policies that contradict
the classical populist recipe. Their neoliberal economic policies based
on privatization and the reduction of the size of the state and the
opening of the economy are so fundamentally different from the policies of their predecessors that many analysts have questioned the use
of the term *populism,* even with the prefix *neo-,* to analyze the governments of Menem, Fujimori, Collor de Mello, or Bucaram (Quijano
1998; Sánchez Parga 1998). However, as Kenneth Roberts (1995) and
Kurt Weyland (1996) have demonstrated, macroeconomic policies that
are exclusionary and antipopular go together with microdistributive

policies that partially include the very poor at the expense of the organized sectors who were the beneficiaries of import substitution.

Whether or not the categories populism or neopopulism are adopted, researchers still have to identify the political, cultural, and material relationships between leaders and led. The study of structural social and economic transformations that explain why these leaders emerge and an analysis of their different economic policies cannot replace the research on more narrowly defined political questions, such as how these new leaders get into office, what are their political styles, and what is their impact on newly installed democracies.

Quoting Gordon Allport, José Nun (1994, 94), asserts that social scientists tend not to solve their research problems, they simply get bored with them and end up submitting the prefix *neo-* when they reintroduce their previously unresolved research questions. The debates on populism and neopopulism illustrate this trend. The attempts by modernization, dependency, and discourse analysis theoreticians to develop an all-inclusive theory of Latin American populism ended in fierce debates without many agreements. The term *populism,* hence, became a contested category that referred to such an array of historical experiences that many objected to its academic usefulness. In the 1990s, after the elections of Collor, Fujimori, and Menem, the concept of populism was reintroduced with the prefix *neo-* to account for the different class alliances and economic policies between classical and new populist experiences. As the concept was offered, the unresolved questions raised by previous debates have reappeared. Some dubious notions—such as a reified idea of crisis, the theory of available masses, and the recourse to the notion of manipulation—that guided previous research on classical populism have reappeared in the debates on neopopulism. This chapter critically reviews these controversies by focusing on how social scientists explain the concrete mechanism that articulates the relationship between leaders and followers, and how they analyze the tensions between liberal-democratic regimes and populist appeals to the people.

On Crises

The thrust of the structuralist argument developed by influential Latin American analysts such as Guillermo O'Donnell (1994), José Nun (1994), and Carlos Vilas (1995a) is that, as in the past, when the crises of the oligarchical order based on an agro-export model of development gave birth to classical populism associated with import substitution industrialization, the transition to a new socioeconomic order is giving shape to new forms of political participation. The crisis of the oligarchical state and the agro-export development model in the 1930s and the crisis of import substitution industrialization, the debt crisis, and the increasing globalization of the economy in the 1980s and 1990s are certainly related to the sense of insecurity and exclusion of the electorate that is used by populist leaders to get elected. But, because, as Alan Knight argues, the notion of crisis "is a vague, promiscuously used, under-theorized concept which defies measurement and lacks explanatory power" (1998, 227), it cannot account for why populist politics and not class politics, for instance, are the vehicles through which common people interpret their perceptions of crises. The appeal of populist or class-based rhetoric or, for that matter, any other type of political discourse in a particular historical conjuncture still cannot be explained by the recurrence of a reified notion of crisis. As E. P. Thompson (1971) argued long ago, economic crises are experienced through common people's values, norms, and prejudices. The economy is always culturally mediated.

The notion of crisis cannot account for the continuous allure of populism in nations such as Argentina, Brazil, Ecuador, Peru, and Bolivia either. In these countries, populist politicians, when allowed by the military, have been strong contestants in local and in national elections from the 1930s and 1940s to the present. Populism has been the norm rather than the exception, as implied by the notion of crisis and has existed "in 'normal,' 'non-critical' times" (Knight 1998, 227).

If populism is reduced to an expression of crisis, it is viewed as a temporary phenomenon. The resolution of the crisis will either bring back what was considered to be "normal" politics or result in a new political configuration. Populism old or new continues to be interpreted as a temporary stage, a transitory phase that will eventually disappear. The critics of modernization theory and orthodox Marxists models of class formation illustrated the dangers of using binary models that artificially divide politics and, more generally, collective action into the normal and the abnormal. In these constructs, the theorist prescribes what he or she considers to be the norm and relegates the abnormal to moral condemnation or explains it as a deviation from the arbitrarily constructed universal norm. Populism, like other political phenomena such as parties, unions, and revolutions, continues to be compared with what Alan Knight calls a "mythical European standard" (1998, 238). These old practices of analyzing Latin America through what Aníbal Quijano (1998) calls Eurocentric lenses by constructing highly idealized models of Western politics that are compared to the Latin American "deviation from the norm" have not allowed us to fully understand what is particular to Latin America or to explain and interpret it in its own right. Instead of analyzing populism or neopopulism by focusing on their "negative characteristics, and deficiencies" when compared to romanticized Western models of politics, we need to focus on what these phenomena are (Mackinnon and Petrone 1998, 44).

By giving too much weight to social and economic transformations, the specificity of politics tends to be lost. The analysis of classical populism as the political counterpart of import substitution industrialization (ISI), for instance, has been shown to be untenable. "ISI is not established as the causal agent of populism" (Perruci and Sanderson 1989, 35). Populism preceded ISI in the classical examples of Brazil, Mexico, and Argentina and, contrary to its premature death sentence, did not disappear with the crisis of ISI. Populism, and politics more generally, cannot be explained as a reflection of supposedly deeper structural forces such as the economy, which does not mean the absolute autonomy of the political because social and economic processes set limits and constraints on politics. For instance, the everyday humiliations of the poor, used by populist leaders in their politically motivated claims to incarnate the underdog, are economic and social in nature. A political reading might offer a better explanation of the continuous resilience of populist movements seeking power.

My hypothesis is that the attraction of populism should be explained by the particular form of political incorporation in Latin America: one based on weak citizenship rights and strong rhetorical appeals to, and mobilization of, el pueblo. In Latin America, there is a duality between the official recognition of rights in constitutions and the rhetoric of state officials and the weak implementation of these same rights in everyday life (Chevigny 1995; Pinheiro 1994, 1997). This differs from the Western pattern of political inclusion, where rights are universal and people are citizens with rights and duties that give them entitlements, protections, and obligations. There is a distinction between common citizens, who are subjects of law, and a few important persons of the community, who, in addition to enjoying their citizenship rights when it is for their convenience, are also beyond or above the law (Matta 1991). Because constitutional civil rights do not protect all people in their everyday interactions as equals vis à vis the state and other citizens, the poor and the excluded have to rely on powerful patrons who can protect them from the arbitrariness of the police or from the rich. "Institutional rules are less important in these situations than personal arrangements and connections based on reciprocities" (Vilas 1997, 19). The schizophrenic coexistence of universal rights in the solemn declarations of the state and the lack of implementation of these same rights in everyday life explain why the poor search for a benefactor. This protector can be an employer, but more commonly, because so many of the poor are self-employed or their patrons are unwilling to protect them, it is a politician. The poor and the excluded have been incorporated as members of political clienteles or, a few, as members of corporatist groups such as blue-collar workers or state officials. "Relational loyalties based on no legal or ideological commitment" (Matta 1987, 321) guarantee access to state resources and the fulfillment of legally prescribed but not implemented constitutional rights. By participating in clientelist networks, common people not only gain access to economic resources, they are also included in networks that generate particular political identities and a sense of community. In many cases these networks have generated plebeian identities that constitute the poor, those at the bottom of society, the nonwhite, as the essence of the real nation (Franco 1990, 46–47).

Strong rhetorical appeals to subaltern groups as el pueblo and as the real nation have accompanied movements that have conceived of democracy as a form of direct popular participation, the occupation of public spaces, the acclamation of their leader, and the booing of opponents (Álvarez Junco 1994, 26–27). This understanding of democracy that does not always respect the norms of liberal-democratic procedures has become part of the political repertoire of popular collective action. These political traditions that express how common people have been incorporated into politics, that are used by most politicians, and that sometimes can be effective in bringing changes in favor of the popular sectors are always present. The populist temptation, or its possibility, is always there. What is needed are particular circumstances where these populist appeals will work over alternative discourses. Times of economic crises, change, and insecurity, or perhaps distrust in models of formal democracy that do not deliver material goods or provide a sense of belonging to the system and that are used by elites to silence and exclude the "other" explain why populism, contrary to the wishes of modernizing politicians and intellectuals, has not disappeared and constantly reemerges.

This emphasis on populism as a specific modern phenomenon that has been the result of particular forms of political incorporation

of ordinary people into the political community and that has been at
best ambiguous for the democratization of Latin America does not
mean that I am writing an apology for populism. On the contrary,
normatively I disagree with these semiauthoritarian, and at the same
time semidemocratic, phenomena. What I am suggesting, following
Carlos Franco, rather is "that those who want to transcend populism
should start by accepting it" (Franco, Cotler, and Rochabrún 1991,
116), and to do so, populism needs to be studied as what it is and not
what it is not (Mackinnon and Petrone 1998, 44).

On "Available Masses"

If the word crisis is the favorite term used to explain why these movements have reappeared, the idea that leaders manipulate "anomic and
available masses" continues to be the standard explanation for their
appeal. Kurt Weyland, for example, argues that the "unorganized,
largely poor people in the informal sector" have become available for
neopopulist mobilization (1996, 10). Kenneth Roberts concludes his
analysis of Peruvian neopopulism with the affirmation that the "fragmentation of civil society, a destructuring of institutional linkages,
and an erosion of collective identities [enabled] personalist leaders to
establish vertical, unmediated relationships with atomized masses"
(1995, 113).

Even Marxists who have rejected the term *neopopulism,* such as
Carlos Vilas and Aníbal Quijano, have returned to Germani's notion
of available masses (1971). Vilas (1995a) argues that unlike the strong
class identities of classical populism, the erosion of collective identities as a result of neoliberal economic policies has resulted in the creation of "available masses" that need to be integrated into the political
system. Aníbal Quijano (1998) also returns to notions of manipulation when he explains Fujimori's success as a result of an economic,
political, ideological, and identity crisis that has left the popular

sectors without the capacity to produce autonomous discourses to intergrate these transformations. "In this condition, with politically dismantled and socially disintegrated masses, the dominant sectors did not have much difficulty in combining the effects of the 'dirty wars' with the discourse of a new 'modernization.' Thanks to their control of communication technology, they have deployed a new political scenario where politics becomes a spectacle, even a scandal (Collor, Menem, Fujimori), to allow for better manipulation and control of the masses" (Quijano 1998, 185).

These comments illustrate, on the one hand, a nostalgia and glorification by Marxist analysts of highly idealized views of past class politics that purposefully forget that many of these working-class political identities were populist. On the other hand, disregarding the research on the informal sector that shows high levels of organization and rational-strategic political behavior, it is assumed that people precariously employed in informal occupations constitute available masses for populist mobilization. Old notions die hard, and the hypotheses developed by Gino Germani (1971) on the availability of disorganized masses for political mobilization continue to reappear, even in highly sophisticated studies. The uneasiness of researchers with the successes of semiauthoritarian-semidemocratic leaders seems to bring back old ideas from mass-society theory of the manipulation and irrationality of followers. Instead of studying the concrete mechanisms that articulate leaders and led, Le Bon's notions of irrational masses and manipulative leaders (1983) have been reintroduced.

Notions of manipulation of available masses have also been reintroduced in studies of the role of television in politics that explain elections by the manipulation of leaders, their advisors, and media elites (De Lima 1993; Petras 1997; Zirker 1998). Undoubtedly television has become central to politics. Thomas Skidmore, in his introduction to a comparative study of the role of television in Latin American politics, notes that "TV is rapidly transforming the way in which political candidates are constructed, marketed, and consolidated. It is also transforming the way politicians govern once they reach office" (Skidmore 1993, 2). The specific role of this medium, however, needs to be assessed. For many authors, television does not allow for open deliberation, dialogue, and the logic of arguments that characterized traditional forms of politics based on language. For instance, Giovanni Sartori (1998, 107–16) forcefully argues that television personalizes politics, presents politics as a spectacle, and is based on emotional appeals rather than the rational discussion of ideologies that characterized liberal parliamentary democracies. Populism has become telepopulism. For Pierre-André Taguieff this is a form of "video demagogy; the demagogue acts on his audience by letting himself be seen more than understood." As a result, "citizens are reduced to spectators, mere consumers of spectacles" (1995, 42, 43).

These interpretations bring back the Old Frankfurt School's apocalyptic understanding of the mass media that concentrated solely on the production of images without analyzing the reception of those messages by researching "how people make sense of the media and what groups and traditions help people mediate media content" (Straubhaar, Olsen, and Cavaliari Nunes 1993, 120). Recent elections in Latin America (Bucaram over Nebot in Ecuador in 1996; Fujimori over Vargas Llosa in Peru in 1990) have shown that those who win have not necessarily had more televised propaganda or that their advertisements have been more sophisticated and expensive. Mario Vargas Llosa, for instance, who spent over twelve million dollars on televised propaganda, lost the election (Poole and Rénique 1992, 145). It is crucial to study the reception of media messages without assuming manipulation or naively assuming resistance and the open and free interpretation of codes by autonomous actors. Given that all politicians use the mass media to get elected, it is important to compare their televised propaganda in particular elections, paying attention to how they interpret existing problems, what their answers are, and what images of themselves and of their rivals they present. To evaluate the success of their messages, we have to connect them to the motifs and forms of representing political problems available in particular political cultures.

In his presidential campaigns of 1988, 1992, and 1996, for instance, Abdalá Bucaram used televised propaganda to deliver a populist message that had been present in the country since the 1940s. It was a message of total antagonism between the people, whose will he claimed to embody, and the evil oligarchy, who needed to be crushed. Unlike other Ecuadorian politicians, who hired foreign experts to devise their political advertisements, Bucaram designed his own propaganda. His commercials had a homemade quality and were based on aspects of popular culture such as ballads. They used the continuous repetition of a simple message in their lyrics, images, and written captions. This style was based on popular religious art that represents the miracles of a particular saint or the Virgin in the form of a comic book with pictures and captions. For instance, when the lyrics of the commercials mentioned the evil oligarchy, the faces of Bucaram's political enemies appeared simultaneously with captions like "corrupt oligarch" or "pampered rich kid."

Collor's electoral success over Lula in 1989 is partially explained by the way in which he articulated existing perceptions that the Brazilian crisis was produced by politicians, and that the solution would come from a nonpolitical savior who would implement pragmatic answers. The role of television in creating this scenario via soap operas and manufacturing Collor as a redeemer however, has been debated. Whereas Venicio De Lima (1993) stresses the role of the media empire Globo in manufacturing Collor's candidacy, Carlos Eduardo Lins da Silva (1993) questions the conspiracy theory implications of De Lima's analysis by showing how there was an elective affinity between how soap operas and Collor interpreted the political circumstances. He argues that the media and Collor used previously existing interpretations of the Brazilian crisis as the product of the corruption of politicians and the need to find an outsider who could save the homeland. Collor, moreover, was not the first choice of the

Globo. He became the anti-Lula candidate only after unsuccessful attempts by the media to manufacture the figures of Mário Covas and Guilherme Afif Domingos (Nascimento 1994, 65).

Television is not the only medium through which leaders get elected. In Peru, for instance, electors rejected Vargas Llosa's overexposure in the media in the 1990 elections to such an extent that Fujimori's strategy in his 1995 reelection campaign was to use fewer spots than his rivals (Salcedo 1995, 42, 95–96). Even in countries like Brazil, where opinion polls suggest that television is the main forum for the transmission of the candidate's ideology and personality (Silva 1993, 143), families, friends, and organizations such as the Catholic Church and neighborhood associations mediate how people interpret the messages delivered by televised propaganda, news, and debates (Straubhaar, Olsen, and Cavaliari Nunes 1993, 124). Television has not replaced clientelism and political machineries, and, in some cases such as in Ecuador, mass political rallies.

The elections of Collor de Mello in 1989, Fujimori in 1990, and Bucaram in 1996 took place in poorly institutionalized and fragmented political systems. These nations have experienced a proliferation of political parties. They realize that many parties lack concrete ideologies, that most continue with the old practice of clientelism, and that parties are still personal vehicles for candidates to win elections. The electoral triumphs of these caudillos took place when there was a simultaneous proliferation of political parties and distrust of politicians among the electorate (Oliveira 1992; Moisés 1993; Conaghan 1995; Isaacs 1991; Panfichi 1997). Whereas in Brazil "twenty-two contenders stood for election during the first round of the 1989 presidential race" (Moisés 1993, 591), nine candidates ran for the presidency in Peru and Ecuador. The two finalists in Brazil, Ecuador, and Peru, who had obtained approximately one-third of the total vote, competed in runoffs. The triumphs of the winners in all these elections cannot be explained solely by their style and rhetoric. These elections must also be interpreted as protest votes against the political establishment. The opposition of many to the candidate of the white, right-wing traditional elites in Peru and Ecuador and to the left in Brazil must also be taken into account. The political style and rhetoric of these candidates and the strength of their political machineries in capturing votes certainly determine why they won, but cannot be seen as the only explanatory variables. Their alliances with other political forces and associations of civil society in runoff elections and the mistakes of their opponents also explained their victories.

Class and ethnicity figure at the center of the rejection of Vargas Llosa and Nebot. In January 1990, when Fujimori appeared as the third contestant in opinion polls, Vargas Llosa was asked to give his opinion about the candidate of Cambio 90 (Change 1990). The novelist replied, "But nobody knows that *chinito* (little China man)." The next day Fujimori opened a major rally in a Lima shanty town with the phrase, "Here we are, the *chinitos* and the *cholitos*" [poor mestizos] (Quijano 1998, 192). In this fashion, the election became a confrontation between the white elite (*blanquitos* and *pitucos*) and the nonwhite common people: chinitos and cholitos (Degregori 1991, 115). Fujimori presented himself as the projection of two decisive experiences of many common Peruvians: migration and racial discrimination (Panfichi 1997). Like many, he is the son of immigrants who had to struggle with a "deficient" Spanish, and he was discriminated against by traditional white elites. Hence the allure of his simple slogan: "a president like you."

Similarly, after Ecuador's former president, Febres Cordero, stated that the voters for Bucaram's candidate for mayor of Guayaquil were a "bunch of prostitutes and thieves," Bucaram transformed the meaning of these insults used to describe his base of support by saying that the only prostitutes and thieves were the members of the Ecuadorian oligarchy, in particular the fellows of Febres Cordero's Social Christian Party. As shown in chapter 3, Bucaram transformed the members of the well-established elites into the embodiment of the effeminate antination. That is why his struggle was against the *aniñado* (pampered rich kid) Nebot.

Collor's, Fujimori's, and Bucaram's electoral coalitions included the marginalized sectors of society. As analyzed in chapter 3, Bucaram was supported by a coalition of a marginal elite of Lebanese descent who had acquired capital but not social standing, and the very poor and middle-class sectors displaced from the labor market and positions of authority. Collor's voters "included sizable sectors of the population that are excluded from Brazilian society, that is, the destitute, the poorest, the functional illiterates . . . [as well as] a proportion of middle income brackets, and factions of the highest income classes" (Moisés 1993, 583). Fujimori's voters in the 1990 election similarly encompassed such excluded sectors as the very poor, the inhabitants of provinces and the Andean countryside, and *cholos* (poor mestizos) and Indians (Degregori 1991,102). His coalition included organized sectors of society such as emergent noncriollo elites of the Asociación de Medianos y Pequeños Empresarios Industriales (Association of Medium and Small Industrial Entrepreneurs), the Protestant churches, and the very poor who made their living in the informal sector (Quijano 1998, 191). All these groups have been discriminated against by traditional white criollo elites because of their class or ethnicity. For instance, the members of the Association of Medium and Small Industrial Entrepreneurs were not considered equals by the members of the white-dominated National Association of Industrialists. Even though they belonged to a national organization, they were not invited to their meetings or their private social events because of their nonwhite cholo ethnicity (Quijano 1998, 191). The visible presence of Protestant and evangelical leaders in Fujimori's team encouraged the right and sectors of the Catholic Church to associate their religion with anti-Peruvian values and to declare a "holy war" against them (Poole and Rénique 1992, 146–48). Unlike Vargas Llosa, who promised only the expansion of the market, Fujimori was also seen as the embodiment of social mobility and success for nonwhites who make a living in the informal sector of the economy (Adrianzén 1998, 299).

Neopopulist leaders such as Collor, Menem, Fujimori, and Bucaram are innovators. Their rhetoric and political style broke with conventions and articulated many of the symbolic and material demands of the electorate. Fujimori and Bucaram represented simultaneously the rejection of traditional white elites and the common nonwhite elite person's dream of social mobility and democratization of caste relations. Collor was successful in presenting himself as the embodiment of a neoliberal modernity; his figure, elegant dress style, and extravagant and expensive taste in sports symbolized a new yuppie Brazil to come (Oliveira 1992, 105). He cultivated the image of a young and energetic political outsider, a messiah acting above and beyond the interests of group organizations such as unions or employer's associations, whose main task was to destroy the privileges of inefficient bureaucrats, the *marajás*, to bring redemption to his descamisados. In the 1989 presidential campaign, "Menem embodied the caudillo who descended from a very poor province to talk to all the excluded and disenchanted in their own language" (Nun 1994, 107). He projected the image of a winner who has triumphed in two mythologized arenas of social mobility: sports and show business. That is why a few months after becoming president he declared, "I am the president of the nation and I play soccer with Maradona. What else can I ask in life?" (Novaro and Palermo 1996, 213). Menem transformed key Peronist political rituals. Instead of using mass meetings, Menem, following the style of the Pope John Paul II, visited common people in their neighborhoods. Traveling in his *menemovil* he encountered them in their everyday and nonpolitical spaces, where he blessed them and kissed their children. His image had more in common with a "religious leader or a show business celebrity, than with a typical campaigning politician" (Novaro and Palermo 1996, 207). He also transformed Peronist rhetoric by replacing the traditional class invocation to "the workers" with generic appeals to "brothers and sisters," references to religious themes, and the phrase "Follow me!" (Nun 1994, 108; Novaro and Palermo 1996, 209).

Clientelist networks also explain the triumphs of these politicians. José Álvaro Moisés reminds us that, unlike the commonsense construction of Collor as a politician without an institutional base of support, it is worth remembering his success in building an electoral machine. This "para-party" had an important role to play. "It defined an image (*marajá* [inefficient, well-paid bureaucrats] hunter); linked it to a program of government (shrinking of the state, modernization of the economy, and the resumption of growth); organized the material resources (i.e., the electronic media) indispensable for communication with the voting public; and, lastly articulated a range of social alliances capable of sustaining Collor's candidacy" (Moisés 1993, 592).

It is important to remember that all political contestants exchange political subordination for material rewards, and that Nebot's political party or Vargas Llosa's electoral coalition, for instance, had built networks as strong as those of Bucaram and Fujimori. Researchers who emphasize the rational instrumental vocation of the electorate sometimes forget that clientelistic networks offer more than utilitarian benefits. Carlos Franco (1990) argues for the need to analytically differentiate "distributive populism" from "identity populism." Whereas the former is explained by the rational utilitarian exchanges of votes for goods and services and is used by most political parties, the latter focuses on how populist discourse gives back to the subordinate and the poor the self-worth and recognition to be at the center of the nation. Clearly the type of clientelistic relationships established by populist parties give more than material rewards. Javier Auyero's ethnography (1998) of how brokers from the Peronist party deliver goods and services at the local level offers a clear theoretical and methodological advantage to reductionist rational choice approaches. He illustrates the importance of analyzing the services given with how they are given. He shows how the performances of local Peronist brokers and their bonds with clients are based on past interpretations of Juan and Eva Perón that create and re-create particular political and cultural identities.

Aldo Panfichi (1997) argues that, whereas the election of neo-populist leaders can be explained by emotional factors that link leaders and followers, their permanence in power is based on their concrete achievements. The reelections of Menem and Fujimori are certainly explained by their capacity to solve concrete problems by building alliances with important institutional players such as the armed forces and the local and international business community. In contrast, the abrupt terminations of Collor's and Bucaram's administrations were caused by their inability to develop alliances with key institutional players. Fujimori successfully disarticulated the guerrilla movement. Like Menem, he developed good relationships with the military by giving amnesty to perpetrators of human rights abuses. He allowed the armed forces carte blanche in their fight against "subversion," and he relied on the military as his institutional base of support. Both leaders could also show economic successes. They were able to get rid of hyperinflation and achieve high levels of economic growth. Kurt Weyland reports that in "subsequent weeks and months, 72 percent to 77 percent of Greater Buenos Aires residents endorsed [Menem's] stabilization plan of July 1989, and 85 percent to 89 percent approved of the president's performance" (1998, 550). In Peru, where Fujimori's adjustment plan of August 1990 raised the price of basic necessities by up to 3,000 percent, 50 to 60 percent of opinion poll respondents supported the plan, and the president was endorsed by 57 percent of respondents in one poll (Weyland 1998, 551). Both leaders counted on the approval of international financial institutions and important sectors of the local business elites. The privatization of state enterprises allowed them to have resources to develop successful antipoverty programs (Roberts 1995; Roberts and Arce 1998; Weyland 1996, 1998).

Menem institutionalized his rule by relying on a reformed Peronist party. He was the first Peronist presidential candidate who had won in primary elections. Marcos Novaro (1998; Novaro and Palermo 1996) has argued that Peronism has been transformed from a movement into an electoral party. Since the 1940s, all social conflicts in Argentina have become politicized as the struggle between General Perón, the embodiment of the Argentinean people, and his enemies, who were the foes of the nation and had to be crushed. Liberal-democratic procedures and the rule of law were not considered important in this total war between the people and their enemies. The Peronist party started its internal reform after the collapse of the last military government. It did so in conjunction with Alfonsín's attempt to redefine the rules of the democratic game by constructing politics as the struggle between the forces of life, who respected the right to dissent and the right of the opposition to exist, and the forces of death. They accepted democracy, publicly denounced the forces of death, and, in the process, started to change their views on political conflicts. Former enemies became adversaries who had a right to exist and express their opinions. These changes in Peronist discourse have not been matched by a new democratic conversion of its leader. Even though the number of "emergency decrees" that bypassed Congress has diminished, Menem has also invoked special executive privileges. Novaro (1998) concludes his analysis by pointing out the tension between a limited conversion of Menem to democracy and the old authoritarian practices that understand the leader as the sole interpreter of the national destiny.

These transformations of Peronist discourse coincided with a crisis of the labor movement, its former base of support. Menem was able to play on their internal divisions and get the support of some union leaders for his economic reforms, which were going to further undermine the collective power of the working class. Menem approached the international financial institutions and the most powerful business groups (Nun 1994). The formerly nationalist movement became a party committed to globalization. This neoliberal party of order that no longer claims to represent the interests of the working class, nonetheless is still supported by the poor. Antipoverty-targeted programs that deliver goods and services and continually re-create Peronist loyalties are the instruments used to obtain popular support. As Auyero (1998) demonstrates, they have preserved the symbols of Peronism but not its policies.

In contrast to Menem, who relied on his reformed political party, Fujimori "quickly demobilized *Cambio* 90 and broke with the leadership of the Protestant and small business groups that had initially supported him" (Roberts 1995, 100). The military, in particular the Servicio Nacional de Inteligencia (SIN; National information service), has become Fujimori's base of institutional support. In the name of a struggle against the political class, Fujimori's 1992 *autogolpe* culminated a series of nondemocratic moves that have profoundly shaken, if not destroyed, Peruvian democracy. Nonetheless, he was reelected in 1995 with a broad range of popular, middle-class, and elite support (Roberts and Arce 1998). Many electors voted for him in an election that represented the collapse of traditional political parties and the party system because of his capacity to deliver concrete results, such as ending hyperinflation and bringing order by neutralizing the guerrilla movements (Lynch 1997; Panfichi 1997).

Unlike these leaders who were reelected, Collor and Bucaram did not finish their terms in office because they did not gain the support of key institutional players. Both antagonized the armed forces. Bucaram challenged the internal unity of this institution by involving them in his government. Collor contested the power of the military by reducing their salaries and dissolving the SNI (Information National Services) (Weyland 1993, 12). They did not secure the support of business elites either. Like Bucaram, Collor was not trusted by entrepreneurs, who resented his populist, antibusiness rhetoric during the campaign. For instance, he did not accept the endorsement of São Paulo's business community; he "scornfully rejected their support and accused them of being selfish profiteers" (9). Collor was seen as the lesser of two evils when compared to Lula. His arrogance did not help him either. After winning the elections, Collor was asked how he was going to reciprocate the bourgeoisie for their support. He answered that he had already repaid them by defeating Lula, "the monster of the bourgeoisie and of all the bureaucratic-entrepreneurial sectors" (Oliveira 1992, 101). His economic policies further divided and alienated these elites, in particular less technologically advanced sectors that would be unable to compete in an open economy (Weyland 1993, 11).[1]

Politicians were eager to reduce the power of these caudillos or, if possible, to topple them. They were afraid that if these leaders were successful, they would concentrate too much influence. They were also antagonized by their arrogant styles and by their inability to sustain alliances. Bucaram and Collor used corruption to build a base of support in fragmented political systems. Given that the only way to obtain support from the legislative branch was to dispense patronage to individual representatives, they abusively and carelessly used state resources to buy political support. When accusations of corruption gave politicians the means to articulate their opposition, they did not hesitate to overthrow these presidents. In Brazil the rule of law and the constitution were the mechanisms used to topple Collor; in Ecuador, politicians used dubious constitutional loopholes. Brazilian democracy was strengthened by the mobilizations against corruption and by the respect of political elites for democratic procedures; Ecuadorian democratic institutions were further discredited.

On New Populism and New Democracies

The relatively optimistic assertions about the possibilities for democratization in Latin America have been replaced by more sober and pessimistic assessments (Loveman 1994; O'Donnell 1994; Petras 1997; Vilas 1997, 1998; Zirker 1998). Carlos Vilas, for instance, convincingly demonstrates that Latin American democracies are less than liberal democracies even within the institutionalist understanding of the term *democracy*. Even though Latin American democracies have been based on free elections, questions as important as "the rule of law, government accountability for its actions, an effective balance between the executive, legislative, and judicial branches, and military subordination to civilian rule" have not been solved (Vilas 1997, 9).

As argued above, Latin American populist movements have ignored, or not always respected, liberal-democratic forms of representation. They have constructed versions of democracy that claim to represent directly the people's will by negating the divisions of modern society and assuming the membership of all social classes, ethnic groups, genders, and other categories in a homogeneous community: the people. But el pueblo, as Alan Knight reminds us, is a "notoriously vague term." He recollects that "Engels reacted brusquely to a reference to 'the people in general' in the 1891 Erfurt Programme, asking: 'Who is that?' " (Knight 1998, 226). El pueblo is not an empirical fact. The term refers to a social relation of positions that, as García Canclini argues, in Latin America theatrically situates certain actors "against the hegemonic group and not always in the form of confrontations" (1995, 203). Because el pueblo cannot represent and constitute itself as a unitary actor, it always needs elites who can speak on its behalf.

In his reflections on Jacobinism, François Furet argues that the French Revolution's claim to legitimacy was in "the people," a founding principle that was "impossible to embody." Power, therefore, was in the hands of those who claimed to "speak for the people" (1985, 51). It belonged to the "individual or individuals who appear to speak on their behalf, who speak in the name of the people and give them their name" (Lefort 1988, 109–10). Politics was constructed in a way that allows only for the existence of politicians who embody the people's will, or enemies of the people. The people, then, became an ambiguous principle of political legitimacy. On the one hand, politicians had to embody the people, they had to deliver material and symbolic goods, and they also had to stage public acts that expressed the people's will, constituting the people as such. But, on the other hand, the people's will is represented and expressed as a homogeneous moral-ethical datum that does not admit differences. Politicians' appropriation of the people's will, has resulted in either Stalinist totalitarianism or populist authoritarianism.

Claude Lefort shows how the roots of totalitarianism are the representation of "the people as one" (1986). This enactment negates the divisions and diversities of modern society. Politics becomes the struggle between the unitary people, represented by the proletariat, the party, or the egocrat, against the enemies of the people, "the other," imagined to be outside society, and who must be eliminated. Authoritarian populism shares this Manichaean representation of politics as the struggle between the people and its leader—who embodies its will—against its enemies constructed as "the other." But unlike totalitarianism, populist regimes have not totally abolished liberal-democratic procedures and the rule of law. Therefore, they have not taken this antagonism to its totalitarian extremes.

The impossibility of embodying the people makes us rethink the notion of representation. David Plotke convincingly argues that "representation is crucial in constituting democratic practices" (1997, 19). Because, as Norberto Bobbio has shown, direct democracy will not work in complex modern societies, representatives need to be elected. "Deliberations which concern the whole community, are not taken directly by its members, but by people elected for this purpose" (1987, 45). A collectivity "authorizes some individuals to speak for it, and eventually to commit the collectivity to what the representative decides" (O'Donnell 1994, 61). Representatives, for their part, are accountable and responsible for their actions.

To avoid populist authoritarian representation based on the "merging and full identity between a representative and those who seek representation" (Plotke 1997, 28), representation should be based on the principle of nonidentity between representatives and their constituency. In a democracy, a substantial number of citizens, directly or indirectly, have the right to be involved in decision-making processes through procedures for arriving at collective decisions that also guarantee the right of minorities to dissent. Because a democracy offers alternatives, it needs to give basic rights to the electors and their representatives. A democracy "is formal in insisting on the nonnegotiable character of rights and procedures" (Plotke 1997, 32).

Guillermo O'Donnell (1994) has shown that newly installed democracies in Argentina, Bolivia, Brazil, Ecuador, and Peru are different from representative democracies. Delegative democracies do not respect civil rights and democratic procedures. They are based on the idea that whoever wins an election has the popular mandate to govern according to his or her interpretation of the people's will and interests. The president claims to embody the nation. He sees himself as the redeemer of the homeland. His policies, therefore, do not need to have any link to his promises during the campaign or to the agreements made with organizations and associations who supported his election. Because his government needs to "save the country" in the context of economic crises that constrain the institutionalization of democracy, he looks for neoliberal technicians who can design economic policies to create this redemption.

As in the past, the entire responsibility for ruling the country is in the hands of the president. He is perceived as the source of the country's ills or of its successes. Because the government needs to save the nation, its actions do not always respect democratic procedures or compromises with the opposition. The opposition also acts without accepting agreements. In the end, as in the past, the military is called to resolve civilian problems. That is why, as the Peruvian and Ecuadorian examples show, it is difficult to escape the populism–military coup cycle. Unlike in past situations, the ruptures of civilian governments do not put the military directly in charge due to new international conditions. In Peru, Fujimori illegally dissolved Congress in 1992, and, in Ecuador, Congress semilegally deposed Bucaram for "mental incapacity" in 1997.

Lefort has shown that "rights are generative principles of democracy" (1986, 260). Rights are not only codified in laws; they are not static, they change historically. Their existence permits the struggle and the creation of new rights. According to Jean Cohen and Andrew Arato, the following rights that correspond to different institutions of modern civil societies can be differentiated: "Focusing on the institutional spheres of civil society, we can isolate three complexes of rights: those concerning cultural reproduction (freedoms of thought, speech, and communication); those ensuring social integration (freedom of association and assembly); and those securing socialization (protection of privacy, intimacy, and the inviolability of the person). Two other complexes of rights mediate between civil society and either the market economy (rights of property, contract, and labor) or the modern bureaucratic state (political rights of citizens and welfare rights of clients)" (1992, 441).

In Latin America, although the rights that guarantee capitalist relations of production have been institutionalized and are respected, political and welfare rights and the rights that guarantee the institutions of civil society are only selectively respected. The poor do not have the power to exercise their constitutional civil rights and have to seek powerful patrons who can protect them from the arbitrary power of laws. Because the powerful offer their protection to the poor in exchange for their loyalty, relations of domination, as in the past, continue to be personalized. Given their daily interactions in personalized relations of domination, the superordinate sectors see themselves as the natural, good-natured, and kind protectors of the poor. They have the power to construct the desired moral characteristics of their subordinates. If the poor fulfill their expectations and stereotypes, they are rewarded with love. As Mary Jackman argues, "There is no need to engage in explicit power negotiations with subordinates if one has an embedded, ingrained understanding that the continued exchange of affection is contingent upon the fulfillment of specific obligations" (1994, 82). The poor and the excluded exchange their loyalty for the access to economic resources and services to which they are entitled, but from which they are marginalized in their day-to-day lives.

Like the well-established members of the elite, politicians offer their protection to the poor in exchange for their loyalty, and the poor look for a patron who can deliver. Discourses of love and friendship mask real relations of domination between politicians and the poor. Politicians offer their love to the poor, and the poor have to accept that love in the terms offered by politicians. Their everyday contact with the poor, whom they claim to love, makes politicians believe that they know their true interests. Clientelism thus continues to operate as one of the main mechanisms of political control and access to resources.

Everyday practices to escape from laws or to use them strategically for one's benefit schizophrenically coexist with what can be called an obsession to legislate. It seems that politicians have a need to constantly invent new laws and constitutions. They need to legitimate politics with legislation that will not be respected for long. These ambiguous relationships to laws are products of Latin America's colonial heritage, when laws were "to be obeyed but not executed" (Stein and Stein 1970, 75). This preoccupation with laws also demonstrates that the rule of law cannot be totally ignored, and that it might, at some point in the future, regulate social behavior. But before this hope is materialized, what is the function of so many laws? It seems that laws are written in such a way that people cannot obey them, so they will be cast outside the rule of law. Because so many people live at the margins of the rule of law, the destitute and the poor are at the mercy of authorities. Laws, therefore, serve a double function: they exclude and marginalize most of the population, and they create "natural" leaders—politicians—who write these laws and can "protect" the poor.

Delegative democracies are not solely the result of democratization under adverse socioeconomic conditions caused by dependency and economic crises, as O'Donnell argues. They are also based on political traditions that have constructed democracy as the direct representation of the people's will. These political cultures are not explained by a supposedly authoritarian tradition of the region or any other form of cultural essentialism. They are rather the product of a specific pattern of political incorporation of common people into the political community. The fundamental differences between liberal and delegative democracies explain the instabilities of civilian-elected regimes in Latin America, and the coexistence of strong invocations to constitutions with practices to escape from the laws. Latin American democracies that are formally committed to the principles of liberal democracies in the juridical-moral declarations of the state and politicians, ignore the rights of most of the population in their daily practices. They are based on the selective respect for liberal-democratic norms and procedures. It is important, therefore, to differentiate between democracy, understood as everyday authoritarian practices, and discourses that exclude and silence broad sectors of the population from a normative notion of democracy as an ideal to be attained. But, for such a normative notion of democracy to regulate everyday practices between citizens and the state, everyday relations of domination must be democratized. Unless personalized relations of domination are altered, and citizens begin to be considered as individuals with rights and duties, authoritarian populist politics will continue to reemerge in Latin America. The populist temptation will be present as long as the poor continue to live in a "régime d'exception" (Pinheiro 1994, 247) without fundamental constitutional human and civil rights. It will persist as long as class differences also become estate differences between common citizens without rights and privileged groups, who are above the law.

The continuous resilience of populism in Latin America should not be a surprise. After all, most people live in poverty and suffer cultural and political exclusions. Populist leaders continue to incarnate the underdog and to give name to their experiences of exclusion by articulating cultural and symbolic challenges to the elites. Moreover, populist movements partially include and "protect" the poor through patronage and clientelist networks. Populist politicians' authoritarian appropriation of the people's will and their Manichaean rhetoric of a fundamental ethical struggle between them as the embodiment of the people against their enemies continue to pose fundamental obstacles to the institutionalization of democracy. The persistence of clientelism, the lack of respect for the rule of law, and the disregard of democratic procedures should not lead us to a totally pessimistic conclusion. Even the demagogic use of a rhetoric of citizenship rights shows that they cannot be fully ignored and implies the possibility of implementing practices and discourses based on a system that guarantees fundamental rights.

Chapter 5

The Resurgence of Radical Populism in Latin America

A SPECTER is haunting Latin America: radical populism. A new brand of radical and nationalist populist leaders has rejected neoliberal guidelines. Instead they are implementing the nationalist, statist, and redistributive economic policies of their classical-populist predecessors. They have also promised to refound their nations and to establish radical participatory and direct democracy as alternatives to "decaying and corrupt" liberal institutions. Former presidents and respectable media analysts have responded by warning us of the dangers for democracy of charismatic and plebiscitary domination, and of the risks of irresponsible economic policies. A holy alliance is trying to exorcize the ghost of populism that periodically reappears, even though its death has been constantly predicted. Scholars, who are not as pessimistic as media pundits and politicians, are also highlighting the authoritarian and undemocratic traits of the radical populist administrations of Hugo Chávez in Venezuela, Evo Morales in Bolivia, and Rafael Correa in Ecuador. They have argued that these countries' governments have concentrated power in the executive, that these leaders' administrations have colonized and not respected the independence of the different branches of government, and have pointed out the dangers for freedom of expression and pluralism under these regimes (Diamond, Plattner, and Abente 2008; Domínguez and Shifter 2008; Krauze 2008; Laserna 2003; Mayorga 2009; McCoy and Myers 2004). Chávez, Morales, and Correa have also been painted as heirs to the left-wing, radical, and authoritarian populist traditions. Their regimes have been depicted as fundamentally different from the pragmatic, moderate, responsible left that accepted liberal democracy and the capitalist market economy (Castañeda 2006).

Unlike the pessimistic and even apocalyptic warnings of mainstream media analysts and politicians, some scholars have seen in these regimes seeds of hope for post-neoliberal and more democratic societies. They argue that these regimes have replaced political systems based on clientelism and corruption with institutions of radical participatory democracy that can correct the deficits of popular participation and representation in previously existing arrangements. They have also noticed that exclusionary neoliberal economic policies have been replaced by state-centered policies that place a major emphasis on social justice, and they argue that nationalism has replaced the opening of the economy under globalization. In sum, and unlike scholars who see a retrocession of democracy in the region, anti-neoliberal scholars see these leftist regimes as democratic innovators and as sources of inspiration for progressive and left-wing policies in the West (Ali 2008; Barra and Dello Buono 2009; Figueroa 2006; Raby 2006; Stefanoni and Alto 2006; Wilpert 2007).

Reviewing the recent literature on radical populism, it can be noticed that, with few exceptions, scholars have tended to reproduce the cleavages produced by populist leaders. What for some are authentic forms of expression of the popular will by leaders who had empowered those previously disenfranchised, are for others forms of charismatic, authoritarian, and messianic domination. Behind the smoke screen raised by the praise for radical national populism or by its condemnation, we can identify important debates over the meanings and interpretations of democracy. Instead of arguing that populism is the negation or the essence of democracy, this chapter draws on current experiences to explore the uneasy and ambiguous relations between populism and liberal democracy. Populism continues to be an important democratizing force that has mobilized those previously excluded from participation in government. It continues to incorporate common people into the political community. However, the precise working of these processes of inclusion and democratization needs to be specified. What are the forms of political participation and representation privileged by radical populism? How is democracy understood by the friends and foes of populism? What are the effects of populist rhetoric for the democratization of society? Why do common folk continue to support populist leaders?

Populist and Liberal Democracy in the Andes

As Nadia Urbinati has argued, "The debate over the meaning of populism turns out to be a debate over the interpretation of democracy" (1998, 16). For scholars such as Margaret Canovan (1999) populism constitutes the redemptive face of democracy. Populist discursive glorification of the people, its critique of elites, and its emotional style aimed at ordinary citizens draws unmotivated and previously excluded people into the political arena. Canovan is undoubtedly right, if we accept the populist self-interpretation that democracy entails the mobilization of those previously excluded. Moreover, populism draws on passions, and on the antagonistic dimensions that, according to Chantal Mouffe (2005b), are constitutive of politics.

Latin American populists have privileged notions of democracy based on the aesthetic and liturgical incorporation of common people in mass rallies more than on the institutionalization of popular participation through the rule of law. However, as critics of populism have been arguing for a long time, mobilization and participation in mass rallies and plebiscites do not necessarily guarantee autonomy. Gino Germani (1971), for instance, has contrasted autonomous collective action with populist heteronomous collective action based on mobilization in the name of a leader instead of on actors' own interpretations of their interests. Critics have maintained that populist redemption tends to be based on the authoritarian appropriation of the people's will. Because populist politicians claim to embody the people, and the people's will is not given institutional channels to express itself, populist regimes have replaced rational deliberation with plebiscitary acclamation. Moreover, due to their Manichaean discourse and the resulting polarization of political and social cleavages, populist movements resemble situations of war. The foes and friends of populism see each other as enemies and not as democratic rivals who seek negotiations and agreements.

To disentangle conflicting interpretations of the relationships between populist mobilization and democratic autonomy, I will analyze examples of what actors have described as authentic forms of democratic mobilization and participation. I will analyze the institutions of participatory democracy created in Venezuela. Then I will study models of direct assembly and indigenous-community democracy advocated by academics and activists in Bolivia and Ecuador.

In speeches and televised talks, Hugo Chávez argues that in Latin America representative democracy has failed. He presents an alternative model, a democracy "that promotes participation, and that moves toward [popular] decision making" (in Lander 2005, 31). In January 2006 in an address at the sixth World Social Forum in Caracas, Chávez asserted, "Representative democracy always ends up being a democracy of the elites and therefore a false democracy. We want a new model, a revolutionary and people's democracy, one that is participatory and protagonist, not defined by an elite that represents the people" (in French 2009, 357). Participatory democracy became enshrined in the 1999 constitution. Additionally, Chávez's Bolivarian government has created a series of institutions to advance participatory and protagonist democracy.

Starting in June 2001, in order to promote the revolutionary process, President Chávez encouraged the formation of Bolivarian circles. Their aims were to organize disorganized supporters and to insert "'the people into administrating the government' in order to 'make participatory and protagonist democracy more effective'" (García-Guadilla 2003, 192). Bolivarian circles in their heyday boasted approximately 2.2 million members and had an active role in the massive demonstrations that rescued President Chávez when he was temporarily removed from office in the coup of April 2002 (Hawkins and Hansen 2006, 103).

Bolivarian circles have been depicted by Chávez as new forms of genuine democratic grassroots participation, and by the opposition as circles of terror that resemble Cuba's Committees for the Defense of the Revolution. Even though the circles have decayed in the last years, they are an interesting case to analyze the tensions between activation and autonomous participation in populist democracy. In an interesting study Kirk Hawkins and David Hansen show that mobilization of the Bolivarian circles is not necessarily based on the "kind of autonomy that democracy requires" (2006, 127). Their study shows that even though Bolivarian circles do constitute forms of participation for poor people, they often worked as cliental networks to transfer resources to neighborhoods where Chávez had supporters. Moreover, they were based on a charismatic mode of linkage that precludes autonomy from the leader.

Other organizations formed under the Chávez government have faced a similar fate. María Pilar García-Guadilla argues that new organizations promoted by Chávez earlier in his tenure, such as those of pensioners, ambulant merchants or peddlers, and people displaced by natural disasters, have "tended to make narrow demands that could be resolved on an individual rather than collective basis and in a clientelistic and populist manner rather than through collective negotiation" (2003, 193). However, Steve Ellner has shown how the *chavista* process has encouraged independent and radicalized workers' action. For instance, during the 2002–3 ten-week general strike against the state oil company, Petróleos de Venezuela, workers restored production levels and "refuted technocratic assumptions by demonstrating the political and technical capacity of non-specialists, at a time when most upper-level employees had abandoned work" (Ellner 2005, 180).

Since 2007, Chávez has radicalized the Bolivarian revolution through a call to build a program of twenty-first-century socialism. The goal is the construction of a revolutionary and socialist democracy that will transcend representative liberal democracy with the "real and quotidian exercise of power by the great majority of common people" (Acosta 2007, 22). According to Chávez, "popular power is the soul, nerve, flesh, bone, and essence of Bolivarian democracy, of a true democracy" (in Sosa 2007, 52). Communal councils have been conceived as institutions to promote popular power and are seen as the foundation for the future establishment of direct and pyramidal democracy. In pyramidal democracy "all delegates are revocable, bound by the instructions of their constituency and organized into a 'pyramid' of directly elected committees" (Held 1987, 130). Even though this pyramidal system has yet to be organized, the Venezuelan government had established sixteen thousand communal councils by 2006, managing roughly 30 percent of the total budget for social services (Wilpert 2007, 60). Critics and supporters of the Bolivarian revolution have agreed that communal councils so far have faced the same problems as the Bolivarian circles, namely the persistence of clientelism in the exchange of social services for political support, and a charismatic style of rule that neutralizes or prevents autonomous grassroots inputs (Sosa 2007; Wilpert 2007, 195–204).

Bolivarian circles and communal councils may have experienced problems of autonomy because they were created from above. Other institutions, such as the urban land committees and technical water roundtables, have accepted more autonomous grassroots inputs. In particular, the government has given squatter settlements collective titles to land on which precarious self-built dwellings are situated. Through this process, "the community forms an urban land committee to administer its new collective property and to undertake and demand support for material improvement such as water, sewerage and electricity services or road paving" (Raby 2006, 188–89). Similarly, local water committees "arrange the distribution of water between neighboring communities which share the same water mains" (189). Nevertheless, urban land committees and water committees lack autonomy from a charismatic leader (García-Guadilla 2007), as Chávez remains a highly visible guiding force for these institutions. Participation has been reduced to a cadre of committed members who have had difficulties involving other citizens (López 2008, 13).

The Venezuelan experience demonstrates that experiments in participatory democracy have indeed increased the engagement of common people in politics at the local and national levels, as "for a large number of the underprivileged, new historical levels of participation and organization have been achieved" (Lander 2007, 28). Chávez's populist discourse and the spaces given to common people's organizations have resulted in an increased "selfconfidence, pride, and a sense of efficacy of groups such as women, Afro-Venezuelans, and indigenous people" (Ellner 2008, 182). As Raby argues, "Popular mobilization in the streets, in mass meetings and in neighborhoods institutions is a vital part of the process" (2006, 193). However, in the absence of institutions, charismatic leaders set the table for the topics that can be debated and the limits to the discussions. Participation thus can degenerate into plebiscitary acclamation. As Francisco Panizza notes, "Participatory democracy can only prosper within an institutional setting that strengthens rather than undermines representative bodies" (2005b, 730). Without liberal democratic institutions, participatory democracy "is prone to capture by special interests or manipulation by populist leaders" (888).

Even though conflicts around Ecuadorian democracy have not had the same drama and media exposure as Venezuelan struggles, three recently elected presidents—Abdalá Bucaram (1996–97), Jamil Mahuad (1998–2000), Lucio Gutiérrez (2003–2005)—were overthrown before ending their terms. These elected presidents were forcefully removed from power through events that combined collective action and an instrumental use of laws by Congress, which used arguments of doubtful legality to remove them from office. Bucaram was removed through claims that he was loco, Mahuad and Gutiérrez with arguments that they had abandoned power, when in fact they did not abdicate. As in the past, civilians put the military as the ultimate arbiters of democracy, but unlike the past the military has not taken over power. The events that led to the overthrow of these presidents illustrates that democracy is still lived as the occupation of public spaces. The belief that "the people" have the power to remove officers directly and without following the norms established in the constitution worked as a mobilizing myth. Crowds wanted to get rid of presidents by taking over sacred symbols of authority and spaces where power resides, such as Congress or the presidential palace. To illustrate the tensions between populist activism and liberal democratic forms of participation and representation, I will focus on how the leaders and intellectuals of the indigenous movement understood democracy during the 2000 rebellion.

The indigenous movement came to power in January 2000 in a coup d'état against President Jamil Mahuad, who had presided over a generalized economic crisis and who was charged with diverting state funds to rescue corrupt bankers. After indigenous demonstrators, in alliance with junior officers of the army, toppled Mahuad, he was replaced by the self-styled Junta of National Salvation, made up of Col. Lucio Gutiérrez; Antonio Vargas, president of the Confederación de Nacionalidades Indígenas del Ecuador (CONAIE); and Carlos Solórzano, former chief justice of the supreme court. After pressure by the U.S. embassy and by the high command of the Ecuadorian armed forces, the junta resigned and Mahuad's vice president, Gustavo Noboa, was elected president by Congress. During this coup, or popular rebellion, indigenous people, who were not seen as belonging to the people, became its new incarnation. The people became associated with indigenous demonstrators who had taken over highly symbolically charged public spaces, such as the buildings that housed Congress and the supreme court as well as the presidential palace.

Like many Ecuadorians, indigenous politicians and intellectuals have disdained liberal forms of representation and rule. Echoing leftist critiques of liberal democracy, many indigenous leaders contrasted formal democracy with real democracy based on inclusive social and economic policies. Luis Macas, an early leader of the movement, declared, "Democracy lies in justice, in equity, and in harmony," while Antonio Vargas (president of CONAIE at that time) maintained that formal democracy should be replaced by "full democracy" (in Lucas 2000, 164–71). Some of the leaders of the indigenous movement agreed with Gutiérrez's view that true democracy is based on direct forms of election and representation that do not require the mediation of institutions. For instance, Gutiérrez characterized the overthrow of Mahuad as "a sovereign election, a direct election, [and] an election of the majorities" (in Herrera 2001, 96). According to Gutiérrez, "Sovereignty lies in the people whose will is the basis of authority, and making use of this right . . . without representatives has elected its representatives," namely the Junta of National Salvation (Gutiérrez in Herrera 2001, 64).

Indigenous leaders have also claimed that indigenous and non-indigenous politics are fundamentally different. They have argued that the principles of direct democracy, community, respect for others, transparency, consensus, equilibrium, and dialogue characterize indigenous politics. "Participation of the community members in decision making takes place at community council (cabildo) meetings. This means that community actions are governed by consent and discussion is held until consensus is reached. . . . The best examples of the full expression of collective effort are the various uprisings and marches" (Macas, Belote, and Belote 2003, 224).

As this example illustrates, indigenous leaders have idealized their communities as institutions free of conflict and domination. Not all voices, however, are equally valid in community council meetings. Economic and educational differences, the relative power of certain families or ayllus,[1] and, above all, gender give authority to some voices in these meetings. Consensus does not always mean the pacific resolution of conflict. Entire families are coerced to act in marches and uprisings even when they do not support the community's decisions. If they refuse to participate they risk ostracism from their community, they could be fined, or they are threatened with the disconnection of basic services such as drinking water.

Ecuadorian indigenous politicians and intellectuals, in sum, have tended to privilege populist understandings of democracy as occupations of public spaces. Their glorification of direct democracy in community council meetings has hindered analysis of power relations in their own communities. By privileging communal values over individual rights, they have not allowed individuals or families the right to dissent, and those who do not follow the mandate of the community council risk different forms of punishment. Their glorification of idealized peasant communities ignores that a large proportion of indigenous people live in cities, and their construct that true Indianness can only be rural silences alternative constructions of indigenous urban identities. Finally, given their lack of faith in liberal democracy their participation in a coup d'état, and their alliance with a populist nationalist such as Colonel Gutiérrez was not a surprise because it was framed as a rebellion against an oligarchic and corrupt government.

Bolivian scholars argue that communal and assembly democracies are based on the norms, traditions, and experiences of miners, indigenous people, other unionized workers such as coca growers, and poor urban dwellers. They contend that their values of communal solidarity, equality, and consensus building differ fundamentally from the individualistic principles that lie at the root of liberal-representative democracy. Scholars have constructed assembly union democracy and communal indigenous democracy as exemplary models of direct un-mediated representation where all deliberate until they reach a con-sensus and a decision is made (Patzi 2004; Tapia 2006). These schemes do not reduce participation to voting and representation to the delegation of power to representatives. Participation is an obliga-tion linked to the economic, political, and ritual duties of the mem-bers of the community. Leadership is considered a duty and rotates among community members. All participants must abide by collec-tive decisions, which are reached through long deliberations aimed at reaching consensus. Thus, individual rights are subordinated to col-lective rights, as "in indigenous communities democratic rules do not apply, but a form of authoritarianism based on consensus" (Patzi 2004, 117). Those who dissent and do not follow collective decisions are considered traitors and can be punished by monetary fines, os-tracism, and occasionally by physical penalties, such as whipping.

The rebellions of 2000 and 2003, according to these academics, il-lustrated that an alternative system based on assembly democracy could replace liberal representative institutions (García Linera 2001; Hylton and Thomson 2007; Tapia, García, and Prada 2004). During these insurrections against the privatization of water in 2000, and gas in 2003, which led to the flight of President Gonzalo Sánchez de Losada from Bolivia, local assemblies elected representatives to higher instances of assembly deliberation. Representatives at all lev-els could be recalled, and during these rebellions assemblies replaced state power. A pyramidal form of democracy hence is advocated as a viable and vibrant democratic alternative to liberal democratic repre-sentation. Even large-scale meetings, where about seventy thousand people participated, were seen as instances of genuine democratic participation.

"At this level of assembly . . . there was an undercurrent of democratic participation and commentary." Although representatives addressed the crowd, the flow of discussion and proposal was not unidirec-tional. "The crowd responded to different proposals by expressing a collective sentiment, either by applauding or making noises such as boos or whistles. Sometimes leaders have to follow the people." (Patzi, in Hylton and Thomson 2007, 104).

Communal democracy is also considered to be a form of government that can democratize racist and colonial forms of domination, including liberal democracy, which is seen as a neocolonial imposition (Patzi 2004; Rivera 1990). Aymara leaders refer to Bolivia's representative democracy as *q'aracracia,* a term that "combines 'q'ara' ('plucked,' 'bare' or 'hairless' in Aymara and Quechua, meaning 'white person') with 'democracia'" (Albro 2005, 434). Building on these understandings of democracy, President Evo Morales claims that Bolivia's "Western democracy" is "imported" and does not reflect the cultural values of most of the population (Morales 2006, 127). Leftist Marxist and Indianist intellectuals have also rejected neoliberal multiculturalism because it allegedly did not address power relations and left capitalist institutions intact.

Following Western dualist models that have romanticized peasant communitarian practices to criticize capitalism (Roseberry 1989), many Andean thinkers have portrayed indigenous communities as untouched by capitalism. Scholars have recurred to dualistic models that dogmatically differentiate between distinct social types that are supposedly juxtaposed to each other without much interaction. René Zavaleta has coined the term *formación abigarrada,* translated by James Dunkerley as multicolored formation, to argue that in Bolivia different historical epochs and social formations are "placed upon each other without very much interaction" (in Dunkerley 2007, 161). "It is as if feudalism belongs to one culture and capitalism to another and yet they are occurring in the same scenario. Or, as if a feudal and a capitalist country are juxtaposed and only slightly combined" (Zavaleta 1983, 17). Building on Zavaleta's work, recent Marxist and Indianist scholars maintain that in Bolivia different types of societies (nomadic, agrarian, modern) are juxtaposed to each other (Tapia 2004, 2006). They have distinct systems of production, social structures, forms of authority, and conceptions of rights, community, society, and the state. The national state in Bolivia has been weak and has not destroyed indigenous cultures in order to build a homogeneous national culture (García Linera 2005, 21). Capitalist development has been uneven and about two-thirds of the population live under traditional and semimercantile economic circuits in the informal economy and in the peasant and communal economies (ibid.). Yet despite the weaknesses of capitalism and of the state, the Bolivian political system has been constructed with Eurocentric values. Even though elites have tried to impose notions based on the capitalist-liberal creed of the individual, they have not been able to do away with communal forms of government or authority. Whereas most people from the popular sectors such as indigenous people, miners, urban dwellers, and union members practice forms of assembly and ayllu communal democracy, only a tiny urban and white-mestizo minority has lived under the pretense of a liberal representative system.

After long-lasting processes of capitalist development, in which indigenous people have become semiproletarians, urban migrants, and so on, it cannot be maintained that these structural processes have not affected indigenous communities. Moreover, it appears these scholars have forgotten the colonial origins of indigenous communities, and communal forms of rule, in the so-called Republic of Indians, and that some practices of communal democracy such as ritualized punishments have an origin in haciendas and not in ancestral pre-Hispanic practices. Perhaps dualism might allow them to criticize capitalism vis-à-vis idealized communal models, but it provides poor theoretical tools for analyzing how tradition and modernity have become hybridized in Latin America's cultural, political, and social institutions and practices (Avritzer 2002).

Following constructs of pristine precapitalist indigenous communities conceived of by intellectuals, Evo Morales frequently idealizes community life in his political discourse. He has reiterated, "In my community [the indigenous] lived in solidarity. In my community of origin there was no private property. In my community of origin there was no individualism. . . . In my community we did not know about money, but we lived well" (in Albro 2005, 444). This romantic portrait of communal life contrasts with Morales's autobiographical descriptions of growing up in his rural community in abject poverty and with his accounts of how as a child he dreamed of the luxury of one day riding on a bus and even eating oranges and bananas (Stefanoni and Alto 2006, 54).

Because of this idyllic view of indigenous communities as egalitarian institutions based on the principles of reciprocity, deliberation, and consensus, Bolivian academics, like their Ecuadorian peers, have failed to properly analyze the extent of class, educational, and gender differentiations in these communities. If power differentials exist, it is logical to assume that some members of the community will have discursive expertise that will allow them to present their cases using technical or educated language in the deliberation process (Fraser 1999). Managing the "correct" discursive expertise that allows one to "speak well" is highly valued in Bolivia's assembly democracy (Lazar 2008, 244). Indigenous people who do not have the same levels of education will have difficulty finding the right words to articulate their ideas. "Women often talk of themselves as lacking the knowledge necessary to speak publicly" (ibid.). When they address assemblies their voices often do not carry the same authority as those of their male counterparts. If these academics want to paint communities as spaces where debates among equals flourish, they will have to acknowledge the disruptive influence of inequalities on processes of deliberation.

Critics of deliberative democracy argue that individuals do not always engage and participate. Whereas participation increases at moments of collective action or when people have to address concrete needs in their communities, it tends to ebb afterward. Moreover, people sometimes get tired of being asked continuously to participate. Unlike the Western right to be "free" from politics (Held 1987, 291), advocates of communal and assembly democracy mandate participation as an unavoidable duty or requirement of group membership that has normative priority over individual rights. Hence, assembly democracy does not face a lack of participation among its members, but members participate at the cost of fundamental principles of the liberal tradition, such as the autonomy of the individual.

In their passionate defense of liberal democracy, many foes of these populist regimes have idealized the democratic nature of the political systems of Bolivia, Ecuador, and Venezuela before the triumph of radical populist leaders. Scholars sometimes have overlooked these systems' exclusionary characteristics. As a new wave of revisionist scholarship of Venezuela has shown, after 1958 the left was excluded, and Democratic Action and the Christian Political Electoral Independent Organization Committee "shared in the exploitation of the country's oil rent. The revenues obtained from the oil economy initially sustained a vast clientelist and corporatist network of interests that were affiliated to AD and COPEI." When this model of development could no longer work and Venezuela entered into a prolonged economic crisis, mechanisms of patronage deteriorated, and traditional political parties "increasingly resorted to violence and electoral fraud in order to maintain authority and dominant party hegemony" (Buxton 2005, 334). The conclusion of revisionist social scientists is that what has remained in place in Venezuela's current political system is its exclusionary and antidemocratic nature. What has changed is that it has incorporated the poor but "has created a zero-sum framework in the view of government opponents" (346).

As in Venezuela, the notion of democracy in Bolivia and Ecuador has been used by elites to differentiate those who rightfully belong to the national community from those who are seen as its barbaric exterior. When newly elected president Evo Morales traveled to Europe, he was advised by a major national newspaper, *La razón*, "to dress as the *gente* (important, white, urban) and not as a *sindicalero* (unionist)" (Ticona 2006, 171). The reactions of the Ecuadorian media and of some white politicians to the indigenous and military alliance of

January 2000 oscillated between racist-paternalistic views that portrayed indigenous people as naïve masses manipulated by the military, to openly racist charges that "Indians had polluted Congress with their bad odor." Ecuadorian and Bolivian white elites continue to see populist followers as uncivilized others and as folk who are not yet ready for democracy. The elites see themselves as enlightened civilizers who will bring ignorant folk slowly toward democratic participation under their guidance and protection.

Populism and el Pueblo

Populism embodies a Manichaean rhetoric that constructs the struggle between the people and the oligarchy as an ethical and moral confrontation between good and evil, redemption and downfall. The term *the people,* however, is profoundly vague and elastic. In order to disentangle its ambiguities, it is important to start with Ernesto Laclau's observation that the people "as operating in populist discourses is never a primary datum but a construct—populist discourse does not simply *express* some kind of original popular identity; it actually *constitutes* the latter" (2005b, 48). The peculiarity of populist discourse is to frame politics as an antagonistic confrontation between the people and the oligarchy. What needs to be researched is, Who is excluded and included in these discursive constructs? Who has created these categories? What are the levels of social and or political polarization produced by populist discourse? How do populists imagine the promised land that will come after the people are redeemed?

In order to analyze the historical shifts of who has been included and excluded in the category called the people, I focus on countries with multiethnic populations, such as Bolivia and Ecuador. In these nations populist rhetoric has historically constructed the people as urban and mestizo (ethnically and culturally mixed) who had an antagonistic relationship with the oligarchy. The exaltation of poor and mestizo people as the essence of the nation repelled white and foreign-leaning elites, who were terrified by populist challenges. The populist creation of a virtuous and mestizo nation, however, excluded those of indigenous and African descent. In order to belong to the people and to the nation, the indigenous and the descendants of Africa were encouraged to adopt national-mestizo values, to reject their cultural specificity, and to whiten themselves culturally and racially.

During the 1952 Bolivian revolution, for example, the "Indian was erased in favor of a *Mestizo* identity," and languages of class were employed to conceal ethnicity (Canessa 2006, 245). In recent years, due to the strength of indigenous organizations, the discursive elaborations of who belongs to the people have changed. Evo Morales and his party, the Movimiento al Socialismo, have replaced "the mestizo as the iconic citizen with the indígena" (255). Morales's success in the 2006 election is explained, in part, by his ability to articulate anxieties provoked by globalization while presenting indigenous people as the essence of the nation. The new confrontation is between those who have struggled to defend Bolivia's natural resources—indigenous people—and the oligarchy, which has transferred those resources to imperialist and foreign powers. The term *indigenous,* as Andrew Canessa (2007) has shown, now signifies a claim to postcolonial justice, and for a broader political project of nationalism, self-determination, and democratization. This new definition has allowed many who previously did not see themselves as Indians to claim an indigenous leftist and nationalist political identity. This inclusionary political definition has emerged simultaneously with a populist idealization of communal life as pristine spaces free from capitalist domination.

Similarly, if the discursive confrontation between the people and the oligarchy has characterized Ecuadorian politics since the 1930s and 1940s, the social groups assigned to these discursive categories have not remained the same. In the 1930s and 1940s the people were conceived by Velasco Ibarra in political terms. *El pueblo* was a political category whose will was not respected in the polls by oligarchic electoral fraud. This political elucidation of the category el pueblo excluded many poor who couldn't vote due to literacy requirements, as well as indigenous people and Afro-Ecuadorians. Since the creation of the populist Concentración de Fuerzas Populares in Guayaquil in the late 1940s until Abdalá Bucaram's populism, the category the people was constructed as the urban and mestizo poor, who had an antagonistic relationship with the oligarchy conceptualized as a social, economic, cultural, and political category. In these discursive elaborations indigenous people and Afro-Ecuadorians continued to be invisible as distinct cultural groups. Since the 1990s the leaders of the Indian movement and of black organizations used the category el pueblo to frame their claims. They demanded their right to belong to el pueblo, at the same time that they requested their recognition as a different group, culture, or nationality. During the 2000 coup, when an alliance of the indigenous movement with sectors of the armed forces under the leadership of Lucio Gutiérrez overthrew President Mahuad, the people became associated with the indigenous people who occupied Congress and other public spaces. Indigenous people became the people's new incarnation, and even their vanguard in the struggle against corruption and structural adjustment policies.

El pueblo, however, does not conjure only positive images. Elite perceptions have varied from paternalistic to openly hostile and racist. In Venezuela, for example, the benevolent paternalistic image of the people as virtuous yet ignorant and naïve masses that were the foundation of democracy changed with the introduction of structural adjustment policies during the second administration of Carlos Andrés Pérez (1989–93). His government ended with state subsidies, protective barriers, price controls, and wage regulations "that had constituted the populist model of development for half a century." The hike in the price of domestic gasoline in 1989 broke the bond between the paternalistic state and the people based on the shared assumption of the birthright of all Venezuelans for oil rents. Massive demonstrations turned into two days of "massive rioting and looting, escalating from neighborhood grocery stores to commercial centers in Caracas and other cities" (Coronil 1997, 376). After these events the people were transformed into "an unruly and parasitical mass to be disciplined by the state and made productive by the market" (Coronil 1997, 378). This rebellion, known as the Caracazo or the Sacudón,[2] conveyed elite nightmares of the savage, uncivilized, disorganized rabble that invaded the centers of civility. These constructions of the rabble as the antithesis to reason and civilized behavior allowed or justified the state's fierce and brutal repression, which ended in at least four hundred deaths.

According to Fernando Coronil, common people had a different reading of these events. They viewed elites as "a corrupt *'cogollo'* [bigwig] that had privatized the state, looted the nation's wealth, and abused the people. . . . The people have been betrayed by their leaders and democracy has become a façade behind which an elite had used the state for its own advantage" (Coronil 1997, 378). Given these constructions of the categories el pueblo and the oligarchy, Hugo Chávez was able to build himself up and to be elevated by his followers as the embodiment of the antioligarchic popular caudillo.

One of the peculiarities of populism is the discursive construction of society as an antagonistic field where the virtuous people confront their enemy, the wicked oligarchy. The degree of social and political polarization produced by populist discourse and rhetoric allows a differentiation between experiences. In some cases, as in *chavismo* or the classical populist experience of *peronismo,* the Manichaean construction of politics ends in a total and fundamental struggle between the people, as a social and political category, and the oligarchy. Chávez's nationalism, anti-imperialism, positive glorifications of el pueblo as *el soberano* (the sovereign), and use of mass meetings and mass mobilization are similar to the radical national populist experience. But most important is that his movement has politicized economic, cultural, and ethnic cleavages (Roberts 2003). In other cases—for instance Alberto Fujimori in the 1990s in Peru or Velasco

Ibarra in Ecuador in the 1940s—the terms *pueblo* and *oligarquía* had political but not necessarily social contents. Political polarization did not lead to social polarization. Finally, there are mixed cases, such as Abdalá Bucaram's and Lucio Gutiérrez's elections and short administrations in Ecuador. Despite their attempts to bring traditional elites aboard their neoliberal project, their personas brought political, social, and even cultural polarization. All their actions, words, and performances were read through class lines and were portrayed by the upper and middle classes as the embodiment of the culture of the rabble (de la Torre 2006).

Contemporary populist leaders, like their predecessors, have glorified the people as the embodiment of the nation against foreign-led oligarchic elites. They have followed narratives based on an us-versus-them logic where "us" "includes all those who have been abused, exploited, or relegated by 'them' the powerful" (Reygadas 2005, 504). These narratives have empowered common people who have to endure humiliation in their daily lives. Also in the heat of confrontation, populist leaders have symbolically dignified the poor and the non-white, who are portrayed by elites and the media as the rabble, the embodiment of barbarism. Populist leaders have used secularized religious symbols to bring redemption and have promised the coming of a holistic and uncontaminated community (Zanatta 2008; Zúquete 2008).

José Zúquete has analyzed Chávez as an emblematic case of "missionary politics," which he defines as a secular "form of political religion that has at its center a charismatic leader who leads a chosen people gathered into a moral community struggling against all-powerful and conspiratorial enemies, and engaged in a mission toward redemption and salvation" (2008, 92). Chávez's goal has not been to reform the system but to create a new Venezuela, a new republic that needed to be baptized again as the Bolivarian Fifth Republic. To bring about a new millenarian order, "a comprehensive moral and spiritual revolution" was required to demolish "the old values of individualism, capitalism, and selfishness" (Chávez in Zúquete 2008, 114). The chosen people, baptized as "the most powerful force that there is between the sky and the earth, sovereign Venezuelan people," have become incarnated in the leader; Chávez carefully reiterates the phrases "I am not myself, I am the people" (100) and "I represent, plainly, the voice and the heart of millions" (104). In this Manichaean struggle, the enemies of the leader are those of the people, as Chávez asserts: "This [struggle] is not about the pro-Chávez against the anti-Chávez but the patriots against the enemies of the homeland" (105). "Infused by a holistic vision of politics as a soteriological tool, this missionary dimension provides a worldview aimed at increasing the followers' sense of belonging and identity and, thus, maximizing their levels of commitment to both to the leader and to the mission of 'saving' Venezuela" (115).

During his first presidential campaign in 2006, Rafael Correa embarked on a mission of developing a citizen's revolution that counted among its goals the total transformation of the economic and political system. To reinforce the idea of a citizen's revolution, at Correa's mass rallies onlookers were encouraged to sing and dance along with Correa to revolutionary tunes. Unlike other politicians who delivered stump speeches, Correa blended popular music and speech making. He spoke to the crowds in sound bites that were interrupted periodically by the campaign's signature songs. The format engendered a festive atmosphere, with Correa lip-synching and dancing alongside musicians and supporters who accompanied him onstage. These gatherings invited the crowd as both entertained spectators and active participants in what seemed more like a street party than a political rally. Drawing on traditions in Ecuadorian political culture, Correa framed his messages in populist terms, building his discourse around the struggle of citizens (embodied in his candidacy) against the cartel of old and corrupt politicians. This classic populist rhetoric was compelling to many Ecuadorians, who were convinced that political parties and politicians were responsible for corruption and all manner of political and economic problems. Correa's message was inclusive, embracing Ecuadorians of all backgrounds who felt disenfranchised by the political system, and who assumed that redemption will come with the destruction of previous institutions and the creation of new order. Like all populist discourse, Correa's rhetoric was Manichean and authoritarian. Those who do not blindly follow him are branded as enemies of the citizenry, extremist right-wingers, and members of the decaying and corrupt oligarchy. For Correa, the term *oligarquía* is elastic, one that encompasses almost anyone who opposes his political project. Thus, in Correa's terms, the oligarchy includes bankers, businesspeople, politicians, and journalists, whom he deems to be servants of the interests of the establishment.

In his symbolic inauguration at the archaeological site of Tiwanaku before a predominantly indigenous crowd, Evo Morales talked about the coming of a new millennium, the Pachakutik. He said, "In Tiwanaku begins a new era for the peoples of the world; only with the strength of the people will we rid ourselves of the colonial state, and with neoliberalism, we will be able to bend the hand of imperialism" (in Stefanoni and Alto 2006, 22). The ending of neocolonial oppression, racism, and the exclusion of indigenous people were also central motifs in his official inauguration address (Morales 2006, 21–43). His electoral campaign was articulated through a reelaboration of the category the people, understood as the indigenous. The goal of Morales's citizens' revolution is the democratic refoundation of Bolivia through ballots, not bullets.

Unlike other contemporary left-wing populist experiences based on top-down leadership styles, Morales's leadership is grounded in social movements. In his Tiwanaku speech he said, "I ask indigenous people to control me, and if I cannot advance, you push me on; we stand before the triumph of a democratic and cultural revolution" (in Stefanoni and Alto 2006, 22). Morales concluded his presidential inauguration address with words reminiscent of communal indigenous understandings of leadership: "I will rule Bolivia by obeying the

Bolivian people" (Morales 2006, 43). Yet like the other Andean experiences, his movement also relies on his charisma (Stefanoni and Alto 2006, 108). The 2006 campaign slogan used by Morales *Evo soy yo* (I am Evo) "followed a predictable script, based on Morales' skills as a charismatic popular leader or caudillo" (Hylton and Thomson 2007, 132).

The empowerment of indigenous people has been evidenced in the symbolic changes in the Bolivian political landscape (Ticona 2006). Indigenous rituals are performed in the presidential palace, previously a center of white power. Indigenous people have served in many ministries, including the Ministry of Foreign Relations. Yet despite all its democratizing accomplishments, as critics have contended, this self-proclaimed citizen's revolution has not respected the rule of law or the independence of the judiciary (Barrios 2008; Gamarra 2008). As in other Andean nations, rivals have been depicted as enemies of the people and of the nation. After winning the elections, Morales's new vice president, Álvaro García Linera, declared, "We have beaten the anti-nation, the anti-history, the inequity that is *Podemos*" (in Dunkerley 2007, 145).[3] Thus, it should not come as a surprise that in the small village of Quilacollo an indigenous leader affirmed, "In our community there was one vote for Tuto Quiroga; we are going to investigate who this is because we cannot tolerate betrayals by our own comrades" (Stefanoni and Alto 2006, 20).

Populism cannot be reduced to the words, actions, and strategies of leaders. The autonomous expectations, cultures, and discourses of followers are equally important in understanding the populist bond. In order to comprehend the appeal of populism, serious attention should be paid to the communication between leaders and followers. As shown in chapter 3, followers had different readings of Bucaram's discourses and performances. Most did not view him as the leader of the poor that he claimed to be. For many he represented an affront to their superiors. Voting for Bucaram was a good opportunity to act on class resentment and even hatred. For brokers (that is, local politicians with clientelist networks), his election meant the chance to be closer to the centers of power to gain access to goods, services, jobs, prestige, and so on. Common people attended his rallies out of curiosity, or in order to enjoy a free show and have a good time, but not because they supported the self-proclaimed leader of the poor.

Leaders and Followers

If the politics of the "new immigrant" and the "new worker" captured the imagination of scholars of classical populism (Germani 1971; Murmis and Portantiero 1971), the politics of the informal sector have seized the minds of students of neopopulism in their neoliberal or radical manifestations. Despite the increasing number of studies that have shown that the descriptions of the informal sector as disorganized are misleading, many sophisticated works on current populism continue to reproduce these images. The endurance of views of populist followers as disorganized masses reflects dominant views of populism as a collection of extraordinary phenomena. Normal politics, based on organization, has been contrasted with populist politics, a disorganized construct produced by rapid social change, crises, and the other social breakdowns that supposedly lie at the roots of populism. Without denying that populism sometimes emerges in conditions of crisis, populism also arises in normal times, and in nations such as Argentina, Bolivia, Ecuador, Peru, and Venezuela has been a recurrent feature of politics.

Unlike the myths of the disorganized poor, ethnographic research on their strategies of survival and on their politics has demonstrated high levels of organization as well as strategic capacities to negotiate with the state and with political parties (Auyero 2001; Cross 1998; Fernández-Kelly and Shefner 2006; Gay 1994; Lazar 2008). Because many of the poor occupy land to build their own houses, or peddle in the streets, or both—thus breaking city ordinances—they live in a state of marginalization and at the border of illegality. Organization is hence a necessity. In John Cross's words, "Organization is necessary for internal regulation in the absence of legal norms. Land invaders must divide land into lots. . . . Street vendors must at least tacitly recognize the 'right' of others to specific locations as well as cooperate in building up their market zone" (1998, 35–36). Organization also allows the poor to avoid regulatory control by the state, and later to negotiate the process of regulation with the state. State agents also promote organization because it is easier to negotiate with a recognized representative of a group than with a whole array of leaders.

Guillermo O'Donnell (1999) has shown that in recently reestablished democracies, with few exceptions, civil rights are not respected. Many common people are both economically poor and have few avenues of legal recourse. They live under conditions of material and legal deprivation, and in environments of dire violence and insecurity. Because their constitutionally guaranteed rights are not respected, the poor rely on politicians and their networks of brokers to have access to a bed in a hospital, a job, or information on where to go and in whose name to request a favor. Brokers are the intermediaries between politicians and poor people. They gather information and resources and are connected to wider networks and cliques of politicians and state officials. Unlike impersonal and objective rights, favors create long-lasting personalized obligations. The distinction between formal and informal organizations is blurred. Formal bureaucratic rules work together with personalist cliques and networks of friends who dispense "favors," including corruption. In situations where social reproduction and even survival is contingent on belonging to personalized networks, it is very difficult to sustain the image of the lonely poor actor.

Because the poor can choose to leave a broker and join a different network, brokers' positions are unstable, and the poor thus cannot be seen as a manipulated and captive voting base. The poor can exit a network, they can also choose to not vote as the broker requested, or they might feel compelled to repay a favor to the broker. If the poor can choose to leave brokers, brokers can also leave their patrons and join another political party. The unreliable nature of political support gives certain advantages to the poor. For the system of exchanges to work, politicians have to at least deliver some resources. They also need to maintain a name and a reputation that can be used by the poor in order to gain power in their dealings with the gatekeepers of their constitutionally prescribed rights (Auyero 2001; Lazar 2008).

Since the informal sector brings to the minds of scholars images of disorganization, they have not researched how populist parties are organized. Many have contrasted formal-bureaucratic party organizations with populist unmediated relationships with the atomized masses. Since organization is assumed to resemble Max Weber's characterization of ideal type, the absence of bureaucracy presumably means the absence of organization altogether, and the reign of charismatic domination. Populist parties do not fit well into these descriptions. The Peronist Party is organized through a series of informal networks that distribute resources, information, and jobs to the poor (Levitsky 2001). Similarly, Ecuadorian populist parties, such as the PRE, also rely on networks to distribute resources and, in unconditional loyalty to Bucaram, their messiahs (Freidenberg 2003). In conditions of poverty and marginalization, participation in problem-solving networks allows access to resources. Involvement in these networks also generates and reconstitutes identities. The resilience of populism among the poor is partially explained by the PRE's networks.

Even outsiders who claim that they were elected due to their unmediated relationships with followers owe their election to political organizations. Hugo Chávez, Lucio Gutiérrez, and Rafael Correa got to power not only due to the nature of their antiestablishment rhetoric. They won elections because of the support of well-organized left-wing political parties and social movements (Freidenberg 2008; López 2003; Quintero 2005).

Populism continues to have ambiguous relationships with democracy. On the one hand, it is a form of protest and resistance to modernization projects that in the name of supposedly universalistic and rationalist projects have excluded the poor and the nonwhite, who have been portrayed as the incarnation of barbarism. Against exclusionary projects, populism has vindicated the worth of the poor and the excluded, so that rather than being considered obstacles to progress they are constructed as the essence of the nation. But because the people is a discursive elaboration of politicians, it is important to analyze who is included and who is excluded in these constructs. The category of the people is constructed by leaders who have claimed to embody it. This authoritarian appropriation of who are the people and what are their values has had contradictory meanings. On the one hand populism has restored and valued the cultural worth of common people. But on the other, leaders have appropriated the meanings of the popular and have tried to impose their versions of popular authenticity.

Even though populist discourse and representation could have authoritarian elements, populism is lived as profoundly democratic. Populism mobilizes passions and incorporates those previously excluded. Populist mobilization, however, does not always respect the norms and institutions of liberal democracy because its norms and procedures are seen as impediments to the expression of the authentic and homogenous will of the people, which is no other than that of the leader.

The resurgence of national populism is no surprise. Populism has historically arisen as a response to the exclusion of many from the polity. The persistence of social and economic exclusions—and, in particular, the difficulty of the poor to have access to their constitutional rights—explains its resilience. Even though the concrete manifestations of populism and the levels of polarization it entails vary in different experiences, populism continues to be a recurrent feature of democracies where common people's rights are not enforced or respected.

The discursive glorification of common people, the symbolic attacks on the privileges of the elites, the symbolic democratization of spaces of white power and privilege, all these explain why the regimes of Chávez, Morales, and Correa are regarded by their social bases as experiments in democratization. These regimes, as did their populist predecessors, search for mechanisms to bring the leaders and the led into close and unmediated contact. Their permanent electoral campaigns, novel modes of communication (such as Chávez's and Correa's weekly television and radio addresses), and the constant movement of presidencies to remote areas that lack the oversight of other authorities bring to the foreground evidence that a democratic revolution is under way and that leaders are in close contact with their electors, particularly those at the margins of state and nation.

Chávez, Morales, and Correa share the use of a populist discourse to represent politics as a Manichaean struggle between two antagonistic poles. But they differ in the type of relationship between leaders and followers. Morales's administration has given spaces of autonomy to movement organizations. Chávez and Correa, on the contrary, have followed a top-down approach to organization (Roberts 2008). They have had little patience with autonomous social movement organizations and have actively tried to directly supervise grassroots organizations. Correa and Chávez have resorted to a leadership style based on unity and command from above, where the leader appears to be the condensation of diverse demands made from below. Evo Morales has followed a different leadership strategy. Like Lula in Brazil, he has pursued convergence and persuasion, allowing his grassroots constituency more autonomy (French 2009, 367).

These Andean experiments are part of a regional turn to the left that has done away with neoliberal orthodoxy. The state has returned to protect common people, and in these mineral-rich nations, to redistribute rent. Yet it would be reductionist to underscore rent redistribution as the sole reason for increasing levels of support from the common people. The combination of redistribution, populist discursive empowerment, and an increasing presence of the state and the nation might explain the popularity of the leaders of these self-described citizens' revolutions.

Chapter 6

Rafael Correa

Between Radical Populism and a Citizens' Revolution

RAFAEL CORREA's political career has been meteoric. After winning the 2006 election, running as an outsider, this former college professor of economics presided over the transformation of Ecuador's political system. Political parties—such as the Izquierda Democrática, Partido Social Cristiano, Democracia Popular, and Partido Roldosista Ecuatoriano—that had dominated politics since the 1979 transition to democracy have decayed and have become regional and local parties at best. Correa's movement, Alianza PAÍS (AP), is the dominant political force. Ecuadorians went through another constituent process and in a referendum in September 2008 approved their twentieth constitution. Rafael Correa was reelected president in April 2009 with 52 percent of the vote and will govern until 2013, when he could run for another term. But the president could not transfer his popularity to the other candidates of his movement. Although the AP is the main force in the new congress, renamed the National Assembly, they do not have a majority and will need the votes of other movements and parties. Correa's movement also controls many local and regional governments. But there are significant exceptions, such as Guayaquil and other local governments where the opposition is in control.

Correa runs for office and governs on promises to transform liberal democracy into participatory democracy and to preside over a "citizens' revolution." Yet the call for new forms of political participation goes hand in hand with a charismatic movement where Rafael Correa has been manufactured as the embodiment of the citizens' revolution. Correa is also an interesting example with which to analyze the hybridization of traditional and modern campaign and governing strategies (de la Torre and Conaghan 2009). Like previous politicians, Correa uses clientelism, patronage, and a populist rhetoric, yet these old strategies have become hybridized with modern uses of the media. Experts in media manipulation and advertisement occupy key positions in his administration and have been in charge of designing his permanent political campaigns (Conaghan and de la Torre 2008). After becoming president in January 2007 Correa campaigned for a referendum to call for a Constituent Assembly (April 2007), then to elect the members of the assembly (September 2007), to vote to approve the new constitution (September 2008), and then to vote for president, members of the new assembly, and local officials (April 2009).

In order to win elections Correa has depicted political rivals as enemies of the nation and of the revolutionary process. He has viciously attacked politicians, journalists, and a few businesspeople. When he ran out of external foes he focused on internal enemies such as indigenous activists, radical ecologists, and former fellow travelers. His government used laws instrumentally to get rid of opposition representatives and to close Congress. Since Correa has not respected the rules of fair campaigning, he has created an uneven playing field for the opposition. Yet Correa's authoritarian excesses coincided with policies that could broaden and expand democracy. The 2008 constitution expanded civil and social rights and gave rights to nature. Democracy could also be broadened, as the new constitution has recognized that communal, participatory, and deliberative forms of democracy both complement and invigorate liberal representative democracy (Larrea Maldonado 2008, 82). State planning, nationalism, government intervention in the economy, and a new commitment to social justice have replaced neoliberal ideologies with a post-neoliberal socialism of the twenty-first century.

The Elections of 2006

On 15 October 2006, Ecuadorians went to the polls to choose among thirteen different candidates. It was the eighth presidential election since the transition to democracy, in 1979. The winner of the first round of the election was Álvaro Noboa, the richest man in the country and candidate of the Partido Renovador Institucional Acción Nacional (PRIAN). Noboa received 26.8 percent of the vote. Rafael Correa, candidate of the Movement Alliance for a Proud and Sovereign Homeland (Movimiento Alianza PAÍS—Patria Altiva i Soberana), came in second, with 22.8 percent. In the runoff held on November 26, Correa bested Noboa by winning 56.7 percent of the vote (Conaghan 2008b).

Noboa and Correa battled for the presidency in an atmosphere marked by relative macroeconomic stability and deep political uncertainty. By 2006 Ecuador had recovered from the 1999–2000 economic crises. In 2006 the GDP grew at a moderate annual rate of 3.3 percent, inflation was 2.1 percent, foreign debt accounted for 37 percent of the GDP (down from 87 percent in 2000), and poverty had been reduced to 45 percent (from its peak of 63 percent in 1999). Despite macroeconomic recovery, middle- and working-class people felt helpless and anxious about their jobs and thus ready to accept an anti-neoliberal rhetoric. In 2006 the unemployment rate was 11 percent and the underemployment rate was 48 percent. Most important, the available jobs were unstable and fell short of people's expectations of dignified work (T. Larrea 2007).

Ecuador had become synonymous with political instability. In less than a decade, three elected presidents (Abdalá Bucaram, Jamil Mahuad, and Lucio Gutiérrez) had been deposed in semilegal coups. The events that led to their removal combined collective action, the maneuvers of politicians in Congress, and the tacit approval of the armed forces (de la Torre 2006). At the heart of Ecuador's unstable politics was an electoral system that created incentives for party fragmentation and personalism (Pachano 2007). Rather than voting for closed party lists or preference voting within a list, voters were allowed to choose congressional representatives across a variety of lists. With few restrictions on inscribing new movements, presidential candidates proliferated. In 2006 thirteen presidential candidates ran for office, the highest number since Ecuador's transition to democracy in 1979. At least nine political parties have had representatives in Congress (Pachano 2002, 73). Political parties are regional and not national, and they work as clientele machines. Even though traditional parties lost considerable ground after the 1998 elections, they continued to dominate Congress until it was closed by the Correa government. Parties distributed patronage and looked after the business and political interests of local and regional elites.

Political parties that survived the crisis caused by the semilegal removal of Bucaram and Mahuad could not endure Gutiérrez's overthrow. After leading a rebellion or coup d'état against Mahuad, Colonel Gutiérrez won the 2002 elections but his party, the Partido Sociedad Patriótica (Patriotic Society Party), had only five representatives in Congress. In order to survive, Gutiérrez had to seek alliances with different political parties. After the center-left Izquierda Democrática and Pachakutik joined the rightist Social Christian Party in announcing that they would impeach the president, Gutiérrez resorted to an alliance with Noboa's PRIAN and Bucaram's PRE. A new pro-Gutiérrez alliance in Congress illegally reorganized the National Electoral Board and the Supreme Court of Justice. The new supreme court allowed Bucaram to return from Panama, and protests in Quito were used as excuses for Congress to overthrow President Gutiérrez in April 2005 (see chapter 3).

The public became increasingly disillusioned and angry with politicians and parties. Crowds in Quito attacked and beat congressional representatives during the protest that ended in Gutiérrez's removal (Ramírez 2005). Journalists and media pundits fanned the flames of the public's disillusion and, in doing so, helped set the stage for the ascent of political outsiders. The term *partidocracia* (partyarchy) has been widely adopted to describe the Ecuadorian political system.[1] In his columns in *Vistazo* magazine and in his weekly television political show *Más allá de la noticia,* Alfredo Pinoargote pilloried the institutions of liberal democracy. He opined, "Ecuador lives the shame of a fictitious democratic system."[2] He excoriated party elites; they were a "partidocracia," "a dictatorship of a mafia," and "responsible for corruption and ungovernability."[3] The journalist decried the party system as perverse, referring to it with the term *febresborjismo.* This neologism implied a wicked complicity between the two major political bosses and former presidents, León Febres Cordero, from the rightist Partido Social Cristiano, and Rodrigo Borja, of the social democratic Izquierda Democrática.[4] The data found in Tatiana Larrea's qualitative study (2007) summarizes citizens' analysis of Ecuadorian democracy and their hopes for the future, before the 2006 election. Politicians and Congress were seen as the cause of the nation's main problem: corruption. Even though a few years before citizens had hoped for a reform of Congress, by 2006 their feelings were summarized in one of the most repeated slogans of the anti-Gutiérrez demonstrations in April 2005 in Quito: *Que se vayan todos* (Throw them all out). With politics and politicians defined as the source of all problems, the solution appeared to be simple: seek an honest, sincere, and strong leader who had not been corrupted by years of politicking.

Given the depth of the public's disillusion with politics, it was not a surprise when voters endorsed two unconventional candidates in the 2006 race. With a billion-dollar fortune, Álvaro Noboa entered politics as a businessman and philanthropist who promised voters unbridled capitalist modernization and economic growth. Using the financial resources and networks of his economic empire, Noboa built an impressive charitable foundation, the Cruzada Nueva Humanidad (Crusade for a New Humanity). After launching his first presidential bid in 1998 with the help of Bucaram's Partido Roldosista Ecuatoriana (PRE), Noboa founded his own political vehicle, the Partido Renovador Institucional Acción Nacional. In Noboa's second run for the presidency, in 2002, he lost to Gutiérrez, but he approached the 2006 race with confidence. In the 2006 elections (held concurrently with the first round of the presidential race in October), Noboa's PRIAN performed well. Winning twenty-eight congressional seats, PRIAN became the single largest caucus in the incoming congress.

Noboa faced a quintessential outsider in the second round, Rafael Correa. Until April 2005, he was a college professor in the faculty of economics at one of Quito's elite private universities, the Universidad San Francisco de Quito. Outside the classrooms, he garnered some attention for his radio interviews denouncing the dollarization of the economy and neoliberal policies. After the overthrow of President Lucio Gutiérrez, in April 2005, Correa became minister of economy and finance in President Alfredo Palacio's administration. Correa quickly became the government's most controversial figure. He was young, charismatic, and sure of himself. He used his office as a bully pulpit for denouncing neoliberalism and showed his independence by taking on the International Monetary Fund. After leaving office, he and a small group of friends organized the Movimiento Alianza PAÍS (Alliance for a Proud and Sovereign Homeland) in November 2005. Using populist appeals, Correa ran against the economic and political establishment. Lashing out against the partidocracia at every opportunity, Correa framed the election as a contest between good and evil: the honest citizenry (embodied in himself and his movement) confronting the corrupt *clase política*. But Correa fell short of his goal of winning the presidency. In the first round of the election, in October, he placed second, with 23 percent of the vote, and was forced into a second round against Noboa.

Since the transition to democracy, in 1979, politicians have increasingly relied on experts in public relations, opinion polling, and image building. Álvaro Noboa's pollster was Augusto Bernal of the Colombian firm Consultar. Noboa's top media and campaign guru was Luis Eladio Proaño, the former presidential advisor of Abdalá Bucaram and strategist for Noboa's two previous campaigns. Correa's media counselor and top campaign advisor was Vinicio Alvarado, the executive of the public relations firm Creacional. Alvarado's previous credits included work on the presidential campaign of Abdalá Bucaram in 1988.[5]

Television became a key medium in the candidates' campaign strategies. Even though there are laws regulating the amount of money that candidates can spend on television, Noboa ignored them, spending over $2.5 million on television advertising, two-thirds of his entire campaign outlay.[6] Correa spent just over $1 million on television, nearly 90 percent of his total budget.[7] The Correa campaign also boasted the most sophisticated and content-laden Web site of the 2006 campaign. In addition to providing texts of the candidate's positions on the issues in Spanish as well as Kichwua, the site allowed users to download television and radio appearances. Young supporters were organized to manage e-mail lists and post campaign videos on YouTube.

Noboa's television advertising campaign sought to evoke two emotions: optimism and fear. The ads telegraphed optimism and modernity through shots of contented Ecuadorians from diverse ethnic and socioeconomic backgrounds delighted to be working in jobs with the latest technology, led by their savvy successful entrepreneur and future president. The campaign song that accompanied the images was corny, but soaring and inspirational, "Ecuador adelante, adelante Ecuador" (Move ahead, Ecuador). Optimism also came in the form of Noboa's wife, Congresswoman Anabela Azín. TV spots showed the attractive and blond physician attending to the poor with the aid of Noboa's charity foundation. These positive ads were "attempts to elicit enthusiasm through warm images and uplifting music . . . to motivate viewers and to embolden supporters" (Brader 2006, 182).

According to Noboa's script, if Noboa and Azín embodied goodness, it followed that Correa was downright evil. Noboa used redbaiting television spots that accused Correa of being a communist and a disciple of Hugo Chávez. The aim of his fear ads was to create uncertainty about citizen's political choices and to influence them to change their political preference (Brader 2006, 182). Whipping up fears about communism and Chávez proved to be effective in rattling some upper-middle-class voters into support for Noboa. The appeal was limited, however, since a majority of Ecuadorians of all social classes held positive views of the Venezuelan president (T. Larrea 2007, 54–55).

Alvarado and his team designed a campaign that represented Correa as an incorruptible, antiestablishment leader. The aggressive thread in the Correa campaign was evident early on in the slogan credited to Alvarado: *Se viene el correazo* (Here comes a whipping); it was a play on the candidate's last name, which in Spanish can mean belt or whip. In another variation, the play on words became *Dale, Correa* (Hit 'em, Correa)—a cry that was supposed to evoke how Correa would smack down the traditional political elite. During campaign appearances in the first round of the election, Correa brandished a belt to make the point (Conaghan and de la Torre 2008, 272).[8] Mockery and the demonizing of opponents were central to the antiestablishment theme of the Correa campaign. In one of the most talked about commercials, entitled *"Ya basta"*(That's enough), legislators were depicted as clowns riding the elevator in Congress. Correa regularly referred to other politicians as *mafiosos,* liars, and dinosaurs headed for extinction.

The media, however, was not the only site where candidates competed. Both also used more traditional campaigning techniques, such as political rallies, car caravans, walking tours, and, most important, clienteles' networks. The car caravan is a relatively cheap campaigning technique that does not require as much coordination as the mass meeting. "Similarly to processions of saints and virgins who are temporarily removed from their shrines and strutted around neighborhoods, candidates abandon stately locations and buildings and are paraded for public observation and adoration" (Waisbord 1996, 5). This is why, drawing inspiration from the *menemóvil* in which Carlos Menem campaigned for the Argentine presidency in 1989, most Ecuadorian candidates use decorated trucks, painted with their portraits and party symbols, to parade through cities throwing T-shirts and other presents to the crowds.

Candidates continue to seek close contact with their followers. It seems that it is not good enough for candidates to visit poor towns and neighborhoods. People also demand gestures of close proximity, such as shaking hands or getting their picture taken with a candidate. Rallies are the opportunity for local leaders and brokers to show their influence. They are responsible for organizing events and bringing large crowds. Rallies have been modernized with lights, music, fireworks, and the like. In order to be broadcast live they are also timed to coincide with prime-time network news shows.

Noboa repeated the same script in his rallies. Car caravans ended in plazas or neighborhood squares, where he gave away computers, free medical assistance, medicines, wheelchairs, and a microloan to transform a poor person into an entrepreneur. These exchanges of material goods for political loyalty differed in their intensity. In places where his party and charity foundation have had a regular and long-term presence, as in Guayaquil and other cities of the coast, Noboa was able to consolidate loyal groups of followers. For people whose survival passes through the intermediation and help of Noboa's networks, these exchanges symbolized that the candidate had a real and sincere preoccupation with their well-being. They felt obliged to give something back to their benefactor. When these exchanges were sporadic, as when Noboa visited poor neighborhoods in Quito just for one day during elections, people might take the presents without feeling any obligation or gratitude to the politician. When these events were broadcast on television they were read as pretentious acts of a pathetic candidate trying to buy votes.[9] As Emmanuelle Barozet (2006, 89) argues, clientelist exchanges have to follow an ethic of discretion, dignity, and moderation. A candidate like Noboa, who seems to ostentatiously give presents, is morally condemned.

Noboa used the paternalistic symbols of the hacienda to offer his patronage and charity to all the poor. He acted as a good patron, who, instead of enjoying his fortune, suffers because of people's poverty, gives them his money, offers his help, and even donates performances by internationally acclaimed musicians. These exchanges were mediated by religious symbols. The candidate, acting as the hacienda owner in a baptism, mixed the exchange of gifts with blessings and prayers. Like a televangelist, Noboa prayed on his knees and embraced and kissed poor people before giving them wheelchairs.

Clientelist exchanges are based on trust. The candidate counts on people's votes in gratitude for his gifts. Common people expect that the candidate will deliver his promises. The worst thing that could happen for the smooth development of exchanges is that people could feel cheated by a politician. And that is precisely what happened just a few days before the closing of the campaign. Television crews discovered that the affiliation cards of hundreds of Noboa's supporters to his housing project in the city of Manta were dumped in the garbage. Journalists and Correa's campaign argued that Noboa was exploiting the poor and that he was only seeking their vote without ever planning to deliver the houses he had promised.

Correa's campaign strategy was also based on mass rallies where common people were in close proximity to the candidate and sang along with him to revolutionary music of the 1960s and 1970s. Correa's political rhetoric was innovative. Unlike the long and boring speeches of his rival, Correa blended music and dance with speech making. He spoke briefly, presenting a simple idea, music was played, and Correa and the crowd sang along to the campaign tunes and danced. When the music stopped Correa spoke briefly again followed by music, songs, and dance. These innovations allowed people to participate and brought feelings that Correa and his followers were part of a common political project, a "citizens' revolution" against the partyarchy. This was also a good strategy for youngsters, who get bored listening to speeches, and for television viewers, who were presented with only a snapshot of his rallies.

The logo of Correa's campaign was that people's dignity was not going to be bought by the fat checkbook of a millionaire. Correa contrasted the dignity of his physically challenged running mate, Lenín Moreno, who uses a wheelchair, with the insincere charity of the billionaire who gives away wheelchairs in exchange for votes. Correa presented his persona as the incarnation of common people's dreams of social mobility. Despite his humble social origins, he won scholarships to do postgraduate work in Belgium and the United States before becoming a college professor. His campaign creatively used the term *patria* (homeland), as in his slogans "The homeland is coming back," or "Passion for the homeland." This term was reappropriated in the name of his political movement as Patria Altiva i Soberana (Proud and Sovereign Homeland, PAÍS). His persona symbolically united a regionally divided nation. Even though he was born and raised in Guayaquil and talks with a *costeño* accent, Correa speaks the indigenous highland language Kichwua, has lived for many years in Quito, and worked as a secular Catholic missionary in the small Andean village of Zumbahua.

Correa launched the Socio PAÍS program, based on promises for housing, health benefits, and increasing state subsidies for natural gas, gasoline, and electricity for domestic consumption. He also gathered the support of old-time politicians and brokers in different cities

(Freidenberg 2008, 221).[10] Correa's strategy worked on many levels. The support of old-time caciques and brokers, along with his promises to increase subsidies, were translated into votes. In Guayaquil, for instance, the poor voted for him because of his Socio PAÍS programs and promises to increase subsidies for utilities.[11] Finally, the endorsements of old-time politicians for Noboa, and the fact that many showed up at his rallies, were read as evidence that Noboa was part of the partidocracia.

Scholars have argued that when television meets politics, rational debate is displaced by melodrama (Peri 2004; Sarlo 1995; Sartori 1998; Schedler 1997). Beatriz Sarlo writes, "Politics in the mass media is subordinated to the laws that regulate audiovisual flow: high impact, large quantities of undifferentiated visual information, and arbitrary binary syntax that is better suited to a matinee melodrama than to the political arena" (1995, 259). These tales of decay and transformation, as Ted Brader (2006) has argued, have a long history in the Western tradition, where reason has been set apart from passions and emotions. Some scholars have idealized past forms of politics based on ideologies, assuming that ideological politics were devoid of emotions. These accounts, which somewhat reflect a European past of ideological and class-based parties, exaggerated the absence of emotional myths and symbols in working-class politics (Álvarez Junco 1987). Other scholars have assumed that the scientificization of politics and the rise of campaign technocrats, together with the deactivation of citizens and their transformation into passive spectators, have transformed rational deliberation into emotional manipulation. Yoram Peri (2004) has analyzed how the logics of television and politics have fused into mediapolitik. According to Peri, the blending of politics and television favors the personalization of politics. When television meets politics, rational debate is displaced by emotions and drama. In addition to journalists and politicians, the managers of mediapolitik become key players in public life: "These are the experts in marketing and voter research techniques, message development, advertising, image building, speechwriters, pollsters, and particularly political strategies and consultants whose expertise lies in media manipulation" (103).

The 2006 Ecuadorian election illustrates that while campaign strategies clearly were designed to play on the emotions of voters, political debate over substance was not displaced completely. The issues at stake in the 2006 election were by no means trivial. Both candidates articulated distinctive views about the future of public policy under their prospective governments. Correa promised to realize La Revolución Ciudadana—a program aimed at revitalizing the role of the state in the economy and writing a new constitution. Correa's agenda stood in stark contrast to that of Noboa. Whereas Noboa promoted globalization and capitalist development, Correa promised the socialism of the twenty-first century, an amalgam of nationalist policies to protect the economy and redistributive measures to spread the wealth. And whereas Correa argued for a constituent assembly as the mechanism to build a new social contract and new political institutions, Noboa expressed interest only in limited political reforms.

While the media was central to the 2006 campaign, it did not displace traditional ways of doing politics. Nor did the media turn the campaign into an exercise devoid of content. The logics of the new media age and old-fashioned politics have merged. Pollsters and experts in media manipulation have an important role in fashioning the images of candidates and the ways that they make appeals to the electorate. Television is the site where candidates spend most of their resources. Yet candidates' use of the media in political campaigning has not eclipsed traditional modes of electioneering. All candidates use clientelist networks and seek the support of local and regional caudillos who can deliver votes. Rallies and other events where candidates seek close contact with voters have continued to be used in campaigns because they strengthen the commitment of loyal followers and are important sites for the formation of collective identities. "The hypothesis is that attending political events in person increases partisanship, to the extent that the speech is a 'good one'—in other words, that it involves the interplay of speaker and crowd that builds up shared enthusiasm; and reciprocally, those persons who already have an identification with the political leader or faction have a stronger desire to take part" (Collins 2004, 60). In nations where politicians use populist discourses that divide society into two antagonistic camps, mass meetings will be difficult to eradicate. They will continue to comfortably coexist with television and other forms of electronic outreach.

The Permanent Campaign: Democratization through Confrontation and Deinstitutionalization?

Rafael Correa won the 2006 elections on a platform that strongly criticized neoliberalism and that promised to give citizens back their sovereignty that politicians had appropriated. He was the self-proclaimed leader of a citizens' revolution against the partyarchy. He promised to convene a National Assembly in which all mobilized citizens could participate to collectively forge a new post-neoliberal and radically democratic social pact. The plan called for the creation of "an active, radical, and deliberative democracy." It aimed to establish a "participatory model that will allow citizens to exercise power, take part in public decisions, and control the actions of their representatives."[12]

This proposal for radical democracy went hand in hand with an anti-institutional stand. Correa ran without presenting candidates for Congress, promising to close that body and replace it with a constituent assembly (Conaghan 2008b). After winning the election, Correa's government jettisoned fifty-seven opposition members in Congress. Later, the National Assembly assumed all legislative powers after declaring that Congress was in "recess." These actions, as Jorge Domínguez maintains, were "an example of the arbitrary, authoritarian presidential behavior in both procedure and outcome" (2008, 344).

Following Chávez's example, Correa wanted to eliminate the existing political class by winning a series of elections and referenda. In

April 2007, 82 percent of the electorate supported his proposal to convene a constituent assembly. In September 2007 his movement won a solid majority of 80 out of 130 seats in the assembly. The new constitution was approved with 64 percent of the vote in September 2008. In April 2009, Rafael Correa was reelected president until 2013 with 52 percent of the vote.

In order to constantly win elections Correa is in a permanent campaign. He proudly said that he has been campaigning in order to boost national self-esteem and that his main job as president is to serve as "motivator" (Dieterich 2007, 57). The term *permanent campaign* was popularized by American journalists to describe situations where "the process of campaigning and the process of governing have each lost its distinctiveness" (Ornstein and Mann 2000, 219). To engage in a permanent campaign, presidents increasingly rely on experts in media manipulation, such as advertisement and pollsters (Peri 2004). Correa is no exception. Publicist Vinicio Alvarado is the most powerful member of his cabinet, and his firm Creacional is in charge of government advertisement. Santiago Pérez is their pollster, and Emilio Espinoza, who served under Bucaram, was in charge of Correa's radio campaign (Conaghan and de la Torre 2008).

Correa has always been featured in the media. His government, like previous administrations, uses *cadenas nacionales* (national networks) to broadcast their accomplishments and to denounce their enemies. Correa has used the media to seek a direct relationship with the electorate. Alvarado and his team have used the symbols and slogans of the campaign to broadcast the impression that despite the conspiracies of their enemies Ecuador is going through profound and revolutionary change. For instance, the term *patria,* used in the campaign to proclaim that "the homeland is coming back," has been inserted into the updated logo *La patria ya es de todos* (Now the homeland belongs to everyone). The patriotic song *patria querida* is broadcasted in their advertisement. If Correa and his movement, PAÍS, represent the interests of the homeland, it follows that those who question or oppose his proposals are not only enemies of his regime but of the homeland itself. They become the antipatriots and hence their claims can be dismissed and devalued.

In addition to using cadenas nacionales, whose services are free of charge and which broadcast during prime television time (around 8 p.m.), Correa's government also uses paid television advertisement.[13] The government owns its own media outlets, such as the newspapers *El telégrafo* and *El ciudadano*. The state controls four television channels: Tevecuador, and the three stations confiscated by the Isaías bankers in order to collect their debts to the state: TC Televisión, Gamavisión, and a cable channel, Cablevision. In addition, the state runs four radio stations, Radio Nacional, Super K 800, Radio Cupido, and Radio Carrusel (Palacio 2008, 13). Despite owning and controlling important media, Correa has been in a war against the privately owned media. He has characterized journalists and journalism as "mafiosos, journalistic pornography, human wretchedness, savage beasts, and idiots who publish trash" (Conaghan and de la Torre 2008, 278).

Perhaps the main innovation of Correa's media strategy is the weekly radio and television program *Enlace cuidadano* (Citizens' connection), broadcast every Saturday morning. This show allows Correa to set the news agenda for Sunday and to have constant media exposure. Correa uses his program to attack the opposition, to take on major privately owned newspapers such as *El comercio* and *El universo,* and to disqualify notorious media figures such as Jorge Ortiz and Carlos Vera. Correa's media show is broadcast from remote and marginal areas of the nation that few politicians had bothered to visit. Correa promises to bring material goods and services to marginalized towns and neighborhoods that suddenly, and at least for a few hours, become the center of the nation's attention. During these "dialogues" Correa enjoys an unmediated relationship with citizens who attend the shows. The show helps create networks of supporters and allows for a constant renovation of the charismatic unmediated bond between leader and followers. Correa, to the dismay of the independent media and the opposition, continued to hold his Saturday program even during his latest campaign as an incumbent president.

In order to win elections, "campaigning and campaigners use the language of war—opponents are enemies to be vanquished. Policymakers use the language of negotiation—today's adversaries may be tomorrow's allies" (Ornstein and Mann 2000, 225). Correa has gradually become a master of confrontational and Manichaean populist rhetoric. He has followed the Concentración de Fuerzas Populares (Concentration of Popular Forces) in its characterization of the oligarchy as *pelucones* (wigs). "We have to defeat the oligarchy, the partyarchy, and the wigs who want to go back to the past."[14] Any politician, journalist, or citizen who opposes or challenges him has been labeled a pelucón. Social movement organizations have also been the target of Correa's belligerent rhetoric. In July 2008 he called ecologists *aniñaditos* (infantile and not fully masculine pampered kids) "with full bellies who oppose everything all the time." He contended that "infantile radical" ecologists are "the main danger to our project."[15] A few months later he corroborated that view: "We have always said that the main danger to our political project, after defeating the right in elections, are the infantile left, ecologists, and Indianists."[16]

According to Correa, "The people is not a conceptual phantom, it is not an empty rhetorical word. It is a palpable reality that demands loyalty, love, commitment, and sacrifice."[17] The Ecuadorian people are living through a revolutionary moment. "The Ecuadorian people have brandished [Eloy] Alfaro's sword" to bring about "change, to fight against the past, for sovereignty, and for dignity."[18]

In order to win the elections he is always running for, Correa also uses political clientelism. His movement has incorporated former politicians and caciques who can deliver votes (Freidenberg 2008). For example, he summoned Ambassador Iza Obando from Spain to work on the 2009 elections in Guayaquil and in the province of Guayas. Many neighborhood leaders have abandoned traditional parties and have shifted their alliance to Correa's movement. In Quito, for instance, former clientelistic networks of Democracia Popular and Izquierda

Democrática became integrated into Correa's AP. Clientelism is also used to deliver social services such as the Bonus of Human Dignity, which is given to families who live below the poverty level. Correa's administration increased the bonus from $15 to $35 a month, and in 2008 they covered 1.3 million people. In some regions, as in indigenous communities of the province of Chimborazo, local activists of the president's movement threatened to discontinue this benefit to families that do not support the president by attending his rallies.[19]

The underlying tensions between populist charismatic leadership and top-down mobilization versus autonomous citizens' activation came into the open during the constituent process. Unlike the constituent assembly of 1997–98, which was perceived by the left as exclusionary and manipulated by right-wing parties who drafted a neoliberal constitution, it was promised that the drafting and the discussion of the new constitution would be transparent and open. Alberto Acosta, a founding member of the AP and the president of the assembly, argued, "This is an opportunity to construct citizenship, for people to participate. . . . We want this new pact, this new project of life in common, this social pact to be reflected in a new constitution that will belong to all of us, the citizenry."[20]

The left had a majority in the assembly. However, and unlike the previous constituent process, in 1997–98, when social movements such as the indigenous movement had the power to stage massive collective actions, the indigenous movement had entered a period of crisis. The Gutiérrez administration played on the divisions within the movement. Indigenous Protestant leaders of the Federation of Indigenous Evangelists of Ecuador (Federación de Indígenas Evangélicos del Ecuador, FEINE) supported President Gutiérrez. The Confederation of Indigenous Nationalities of Ecuador (La Confederación de Nacionalidades Indígenas del Ecuador, CONAIE) was weakened and could not mobilize its rank and file in the demonstrations against Gutiérrez's regime. Indigenous people felt alienated from the leaderships of CONAIE and Pachakutik. Many did not even vote for their historical leader, Luis Macas, in the presidential elections. In 2006,

Macas got only 2.6 percent of the total vote, and most indigenous people voted for Correa or for Gilmar Gutiérrez, the candidate of the Patriotic Society.

Despite the inability of weak social movements to stage collective action, the assembly incorporated many of their demands. Perhaps the most innovative was to grant rights to nature, as in the following passages from the constitution:

> Nature, or Pachamama [Mother Earth], where life is reproduced and exists, has the right to exist, persist, maintain and regenerate its vital cycles, structure, functions, and processes in evolution.
>
> Every person, people, community, or nationality will be able to de- mand the recognition of rights for nature before public institutions.
>
> Nature has the right to integral restoration. This integral restora- tion is independent of the obligation on natural and juridical persons or the state to indemnify the people and the collectives that depend on natural systems.

The constitution also prohibits the "introduction of organisms and organic and inorganic material that can alter in a definitive way the national genetic patrimony."

The constitution recognizes that Ecuador is an intercultural and plurinational state and gives indigenous and Afro-Ecuadorian people the right to control their ancestral territories, including their own sys- tems of justice (Larrea Maldonado 2008). Even though the women's and gay and lesbian movements are not allowed to advance their rights to abortion and gay marriage, the new constitution allows people to de- fine their own sexual identity and has paved the way for same-sex cou- ples to have the same rights as heterosexual couples (Ospina 2008, 134).

The Contested Meanings of Democracy in the "Citizens' Revolution"

Different projects of democratization coexist under Correa's admin- istration. Rafael Correa, who was never a militant of a left-wing party, maintains the old leftist distinction between "formal" bourgeois democracy and "real" democracy. The latter is based on "equity, justice, and dignity."[21] Correa defines revolutionary democracy simply as "equity."[22] Because Correa does not have much respect for formal bourgeois liberal-democratic principles, such as pluralism, civil rights, and the separation of powers, he said in Havana that Cuba is an example of real democracy and human rights. The Cuban revolution "is extraordinary because it secured the reestablishment of human rights for all Cuban men and women. It is the recognition that the first constitutional right of all human beings is their full dignity. . . . The Cuban revolution has no skeletons hidden in the closet of history, and has never practiced torture or 'disappearances.' The Cuban revolution has eliminated racial and gender discrimination."[23]

In order to achieve a more equitable society, Correa's administration has followed typical national populist policies, which are supported by the high prices of oil. Spending in social programs increased from 5.3 percent of the GDP in 2006, to 6.1 percent in 2007, to 7.4 percent in 2008 (Ramírez and Minteguiaga 2007, 96; Machado 2009, 11). The minimum wage was increased from $170 to $200 a month, and the new constitution got rid of subcontracted labor. The government continues to subsidize natural gas for domestic consumption, gasoline, and electricity for the poor. The government also reactivated state planning of the economy to promote a strategy of national development (Ramírez and Minteguiaga 2007). Public credit increased by 97 percent in 2007 and 58 percent in 2008 (Machado 2009, 10). It is doubtful that these levels of spending can be sustained in the long run, especially if oil prices fall (Weyland 2009).

Some prominent members of Correa's movement have argued that deliberative radical democracy is an alternative to liberal democracy. They have advocated for the destruction of previously existing institutions and for the creation from scratch of a new institutional order. It is difficult to see how deliberative democracy could be constructed without strong institutions and the rule of law. In their absence deliberation might degenerate into plebiscitary acclamation. Moreover, even though their movement, Alianza PAÍS, is leading a citizens' revolution in which Correa could be just another citizen, they chose to follow the populist traditions, manufacturing Correa as the embodiment of the revolutionary process. Thus it was not a surprise that their project of deliberative democracy clashed with Correa's charismatic leadership in the constituent assembly. Correa became impatient with debates in the assembly that might cost votes in the referendum to approve the constitution. The president prioritized what opinion polls were telling him over demands of social movement organizations and of some of his assemblymen. He disapproved of Indianist proposals to make Kichwua an official language, ecological protectionist plans to forbid open mining operations, and feminist discussions about abortion and gay rights. He accused his own assemblypeople of delusion through "left-wing infantilism." He also worried that the assembly would not have a constitution ready by a previously promised date. Correa viewed the delays—explained by Alberto Acosta, president of the assembly, as necessary for the job of drafting a new constitution—as signs of an overly democratic, naive, and inefficient leadership in the assembly. In the end, Correa asked the political bureau of the AP to request Acosta's resignation from the presidency of the assembly, and Acosta acceded to the demands of the party. After naming Fernando Cordero its new president, one more in tune with Correa's wishes, the assembly completed its job on schedule. In a referendum the new constitution was approved with 64 percent of the vote, but at the cost of limiting deliberation on its content and of not following its own institutional procedures.

Correa is leading a citizens' revolution by urging his supporters to take up ballots rather than bullets. He has not limited himself to changing the course of neoliberal economic policies or to modifying existing institutional arrangements. Reform has certainly not been his goal. The term *citizens' revolution* has allowed Correa to legitimize his regime with Marxist notions of the need for a total rupture with the existing order to bring meaningful and long-lasting change. In front of an audience of policemen he said, "Nobody takes a step backward. This revolution will not be sold, nor will it surrender. We are deepening the citizens' revolution."[24] The notion of a total rupture with the immediate past helps paint elections as Manichaean struggles between historical projects. "We are infringing on the interests of the powerful (thus) we are confronting a virulent reaction."[25] He also said, "Few governments in history have had to confront such a stubborn and irrational opposition as the one we have had."[26] Revolutions also require new social pacts, expressly new constitutions, to begin the construction of a new order. But revolutions, even when they are depicted as peaceful and based on electoral legitimacy and the rule of law, also call for special measures that will bypass legal norms and procedures. Because their goal is to construct a new regime, the tools used to implement change are not necessarily required to respect procedures or the rule of law. Living under a revolution justified Correa's administration's illegal closure of Congress, the war against the media, and the defamation of former allies.

Revolutions signify active participation of the common people, their politicization, and their presence in the streets and in the plazas. Polarization in permanent elections helps create a revolutionary atmosphere in which people feel they have embarked on an extraordinary project. Revolutionary moments have the particular quality of making people feel part of a project and a moment when a new chapter in history is being written. It forces people to take sides and does not allow for skeptical bystanders. Society becomes polarized and simplified into two antagonistic camps: history and antihistory. Politics "ceases to be seen as an instrument for the incremental adjustment of conflictual interests and becomes instead a politics of 'ultimacy,' where ultimate issues are at stake in a once-and-for-all confrontation" (Michael Barkun, in Zúquete 2007, 203).

The term *revolution* also grounds Correa's government's feats in previous popular struggles for national and popular liberation, and in new interpretations of their nations' history. Like other populists, Correa considers "select historical figures to be avatars of the 'essence' of the respective nations" (Zúquete 2007, 194). Perhaps the most dramatic example is the chavista resuscitation of the figure of Simón Bolívar, the generally acclaimed liberator of South America, from conservative historians in order to cast him as an anti-imperialist revolutionary model. Correa sees himself also as the follower of Eloy Alfaro Delgado, his distant relative. At the turn of the twentieth century Alfaro lead the liberal revolution and the separation of church and state. Under the new revisionist history, Alfaro is also painted as an anti-imperialist and a radical democrat, even though he is rumored to have said, "What we won with bullets we will not lose with ballots." Correa's citizens' revolution is pursued in the names of Bolívar and Alfaro. In Havana, Correa finished his speech by invoking "the protective shadows of Bolívar and Martí. With this renascent entry of Fidel into the Ciudad Libertad. . . . And with the memory of Che, we say with dignity and with all our heart . . . ¡Hasta la Victoria Siempre!"[27] These words, reminiscent of the Cuban revolution and of Che Guevara's struggles, are used by Correa to end all his orations. By so doing, he not only presents himself as the inheritor of revolutionary movements, he conveys to his followers the notion that they are all embarked on a radical struggle against imperialism and its national cronies.

Correa privileges notions of democracy as social justice, while some of his followers are seeking to construct better and more meaningful forms of participation and representation through radical participatory democracy. Because they argued that previous institutions were corrupt, Correa's administration decided to build new democratic institutions from scratch. In order to transform the political system, they used laws instrumentally. It remains to be seen if Correa will feel constrained by the new institutional order created by his administration. So far he is changing the articles of the new constitution that he does not approve. The transitory National Assembly, where he had a majority, reformed constitutional provisions that forbid open mineral exploration and the import of transgenic food. Like previous populists, he considers himself the incarnation of the will of the people, which goes beyond constitutional and other institutional constraints.

Correa has not respected pluralism either. He is very uncomfortable conversing with people who divert or dissent. He claims an exclusive grasp of the truth and paints opponents as allies of the oligarchy or as naive left-wing infantile radicals. He also dislikes autonomous social movement organizations when they push for demands that differ from his interpretation of what social change should entail. He has requested, "Indian brothers, do not fall into the traps of irresponsible leaders . . . of social organizations that do not represent anybody but that act as if they represent all of us."[28] It remains to be seen if this project for autonomous citizens' participation could be realized under a populist charismatic leadership that favors mobilization from the top down.

In sum, as in previous populist movements, the leader appropriates the will of the people, which is considered to have one meaning and identity. Because rivals are considered to be enemies of the revolutionary process, their opinions are dismissed. Yet unlike previous populism, Correa's government is based on technocratic rationality. He reiterates in his speeches, "This president, this government, does things without selfish motivations. With clean hands, passionate hearts, and lucid minds we work for the benefit of the homeland. And we do it in a technical way, to reach equality and justice."[29] Experts in media manipulation are in charge of designing his permanent campaign. Technocrats have been appointed to several levels of the administrations. All of them have one goal: to accumulate all political power in order to build a revolutionary society. Yet how authoritarian or democratic it will be remains an open question.

Conclusion

Between Authoritarianism and Democracy

THIS BOOK has illustrated that Latin American populism is neither a temporary political phenomenon linked to the transition to a modern society nor a phase of dependent development linked to import substitution industrialization. Despite the wishes of intellectuals and politicians, populism refuses to disappear but continues to be a recurring political reality. This book has also demonstrated that populism is not the expression of circumstances of social, economic, political, and ideological crises associated with the transitions to different systems of accumulation, such as the transition from export-led development to import substitution, from nationalism-protectionism to neoliberalism, or to the crisis of neoliberal policies. Populism has existed in "normal," noncritical times as well as during periods of crisis and rapid social change (Knight 1998, 227). I have also joined others in arguing that populism cannot be reduced to the enactment of economic policies linked to import substitution industrialization, and that this political phenomenon has adapted itself to new economic situations. During the 1990s populism comfortably coexisted with neoliberal market-oriented policies (Knight 1998; Novaro 1994, 1996, 1998; Novaro and Palermo 1996; Roberts 1995; Roberts and Arce

1998; Weyland 1996, 2001, 2003). Nowadays radical left-wing national populism has returned to the Andean nations of Bolivia, Ecuador, and Venezuela. It has reversed neoliberal policies by implementing a program of socialism of the twenty-first century that, so far, resembles more classical populist than socialist policies (Weyland 2009).

I have drawn on the rich literature on Latin American populism to present a multidimensional approach to its study. I have developed a theory and methodology to study political leadership as a social relationship. This approach integrates the analysis of how populist leaders have been socially created with the study of their innovations and actions that allowed them to become outstanding figures at particular historical junctures. This method combines the analysis of material exchanges between leaders and the led with an analysis of discourses, symbols, myths, and rituals. My aim has been to transcend the false dichotomy between models that explain political leadership by solely using categories of instrumental rationality, such as clientelism, and those models that concentrate only on symbols, discourse, and charisma.

I understand populism, old and new, as a political phenomenon characterized by the following traits: (1) It is Manichaean discourse that presents the struggle between the people and the oligarchy as a moral and ethical fight between good and evil, redemption and fall. Because the categories "people" and "oligarchy" are extremely vague, we have to analyze who is included and excluded in these rhetorical categories in different historical circumstances. We also have to explore the levels of polarization and confrontation provoked by populist discourse and to study how it politicizes existing class and ethnic inequalities. (2) A leader is socially constructed as the symbol of redemption, whereas his enemies are created as the embodiment of all the problems of the nation. The leader claims to be an ordinary human being who, due to his effort and strong will, has climbed from the bottom to become an extraordinary figure. The leader asks the led to believe in his honesty and commitment to the people and the homeland. The ambiguities of ethical discourse also facilitate the

creation of foes. "Enemies are characterized by an inherent trait or set
of traits that mark them as evil, immoral, warped, or pathological,
and, therefore, a continuing threat regardless of what course of action
they pursue" (Edelman 1988, 67). (3) Populist movements are coalitions of emergent elites with the popular sectors. The nature of these
alliances differs in each experience. Peronism and Varguism, for instance, included the national industrial bourgeoisie with organized
workers, sectors of the middle class, and state employees. Neoliberal
neopopulist movements incorporated the very poor with emergent
elites, excluding sectors of the national industrial bourgeoisie and the
organized working class and state employees, who were the beneficiaries of classical populist policies. Radical nationalist populist movements appeal to people who made a living in the informal sector, as
well as to elites and middle-class people who opposed neoliberal
globalization. In some cases, as in Morales's Bolivia, indigenous people, understood as the defenders of national natural resources and as
a political project against neoliberal globalization, are becoming the
center of the nation. (4) Populism is characterized by attempts at top-
down mobilization. At the same time that it opens spaces and venues
for common people to present their grievances, top-down mobilization could clash with the autonomous demands of social movement
organizations. (5) Populist politics has an ambiguous relationship
with democracy. On the one hand, populist movements partially include people previously excluded from the political community. On
the other hand, these movements do not respect liberal-democratic
norms and procedures. Populism rejects mediated politics, seeking
instead the direct, unmediated relationship between leaders and followers. Populists have favored plebiscitary acclamation as spaces
where the unified and homogenous populace acclaim their leader-
savior. Populists have also seen elections as constitutive of their legitimacy (Peruzzotti 2008). Classical populists have expanded the popular
franchise and struggled against electoral fraud. Contemporary radical
populists have embarked on permanent elections as tools to certify
their legitimacy and to destroy existing political elites.

The uneasy relationship between populism and liberal democracy is explained by the particular process of political incorporation of common people into the political community in Latin American countries. Unlike the Western pattern of inclusion via the progressive extension of citizenship rights, the inclusion of common people in Latin America has not been based solely on citizenship. Common people's citizenship rights are not always respected or enforced, and political and limited social rights have been given priority over civil rights. Populist politics, understood as a particular rhetoric and style of political mobilization, therefore, has become the main form of mediation between the state and civil society.

Classical and contemporary Latin American populism is better understood as a political phenomenon. Populism is the result of a particular form of political incorporation of common people into the national community. This incorporation is based on a rhetoric that places the people at the center of national life. The people represent the incarnation of the authentic nation, which antagonistically confronts the oligarchy, which represents the foreign-dominated antination. The struggle between the people and the oligarchy is Manichaean and ethical. Democracy is understood as crowd action and mobilization on behalf of a leader rather than as the respect for liberal-democratic norms and procedures. Strong appeals to the people and the mobilization of common people on behalf of a leader coexist with weak and not-always-enforced citizenship civil rights. Socioeconomic and political distinctions between a few citizens, who not only enjoy all the privileges of living under a state of law but who can also be above the law, and the majority, who are excluded from the benefits of their rights, explain the appeal of populist politicians. Like other politicians, populists have built political machines that exchange votes for goods and services. But, in addition to what other political parties have offered, populist politicians have given back dignity and self-worth to those who are constantly discriminated against in their daily lives.

In the 1990s scholars showed the elective affinities between neopopulism and neoliberalism (Novaro 1994; Roberts 1995; Weyland

1996). The regimes of Chávez, Morales, and Correa illustrate the hybridization of Marxism and populism. These traditions despise liberal mediations, seeking instead mechanisms to allow the people to express their sovereignty directly and without intermediaries. Because Marxists and populists have conceived of politics as an antagonistic confrontation between two camps, they have assumed that diverse interests, identities, and demands could be homogenized and simplified in moments of rupture and struggle. Both traditions look for authentic values and traditions of "the people" in idealized precapitalist pasts. "The unpretentious simplicity of the lower orders and their staunch loyalty to native traditions and ancestral virtues are believed to foster uncompromising opposition to and insurrectionary resolve against foreign invaders and masters" (Talmon 1991, 2–3). Even though Marxists have assumed that a promised land lies in the future, they search in precapitalist and primitive social formations for clues of how it might look. Despite advocacy of nonmediated and direct representation and participation by populists and Marxists, both the populist leader and the Leninist parties, respectively, have assumed the roles of embodying the interests and demands of the people and of the proletariat. Both traditions have demonstrated little tolerance for pluralism, and civil rights have finally been understood as facades for the domination of the oligarchy or of the bourgeoisie.

This book has analyzed current proposals for democratization in the Andean nations based on substantive visions of democracy that promise the authentic presence of the represented and for the genuine enactment of popular sovereignty. As Andrew Arato has warned, "The radical pursuit of substantive values of democracy—popular sovereignty, genuine representation, community or their combination—at the cost of democratic procedures" could lead to authoritarianism or even to "revolutionary dictatorships that will use substantive democratic claims of legitimacy to justify their creation of entirely new political regimes" (2000, 942). In contrast to Arato's catastrophic warnings, the search for substantive models of democratization in Venezuela, Bolivia, and Ecuador have not fully dispensed with liberal republican institutions and are not leading necessarily to authoritarian outcomes. On the contrary, these nations are trying to improve and to correct the participatory and representative deficits of liberal procedural democracies. Indigenous communal models could lead to deeper democracy if communities are democratized with the values of pluralism, individual freedoms, and human rights. Radical participatory projects might democratize their societies if they do not dispense with liberal institutions. But, and Arato's suggestion is very pertinent here, in the absence of strong liberal institutions these experiments aiming to deepen democracy could be used for authoritarian plebiscitary acclamation and the clientelist redistribution of resources for political support.

The self-understanding of current radical populist processes as electoral revolutions encapsulates well what supporters and critics of these regimes have observed. That is the empowerment and participation of common people via authoritarian practices. These regimes can be simultaneously seen as episodes of democratic retrocession and of democratic renaissance. The call for revolutionary transformation at the same time that increases the level of participation of common people in politics presents politics as zero-sum struggles between antagonistic camps. The search for a rupture with the past, in line with Marxist and populist traditions, has the virtue of involving people in politics and the danger of bypassing institutions, leading to personalization and authoritarianism.

Populist rupture has also implied the creation of a new order. As Laclau maintains, "Populism presents itself both as *subversive* of the existing state of things and as the starting point for a more or less radical *reconstruction* of a new order whenever the previous one has been shaken" (2005a, 177; emphasis in original). The preambles to the new Venezuelan, Ecuadorian, and Bolivian constitutions illustrate how seriously these regimes have taken their tasks of refounding their nations. The Venezuelan constitution of 1999 changed the name of the nation to the Bolivarian Republic of Venezuela, citing as its main goal the refounding of the republic and the establishment of participatory and protagonist democracy. The Ecuadorian constitution of 2008, drafted only ten years after the recognition of indigenous and women's rights in the constitution of 1998, aims to "construct a new way in which all citizens will live together in diversity and in harmony with nature to reach the 'good life' the *sumac kasay.*" The Bolivian constitution of 2009 contains the longest and most radical preamble. This document, at least through language, refounds the nation, "leaving in the past the colonial, republican, and neoliberal state." The constitution also tasks Bolivians with the "historical challenge to build collectively a social unitary state of plurinational and communitarian law."

Based on ethnographic analyses of the political campaigns of Abdalá Bucaram, Rafael Correa, and Álvaro Noboa, I have analyzed political discourse as political rituals that create identities in moments of intense polarization. As Pierre Ostiguy (2007) has shown, populist discourse takes place in moments of intense conflict and polarization. Populist discourse is built, in part, as responses to the accusations of its detractors. Perón, like Chávez and Bucaram, for instance, reversed the negative images of their followers as barbarian masses, arguing that they were the embodiment of authentic national values. Populist discourses are spectacles centered on a leader who celebrates the values and culture of his followers allegedly embodied in his persona. Bucaram entertained his followers with the music of the pop band Los Iracundos and by mocking the oligarchy. Similarly Rafael Correa's performances resembled street celebrations where all participants and bystanders sang along, danced, and celebrated the coming of a citizens' revolution against the partyarchy. Populist discourses are also collective elaborations insofar as the leader tends to repeat the words that have been successfully received by his followers. Thus Bucaram used almost the same words in all his performances during his 1996 electoral campaign. Instead of giving scholarly speeches, Correa learned to speak in sound bites. Yet populist discourse is not always successful. As the example of Álvaro Noboa during the 2006 campaign illustrates, neither his words promising to redeem the poor nor his giveaways were read as examples of generosity toward the poor. Media analysts, as well as common people, interpreted his actions as the desperate attempts of a millionaire trying to buy poor people's votes.

This book challenges arguments that television has replaced traditional electoral mechanism, and that it explains the appeal of populist leaders to atomized masses that make a living in the informal sector of the economy. This book has analyzed the hybridization of tradition and of televised postmodernity. The analysis of the 2006 presidential election in Ecuador shows that while the media is central to campaigns, it has not transformed the political arena completely by displacing traditional ways of doing politics. Nor did mediapolitik turn the campaign into an exercise devoid of content. The logics of the new media age and old-fashioned politics have merged. Pollsters and experts in media manipulation have an important role in fashioning the images of candidates and the ways that they make appeals to the electorate. Television is the site where candidates spend most of their resources. Yet candidates' use of the media in political campaigning has not eclipsed traditional modes of electioneering. In a political culture long steeped in personalities and Manichaean appeals, television alone cannot be blamed for the personalization of politics. Candidates have always worked hard to invent appealing characterizations of themselves (as saviors) and off-putting caricatures of their rivals (as devils) and popularize those views through regular media coverage and paid advertisements. But the personal dimension of political campaigns does not mean that the choice between candidates is reduced wholly to a contest over the likeability of competing media images. When candidates opt to present clear and polarizing choices to the electorate, as for instance Correa's socialism of the twenty-first century versus Noboa's capitalist modernization, the ensuing political debate and the stakes of an election are anything but trivial.

Taylor Boas (2005) has demonstrated that media bias, not televised populist appeals, explains the elections of Fernando Collor de Mello in Brazil in 1989 and Alberto Fujimori in Peru in 2000 and 2001. His study illustrates the need for more research on the reception of media images, and it is important because it challenges the common-sense view that television is the main mediation between a neopopulist leader and atomized masses of followers in the informal sector. In addition to survey studies, we need more ethnographic work to explain how people receive media images. Instead of understanding poor citizens as isolated individuals, we should study how their immersion in family, neighborhood, religious, and other networks influence how they perceive media images (Straubhaar, Olsen, and Cavaliari 1993; Porto 2007). In sum, we are in front of a rich research agenda to analyze how the new media interacts with traditional forms of getting elected to office and to explain how media images are perceived, especially by common people.

By analyzing populism as a modern political phenomenon that is the result of a distinct process of political incorporation and that has produced a particular implementation and understanding of the word *democracy,* the continuities and discontinuities between historical and contemporary experiences can be better analyzed. The case studies of José Maria Velasco's populism in the late 1930s and 1940s, Abdalá Bucaram in the 1980s and 1990s, and Rafael Correa from 2006 to 2009 illustrate these similarities and differences.

Velasco's populism was built around a political and ethical understanding of the political cleavages of his times. During the late 1930s and early 1940s, the old practices of electoral fraud and the politics of notables could no longer work. Common citizens such as artisans, state employees, professionals, and a numerically small proletariat demanded their political incorporation. Velasco struggled for these demands and symbolized the democratic ideal at the same time that he inaugurated a new political style. He took politics out of the salons and the cafés of the elites and into the public plazas. He visited most of the country during his political campaigns, delivering speeches heard by voters and nonvoters. Crowds, many of whom were addressed by a politician for the first time, started to feel that they were participants in the political process, even if they only participated in mass meetings and demonstrations on behalf of their leader.

Velasco transformed political problems into ethical and moral struggles. The ambiguities of an ethical discourse allowed Velasco to claim to be above political parties and the organizations of civil society. After all, he claimed to embody the ethical virtues of honesty, sincerity, patriotism, and good will that were demanded of him by many of his followers. Velasco's adversaries were transformed into villains who needed to be crushed before redemption could be achieved. The demonization of political rivals and the ambiguities of Velasco's moral discourse facilitated the formation of political alliances. Because the nature of the struggle was ethical and Manichaean, the respect for liberal-democratic procedures and norms became secondary to the fulfillment of the will of the people, which the leader claimed to embody. Velasco's regimes were semidemocratic because they partially included previously excluded people and because they demanded honest and free elections. They were simultaneously semiauthoritarian inasmuch as they did not respect the rights of his opponents and disregarded constitutions and liberal-democratic procedures.

Velasco was an austere and ascetic caudillo who epitomized the image of a Catholic saint. It is important to stress that in Ecuador the incorporation of common people into the political community was carried out through Catholic-inspired symbols and a Christian ethical language. If Catholicism was the idiom used by a democratizing movement, it is because religion offered the poor and the excluded the symbolic dignity and humanity that was denied to them in their everyday lives (Cueva 1988, 150–56). Also, it is worth remembering that this religious idiom was selectively appropriated by the left in their myths of communism as an earthly paradise and their image of the proletariat as the new Christ (Álvarez Junco 1987).

If Velasco's elaboration of the categories "people" and "oligarchy" was purely political and ethical, Bucaram's was more social. Starting with the founding of the CFP in Guayaquil in 1949, the notion of el pueblo has increasingly referred to social, political, and ethical distinctions. This profoundly vague term—*the people*—nowadays refers primarily to the poor, the precariously employed, the marginalized, and the excluded. Obviously this is in part a reflection of the increasing number of poor urban dwellers who make a living in the informal sector of the economy. Unlike a class-based discourse, however, its counterpart, the term *oligarchy,* does not refer only to the well-established "white" elites. This moral category has been used to denounce any opponent or political rival of Bucaram and has not been applied to millionaires, who supported the populist leader.

Following the style of his uncle and leader of the CFP, Assad Bucaram, Abdalá Bucaram has been able to elaborate discursively on the everyday experiences of exclusion of the urban mestizo poor, transforming their humiliations into a source of pride and self-respect. By consciously embodying the dress style, language, mannerisms, and masculinity of common people, who are despised by elites and their middle-class imitators, Bucaram presented himself as man of common origins who had ascended socially and who deserved to be the leader of the nation. He claimed to embody the authenticity of common mestizo Ecuadorians, who were ridiculed and humiliated by effeminate elites, who aped Americans and Europeans. The success of Bucaram's electoral style was explained by his politicization of everyday interactions. Many voted for him to reject the candidate of their bosses. They also voted for a candidate who symbolized plebeian mestizo culture and mannerisms.

While in power, Bucaram could not develop alliances with key institutional players such as the Catholic Church, the armed forces, the press, and political and economic elites. Many businesspeople and sectors of the armed forces opposed his drastic plans for privatization and the opening of the economy because they felt that these plans were going to exclude them. Others resented his arrogant and authoritarian style and the danger that, if successful, he could have been reelected like, Menem or Fujimori. Important institutional players did not tolerate the eruption of street speech and "vulgar" behavior in the presidential palace. Bucaram was isolated from the centers of power. An alliance of organizations of common people with politicians, business elites, and the military that rejected the drastic increases in the price of basic services toppled the populist caudillo even at the risk of further delegitimizing Ecuador's fragile democracy.

If Velasco represented an ascetic and religious ideal, Bucaram embodied the struggles of people precariously employed in the informal sector. He was committed to the market as a democratizing force that he claimed would erase the caste privileges of the well-established elites. He demanded the right of all entrepreneurs to benefit from the alleged opportunities of an open and unprotected market economy. He also saw the state as booty to distribute among his followers by allowing his close collaborators to charge fees to do business with the state and allowing his party to strengthen clientelist networks. He also adopted the religious style of televangelists and Pentecostals. His performance blended mockery of the elites with redemption. This explains why he ended his orations by allowing the crowds to touch him in order to be blessed by his charisma.

The increasing importance of clientelism to win votes reflects the accelerating urbanization and continuous marginalization of most of the population. At least since the 1950s, poor people, who are precariously employed in the informal sector, and common people, who live in neighborhoods without basic services, have been organized into networks that exchange votes for services (Menéndez-Carrión 1986). Local neighborhood brokers use discourses of the unmet needs of common people, understood as the deserving poor, who have been abandoned by oligarchic politicians. To be successful, all parties, regardless of their ideology, need to build networks that exchange votes for services (Burgwal 1995; Freidenberg 2003). These clientelistic exchanges re-create and constitute popular identities of el pueblo as the poor (*los pobres*), who need a patron who can deliver, who can protect them from the police and from the law, and who guarantees their access to constitutionally prescribed but unmet rights. Popular demands for access to basic social services such as electricity, drinking water, and sewerage continue to be articulated politically. Politicians from a middle- or upper-class background have contacts with important people and the networks to deliver their promises and to act as the gatekeepers of constitutional rights that are selectively enforced.

Rafael Correa came to power in 2006 running as the foremost political outsider who, to show that he was not linked to the corrupt institution, did not even present candidates for Congress. His appeal was successful because most Ecuadorians of all social classes and ethnic backgrounds blamed politicians and Congress for all the political, social, and moral problems of the nation. According to opinion polls most Ecuadorians had strong negative views of political institutions after three presidents were not allowed to finish their terms in office. Whereas in 1994, 69 percent of Quito residents trusted Congress and political parties, their level of confidence in 2006 was measured in negative numbers. The level of confidence in political parties in June 2006 was −48 percent in Quito and −61 percent in Guayaquil. Trust in Congress was −41 percent in Quito and −51 percent in Guayaquil (T. Larrea 2007, 109, 111). Congress and political parties were seen as mafias, exemplifying "everything that people hate: corruption, lies, demagogy, fat salaries, inefficiency, and arrogance" (ibid., 82). An antipolitical stance was also adopted by the media. As in the case studied by Mauro Porto, journalists "disseminate distrust in politics, and a rejection of politics and its institutions" (2000, 29). Ecuadorian journalists tended to collapse any distinction between corrupt representatives and the institution of Congress itself, depicting the legislature as the site of all that is wrong with the nation's politics.

Once in power Correa embarked on a permanent political campaign and war against traditional politicians, the privately own media, and some businesspeople. He used the term *pelucón* (wig) to differentiate between those who were with the past and his followers, who believe in his program of political and economic transformation. Correa also tapped into nationalist feelings. Ecuador abandoned its national currency and adopted the U.S. dollar to stop hyperinflation in 2000. Ecuador also hosted a U.S. military base. Correa argued that the nation had been betrayed by antinational political and business elites and promised to bring it back to all Ecuadorians. Building on his promises the state returned to manage and direct economic policy, and to redistribute oil wealth to the poor and the middle class. His policies of socialism of the twenty-first century, as in Venezuela (Weyland 2009), so far resemble more populist classical redistributive and nationalist policies based on oil rent distribution than what used to be considered a socialist program of social and economic transformation.

Correa's leadership style blends technocratic rationality with populist promises of redemption. The president holds a PhD in economics and his regime has attracted the support of experts in media manipulation and of left-leaning technocrats and social scientists. Yet like the regimes of his predecessors, it also uses a populist rhetoric to build the image that the nation is going through revolutionary times, and to charge that all who are not in agreement with his policies are serving, willingly or not, the interests of the oligarchy. Yet unlike the intuitive populism of his predecessors, public opinion polls and focus group interviews guide Correa's strategy of accumulating power through winning elections. Because Correa, like Velasco and Bucaram, sees himself as the embodiment of the undifferentiated and homogenous virtuous people, he has attacked social movement organizations when they have tried to push for their own agendas. The president has called his left-wing critics infantile. His regime created a secretary of the people, social movements, and citizen participation. It seems that one of the aims of this state institution is to get rid of autonomous leaders of social movement organizations and to replace them with cadres close to Correa. The government closed state institutions that were managed by organizations of social movements such as women, indigenous people, and Afro-Ecuadorians. While Correa was in office, the government also took away the management of bilingual education from the leadership of the indigenous movement and transferred it to the Ministry of Education.

Because the term *the people* is ambiguous, it is important to see who has been included and excluded. Velasco and Bucaram shared a mestizo construction of the category el pueblo. Like most Ecuadorian politicians, they assumed that to belong to this category Afro-Ecuadorian and indigenous people have to adopt mestizo cultural values. It can be argued that Velasco did not include Afro-Ecuadorians and indigenous people in his rhetorical construction of the people because most were still tied to the hacienda system and were excluded from the vote by literacy requirements that were lifted only in 1979, the year of his death. But, given the strength of *indigenista* discourses in the populist rhetoric of the Alianza Popular Revolucionaria Americana (American Popular Revolutionary Alliance, APRA) in Peru and in the Mexican revolution, this peculiarity needs to be explained. In his book *Conciencia o barbarie,* Velasco explained the notions of Indian and "authentic" pueblo as opposite poles. His argument was based on the racist commonsense assumption that links the Indian with the uncultured countryside and the city with urban white and mestizo culture and civilization (Radcliffe and Westwood 1996). Velasco assumed that the Indians of the countryside, who lived under the paternalistic tutelage of landowners, were totally marginalized from the nation and that they were absolutely uncivilized, even though they fed the nation. Because the Indian culture is seen as the opposite of civilization and urban life, their integration into national culture has to be a gradual process based on cultural, moral, and economic reform. If Indians are not carefully incorporated, they can become, Velasco argued, uprooted, dangerous masses and a threat to civilization. "In Ecuador, the Indians of the countryside are idolaters, almost naked, tyrannized. . . . The Indian of the countryside is . . . situated on the margins of national life. He does not participate in the life of the state, or even in its general path. He delivers the fruit of his work and he retires to his shack, depressed and sad, to look for *aguardiente* or *chicha* [liquor]. Until the Indian is incorporated into the Ecuadorian nationality, there will be no democracy. It will be a farce. . . . But the Indian of the countryside does no harm. He feeds the nation" (Velasco Ibarra 1937, 156).

This quote illustrates Velasco's ambivalence toward indigenous people and his silence about Afro-Ecuadorians, who are absent from his view of the nation. On the one hand, he was aware that indigenous people were tyrannized, but he did not mention the hacienda system, the cardinal institution that exploited Indians. Large haciendas not only monopolized more than three-quarters of the total area of the highlands, according to the 1954 census, they were also institutions that politically, ethnically, and economically dominated the rural indigenous population (Zamosc 1994). On the other hand, like other intellectuals from the elite, Velasco described Indians as "sad," alcoholic "idolaters" and as totally marginalized from national life. Because Indians in his view are totally "uncultured and uncivilized," they need to slowly be transformed into citizens by religious, moral, and economic reforms. Like other white and mestizo elites, Velasco feels the burden of noblesse oblige to uplift Indians (Guerrero 1997, 556). If Indians are gradually integrated through Catholic religion and social and moral reforms, they can become part of the "authentic" people: "the crowds who are aware of their own objectives." The people are "the artisan, the worker, the mestizo who modestly works and is rooted in his class, who progresses gradually due to his honest efforts, who has a clean soul, and hence a penetrating intuition" (Velasco Ibarra 1937, 208). Otherwise the Indian can become an uprooted person in the cities, or the "abruptly rootless mestizo without consciousness" (108). "The Indian of the cities is extremely dangerous. He has read books. He has abruptly climbed the social ladder. He has invaded public administration. He has not cultivated his spirit. . . . De-Christianized since 1895, no morality of sacrifice limits his tendencies, nor orients his intentions. He is profoundly antireligious. . . . He hates the clergy. . . . He does not respect other people's property. He is a small-time thief. He is rarely a serious thief. But he wastes and squanders public moneys" (156).

Velasco's writing is illustrative of the ambiguities of populist discourse between authoritarianism and democracy. He was aware that without the incorporation of Indians into the national community, "democracy will be a farce." But his understanding of the "authentic" people revealed his elitism, despotism, and racism. If the truthful people were the humble and respectful artisans and urban workers who have accepted their rightful place in a hierarchical society but who nonetheless have the right to vote, the uprooted Indians of the cities that demanded social equality and mobility were seen as dangerous and immoral mobs. Unlike Indians of the countryside, who fed the nation, the Indians of the cities have read books and have lost fundamental Christian values. Velasco assumes that his duty is to civilize and Christianize Indians. He is aware that the hacienda system would no longer work as a mechanism of social control that integrated Indians under the paternalistic authority of landowners. Because Indians moving to the city could become dangerous, uprooted mobs, his role was to teach them a hierarchical view of society. Even though Velasco aimed to expand the franchise and make sure that elections were free and honest, he saw the need to educate and maybe repress uprooted and immoral Indians in the cities.

In a change from the recent past, nowadays haciendas have lost some of their power as institutions of economic, political, and ethnic domination. Agrarian reform laws, the expansion of the franchise to illiterates, state policies toward the Indian population, the emergence of Indian intellectuals, and Indian collective action have modified the white-mestizo representations of the Indians (Guerrero 1997, 1998; Zamosc 1994). In this context, Bucaram's rhetoric and presentation of self, based on a mestizo construction of the people, were resented by some indigenous leaders. His only specific electoral promises or governmental policies on behalf of indigenous people were the exchange of patronage for political support with the numerically smaller organizations of Amazonia. Bucaram appointed Shuar Indian leaders of Amazonia to the newly created Ministerio de las Étnias, antagonizing powerful organizations of the highlands who were at the forefront of massive demonstrations demanding his resignation. Bucaram's paternalistic view of indigenous issues, however, is shared by most white-mestizo politicians (Frank, Patiño, and Rodríguez 1992). Even though, unlike Velasco, he mentioned Afro-Ecuadorians, his views about them oscillated between racist and sexist images about the sexuality of black women and the acknowledgment of the role of Afro-Ecuadorians in the nation.

Unlike Velasco and Bucaram, Correa has accepted the notion that the Ecuadorian nation is multicultural. After all, the 1998 constitution ratified after Bucaram's overthrow changed the image of the nation to pluricultural, and included rights of cultural recognition. Correa also speaks some Kichwua, and the 2008 constitution expanded indigenous and Afro-Ecuadorian rights. Yet, he is very critical of the autonomy of the indigenous movement, particularly when they oppose open mining and oil drilling. Also, and in order to not antagonize mestizo voters, he opposed plans to make Ecuador a bilingual nation. Correa has accepted some demands of the indigenous and black movement for cultural recognition, and he especially shared their demands against neoliberal economic policies. Yet all spaces of social movement autonomy are viewed with suspicion as the legacy of neoliberal multiculturalism. Correa came to power at a juncture when the indigenous movement was experiencing a crisis and when their organizations could not mobilize their rank and file. In a context of limited capacity for indigenous autonomous collective action, he has contributed to further erode autonomous indigenous organizations, bringing to his movement a younger leadership not tied to the past struggles for agrarian reform and for cultural recognition.

Historically, populism has brought instability to democracy. The rhetorical construction of the people as a unitary actor in their Manichaean struggle against the oligarchy could not hide the diverse political and class interests behind the coalitions that brought these politicians to power. Because *el pueblo* is a rhetorical construction that does not exist in reality, it could not be reduced to the interpretations of what constitutes its character, according to the whims of leaders. The particular political organizations and social classes of these populist coalitions struggled against each other and with the leader to impose a "correct" interpretation of the meaning of *the people.*

Past populists ended up in military interventions that nominated the armed forces as final referees of political conflicts, and as the self-appointed judges of what is moral for the nation. However, populists also questioned closed and authoritarian versions of democracy, even if their critiques have been carried out through nondemocratic means. Their style, based on direct crowd action and a rhetoric that constructs the excluded as the bearers of the true nation, has partially empowered and given dignity to the common people. If Velasco articulated the aspiration for honest elections, which were seen as the precondition for moral and social reform, Bucaram articulated the daily humiliations of common people, relocating those at the margin to the center of national life. Correa has gone beyond Bucaram and has delivered material benefits during an oil bonanza. He has also given symbolic redemption by attacking media personalities who populate tabloids and TV shows about the rich and famous. The continuous distinction between common people, who are marginalized in their daily interactions and who are at the fringes of the rule of law, and a few citizens that exist above the law will continue to allow for the resilience of populist politicians. Populism will continue to challenge closed versions of democracy by authoritarian means that will further weaken democratic institutions. Yet how viable populist redistribution is over the medium and long term continues to be an open question. It is unclear if Correa's economic policies, like those of Chávez and Morales, could work with cheaper oil and natural gas prices, or if they will survive an economic downturn (Weyland 2009).

The debates on Latin American populism continue to have normative implications. Because our normative aim is to contribute to the creation of more equitable and democratic societies, populist experiences in all their ambiguities need to be explored. A positive understanding of what populism is, not what it lacks when compared to idealized Western patterns, is needed to comprehend these phenomena. Populism marked the entrance of common people into politics and continues to appeal to the disfranchised. However, these patterns of political incorporation, and the styles of contemporary populist leaders continue to be authoritarian and delegative and are not committed to liberal-democratic norms and procedures. To supersede populism, in sum, we have to understand it as what it is. Populism has been and continues to be a powerful semidemocratic and semiauthoritarian means of mobilization of common people.

Notes

Preface

1. See Aibar 2007; Arenas and Gómez 2006; Barr 2009; Canovan 2005; Conniff 1999; de la Torre and Peruzzotti 2008; Demmers, Fernández, and Hogenboom 2001; Hermet, Loaeza, and Prud'homme 2001; Laclau 2005a; Mény and Surel 2002b; Panizza 2005a; Raby 2006; Roberts 2003, 2008; Weyland 2001, 2003; Weyland et al. 2004; Zanatta 2008; Zúquete 2007, 2008.

2. Carlos de la Torre, "The Resurgence of Radical Populism in Latin America," Constellations 14 (3) (2007): 384-97.

Chapter 1

1. Gamaliel Perruci and Steven Sanderson analytically distinguish between "a *populist order* (under which populists shape the political system while in power), *populist appeals* (the attempts by state managers to secure legitimacy, as well as the attempt of outsiders to gain support from the masses), and *populist contending for power* (the role and dynamics of populist as outsiders seeking entry into the political system)" (1989, 45; emphasis in original). Similarly José Nun writes, "it is one thing to call populist a movement that is seeking power, another to name as such a movement that has become a government" (1994, 96).

2. However, as Alvarez Junco (1987) points out, Manichaeism, moralism, and salvationism are not the exclusive property of populism, but rather characterize a wide range of sociopolitical movements, including liberalism, nationalism, and socialism.

3. Braden, the U.S. ambassador who took an active role in the electoral campaign of 1945–46, compared Perón to fascist leaders in Europe.

4. Carnival in the sense that Bakhtin (1984) gives it, as the world turned upside down.

5. Of course, populist regimes are not the only ones that do not recognize the rights of opponents. Dictatorships as well as elected regimes have repressed, silenced, and, at times, murdered their adversaries.

Chapter 2

1. For descriptions of La Gloriosa by participants see Girón 1945; Muñoz Vicuña 1984; Naranjo 1945; Pérez Castro 1990; Velasco Ibarra 1946. For subsequent analyses of La Gloriosa see Blanksten 1951; de la Torre 1993, 1994b; INIESEC 1984; Quintero and Silva 1991; Vega Ugalde 1987; Ycaza 1991.

2. For studies of Velasquismo, see Arízaga Vega 1985; Burbano and de la Torre 1989; Cárdenas Reyes 1991; Cueva 1988; de la Torre 1993; 1994b; Hurtado 1988; Maiguashca 1991; Maiguashca and North 1991; Menéndez-Carrión 1986; Quintero 1980; and Paz y Miño 1992.

3. Marxism has been the principal paradigm for the study of Ecuadorian populism. Some of the authors who have used Marxism for the study of Velasquismo are: Quintero 1980; Quintero and Silva 1991; Vega Ugalde 1987; and Ycaza 1991. Agustín Cueva's *El proceso de dominación política en el Ecuador* (1988), although situated within the Marxian paradigm, differs from the other studies. He not only analyzes class formation, but, more interesting, also studies the almost mythical relationships between Velasco and his followers.

4. Ecuador was the world's largest cacao producer in the late nineteenth century. In 1894, a year before the Liberal Revolution, the country produced 28.3 percent of the world's production. By the mid-1920s, due to a combination of rising international competition and plant diseases, Ecuadorian production declined to 6.8 percent of world production. This situation was aggravated by falling international prices due to the world crisis of the 1930s (Rodríguez 1985). Cacao exports, which in 1913 represented 63 percent of total export value, by 1933 had declined to less than 20 percent (Unión Panamericana 1954, 30).

5. For analyses of Ecuador's modest import substitution industrialization, see Deler 1987 and Fischer 1983. There are no reliable statistics on the occupational structure of Ecuador in the 1930s and 1940s, but see de la Torre (1993, 66–72).

6. Churrasco is an Ecuadorian dish that includes meat, rice, potatoes, vegetables, and a fried egg.

7. The text of Velasco's speech is taken from *Discursos,* vol. 12 of *Obras completas* (1974, 32–40; emphasis in original).

8. In Sigal and Verón's analysis of Perón, a redeemer is characterized as "he who arrives from outside, who asks from his people confidence and faith because his actions would speak for him, and who conceives his arrival as the fulfillment of a superior mission: the well-being of the homeland" (1986, 34).

Chapter 3

1. For studies of Abdalá Bucaram see Acosta 1996; Burbano 1992; 1997; Cuvi and Martínez 1997; Cornejo 1997; de la Torre 1994a, 1996, 1997, 1998; Fernández and Ortiz 1988; Freidenberg 2003, 2008; Ibarra 1997; Pachano 1997; and Sánchez Parga 1998.

2. Jaime Roldós was president of Ecuador from 1979 until 1981, when he died with his wife Martha Bucaram in a plane crash. Roldós was a member of Concentración de Fuerzas Populares (CFP), a populist party led by Abdalá's uncle Assad Bucaram (1916–81). Under Assad's leadership, the CFP dominated Guayaquil's politics from the 1950s to the early 1980s. For studies of the CFP, see Menéndez-Carrión 1986; Martz 1989; and Rafael Guerrero 1994.

3. For analyses of the nationalist reformist military government of Rodríguez Lara (1972–76) and the conservative and more repressive military regime of the *triunvirato* that followed (1976–79), see Argones 1985; Conaghan 1988; Isaacs 1993; Martz 1987; and Quintero and Silva 1991. For studies of Ecuador's pacted transition to democracy, see Argones 1985; Conaghan 1988; Hurtado 1988; Isaacs 1993; and Martz 1987.

4. Jaime Roldós, 1979–81; Osvaldo Hurtado, 1981–84; León Febres Cordero, 1984–88; Rodrigo Borja, 1988–92; Sixto Durán Ballén, 1992–96; Abdalá Bucaram, August 1996–February 1997; Fabián Alarcón, February 1997–August 1998; Jamil Mahuad, August 1998–present.

5. In a recent study of Lebanese and other Middle Eastern immigrants in Ecuador, Mónica Almieda (1966, 104) writes: "The elite of Guayaquil denied this class of nouveau riche membership in the city's most prestigious social club, the Club de la Unión, until the 1970s and 80s." See also Crawford de Roberts 1997.

6. All quotes from Bucaram come from recorded public speeches of his 1996 campaign.

7. It is interesting that Mussolini maintained that the bourgeoisie is "primarily a moral category: it is a state of mind, a temperament, a mentality clearly contrary to the fascist mentality" (Taguieff 1995, 16). I do not think, however, that Bucaram was aware of Mussolini's remarks.

8. Carmen Martínez and I did ethnographic research of the following mass rallies of Bucaram's 1996 campaign: San Carlos, Quito, 14 June; Santa Elena and Libertad, Guayas province, 15 June; La Michelena, Quito, 17 June; Loja, 21 June; Otavalo and Ibarra, 24 June; Riobamba, 25 June; Plaza de San Francisco, Quito, 30 June; Portoviejo, 3 July; the Cinco Esquinas, Guayaquil, 4 July. I also attended his spectacular return to Guayaquil by helicopter from his exile in Panama on 7 October 1990, and several electoral rallies during his presidential campaign of 1992.

9. For descriptions of the events by participants see Arteaga 1997; Bucaram 1998; and Miño and Macas 1997. For journalist and social-scientific accounts see Baéz 1997; and Cornejo 1997.

10. Unlike the accepted view that, like Menem and Fujimori, Bucaram had switched platforms after assuming the presidency (Zirker 1998), he never rejected neoliberalism.

11. The Ecuadorian case confirms Weyland's argument (1998) that draconian neoliberal reforms tend to be supported by the population only in conditions of deep crisis, such as hyperinflation (defined as inflation exceeding 50 percent per month).

12. National public opinion polls illustrate important regional differences in relation to the level of acceptance of President Bucaram. On 14 December 1996, after he announced his economic program, 50.4 percent of the respondents from the coast held a favorable image, while only 38 percent of the respondents from the highlands supported the president. After he was deposed and following the media campaign that represented Bucaram as the embodiment of corruption, 21.1 percent of respondents from the coast still had a positive view, while 92 percent of highlanders rejected the former president (Informe Confidencial 1997).

13. Bucaram's level of popularity in Quito deteriorated rapidly. On 17 August 1996, 53 percent had approved of his government. By 19 October, he was rejected by 64 percent of respondents, and on 11 January 1997, by 90 percent of Quito's residents (Informe Confidencial 1997).

14. This section is based on ethnographic material gathered in April 2005.

Chapter 4

1. At least at the beginning of his term Collor fared better than Bucaram in public opinion polls. Due to the severity of Brazil's hyperinflation, Collor's popularity rose "from 58 percent to between 71 percent and 81 percent

during the first weeks after [the announcement of] his stabilization plan of March 1990" (Weyland 1998, 551). Bucaram's economic plan was endorsed by only 50.4 percent of public opinion respondents on the coast and 30.8 percent in the highlands (Informe Confidencial 1997).

Chapter 5

1. "The *ayllu* is the basic cell of Andean social organization, dating back to pre-hispanic times" (Rivera Cusicanqui 1990, 100).

2. *Caracazo* derives from the city name plus the suffix *-azo,* implying a blow. *Sacudón* means intense jolt or shake-up.

3. Perhaps Bolivia's vice president has not fully abandoned the Manichaean ideology of his guerrilla past. He was part of the short-lived Ejercito Guerrilero Túpaj Katari (Túpaj Katari Guerrilla Army). After participating in a plot to assassinate George Shultz with a remote-controlled bomb when the U.S. secretary of state visited La Paz in 1988, García Linera was incarcerated for three years (Dunkerley 2007, 145).

Podemos (Social and Democratic Power) was a conservative coalition formed to support Jorge "Tuto" Quiroga. He served as vice president of former dictator Hugo Banzer (1977–2001). After Banzer died of cancer, Quiroga became president of Bolivia (2001–2).

Chapter 6

1. The term *partidocracia* has been used in other national contexts, such as Venezuela and Peru (Conaghan 2005, 267).

2. *Vistazo,* no. 914 (15 September 2005).

3. *Vistazo,* no. 940 (19 October 2006); no. 943 (1 December 2006).

4. Pinoargote's terminology for the party system came to be widely used in the media. Afro-Ecuadorian intellectual Juan Montaño Escobar defined *partidocracia* in criminal terms: "It is a mafia. These parties defend the Cosa Nostra." Montaño, "Revolución verde limón," *Hoy* (Quito), 2 December 2006. *Vanguardia,* a weekly magazine, explained the defeat of the candidates of the main parties in 2006 as a rejection of the partidocracia. And though journalists challenged the existence of a partidocracia, they still clung to the term. See, for instance, the editorial by Diego Araujo, "¿Existe la partidocracia?" *Hoy,* 9 October 2006.

NOTES TO PAGES 180–190

5. Emilio Espinoza, a radio expert who had also worked for Bucaram, headed Correa's radio operation. Marisol Cadena was Correa's image consultant, coordinating his wardrobe and staging his public appearances. Correa's pollster in the second round was Santiago Pérez.

6. To be precise, Noboa spent $2,582,803.71 on television, out of a total campaign expenditure of $3,849,782.57. These figures come from Participación Ciudadana, an NGO that monitors electoral spending. Participación Ciudadana, "Monitoreo de la cobertura de los medios a los candidatos presidenciales. Segunda vuelta electoral 25 octubre–23 noviembre 2006" (unpublished document).

7. Correa spent $1,008,475.32 on television, out of a total budget of $1,130,654.15. Participación Ciudadana.

8. Because of its obvious association with domestic violence, feminists decried the belt wielding at campaign events. Correa denied that it was symbol of machismo but backed off of the belt imagery in the second round of the campaign.

9. See, for instance, the analyses in *Vanguardia* 17 (October 2006): 40–41; and the opinion piece of communications scholar Pepe Laso, "Profetas de la desventura," *Hoy,* 3 December 2006.

10. The well-known *guayaquileño* politician Nicolás Iza Obando actively worked for Correa's campaign. He was later rewarded with an appointment as ambassador to Spain. Among the other local caciques who collaborated with Correa, two are worth mentioning: Vicente Izurieta, former governor of Manabí for the Partido Sociedad Patriótica, and Trajano Andrade, a former congressman for Izquierda Democrática, from Manabí.

11. "Socio País captó militancia de otros partidos," *El universo* (Guayaquil), 6 December 2006; "El voto práctico predominó en el Guayas," *El comercio* (Quito), 1 December 2006.

12. Plan de gobierno de Alianza País, 2007–11, p. 19; at the Web site Gobierno nacional de la República del Ecuador, www.presidencia.gov.ec.

13. In 2007 the government spent, with discount, an estimated $6.9 million on advertisements on television and radio. Without the discount the estimated cost was $16.7 million (Conaghan and Torre 2008, 276).

14. Intervención presidencial en el Aromo, Manabí, 15 July 2008, www .presidencia.gov.ec.

15. Ibid.

16. Informe a la nación en el inicio del tercer año de la revolución ciudadana, Quito, Plaza de la Independencia, 19 January 2009, www.presidencia .gov.ec.

17. Intervención presidencial en acto de entregas de armas en el comando provincial de Manabí, Portoviejo, 12 March 2009, www.presidencia.gov.ec.

18. Intervención presidencial en el Aromo, Manabí, 15 July 2008. Alfaro was president of Ecuador (1895–1901; 1906–11) and leader of the Ecuadorian Liberal Revolution.

19. Father Luis Alberto Tuaza, pers. comm. The Bonus of Human Dignity means a great deal to people who do not earn even the minimum wage of $200 a month. In rural areas it might be equivalent to a week's earnings. In cities it helps poor people pay for transportation, food, and other necessities.

20. "Será indispensable la movilización social," *Expreso* (Guayaquil), December 2006, http://www.expreso.ec/html/political.asp.

21. *El ciudadano,* 26 April 2009.

22. Intervención presidencial en acto de entregas de armas en el comando provincial de Manabí, Portoviejo, 12 March 2009.

23. *Digital granma internacional,* 9 January 2009, http://www.granma.cubaweb.cu/2009/01/09/nacional/artic10.html. In a speech he delivered at Oxford University on 26 October 2009, he defined "true democracy" as the "right to education, to health, to housing." Correa, "My Experience as a Leftist Christian in a Secular World," www.presidencia.gov.ec.

24. Intervención presidencial en acto de entregas de armas en el comando provincial de Manabí, Portoviejo, 12 March 2009.

25. Ibid.

26. Informe a la nación en el inicio del tercer año de la revolución ciudadana, Quito, Plaza de la Independencia, 19 January 2009.

27. *Digital granma internacional,* 9 January 2009, http://www.granma.cubaweb.cu/2009/01/09/nacional/artic10.html.

28. Informe a la nación en el inicio del tercer año de la revolución ciudadana, Quito, Plaza de la Independencia, 19 January 2009.

29. Intervención presidencial en acto de entregas de armas en el comando provincial de Manabí, Portoviejo, 12 March 2009.

References

Newspapers, Fliers, and Diplomatic Reports

El comercio, Quito.

El día, Quito.

El diario del sur, Cuenca.

El país, Madrid.

El universo, Guayaquil.

El telégrafo, Guayaquil.

La prensa, Guayaquil.

La patria, Quito.

La voz del pueblo: Una auténtica expresión democrática ecuatoriana, Quito.

Hoy, Quito.

New York Times.

Surcos: Organo de la Federación de Estudiantes Universitarios del Ecuador, Quito.

Hojas volantes, Biblioteca Aurelio Espinosa Pólit, Cotocollao.

British Foreign Office, General Correspondence, Political FO 371, Archivo Histórico del Banco Central del Ecuador, Quito.

Books and Articles

Abts, Koen, and Stefan Rummens
    2007 "Populism versus Democracy." *Political Studies* 55:405–24.

Acosta, Alberto
    1996 "Ecuador: El Bucaranismo en el poder." *Nueva sociedad* 146 (November-December): 6–16.
    1997 "Todo o nada: La convertibilidad y la reforma neoliberal de Bucaram." In *¡Que se vaya! Crónica el Bucaramato,* edited by Diego Cornejo, 41–56. Quito: Edimpres-Hoy.

Acosta, Vladimir
2007   "El socialismo del siglo XXI y la revolución bolivariana: Una re-
        flexión inicial." In *Ideas para debatir el socialismo del siglo XXI,*
        edited by Margarita López Maya, 21–31. Caracas: Editorial
        Alfa, 2007.

Adrianzén, Alberto
1998   "Estado y sociedad: Señores, masas, y ciudadanos." In *Pop-
        ulismo y neopopulismo en América Latina: El problema de la
        Cenicienta,* edited by María Moira Mackinnon and Mario Al-
        berto Petrone, 257–79. Buenos Aires: Editorial Universitaria
        de Buenos Aires.

Aguirrc, Manuel Agustín
1946   *Una etapa política del socialismo ecuatoriano: Cuadernos doctri-
        narios.* Quito: Editora Ecuador.

Aibar, Julio
2007   *Vox populi: Populismo y democracia en Latinoamérica.* Mexico
        City: FLACSO.

Albro, Robert
2005   "The Indigenous in the Plural in Bolivian Oppositional Poli-
        tics." *Bulletin of Latin American Research* 24 (4): 433–53.

Ali, Tariq
2008   *Pirates of the Caribbean: Axis of Hope.* Rev. ed. London: Verso.

Alianza Democrática Ecuatoriana
1981   *Los postulados de la Revolución de Mayo: Programa de Alianza
        Democrática Ecuatoriana, difundido por la sección provincial
        del Guayas.* Guayaquil: Facultad de Ciencias Económicas.

Almeida, Mónica
1996   "Phoenicians of the Pacific: Lebanese and Other Middle East-
        erners in Ecuador," *The Americas* 53 (1): 87–111.

Álvarez Junco, José
1987   "Magia y ética en la retórica política." In *Populismo, caudillaje, y
        discurso demagógico,* edited by José Alvarez Junco, 219–71.
        Madrid: Centro de Investigaciones Sociológicas.

1990   *El emperador del paralelo: Lerroux y la demagogia populista.*
   .   Madrid: Alianza Editorial.

1994   "El populismo como problema." In *El populismo en España y
        América,* edited by José Alvarez Junco and Ricardo González
        Leandri, 11–39. Madrid: Editorial Catriel.

Angell, Alan
1968   "Party Systems in Latin America." In *Latin America and the Caribbean: A Handbook*, edited by Claudio Véliz, 356–64. London: Anthony Blond.

Arato, Andrew
2000   "Good-bye to Dictatorships?" *Social Research* 67 (4): 925–55.

Arcos, Carlos
1984   "El espíritu del progreso: Los hacendados en el Ecuador del 1900." *Cultura* 19:107–35.

Arcos, Carlos, and Carlos Marchán
1978   "Apuntes para una discusión sobre los cambios en la estructura agraria serrana." *Revista ciencias sociales* 2 (5): 13–51.

Arenas, Nelly, and Luis Gómez Calcaño
2006   *Populismo autoritario: Venezuela 1999–2005*. Caracas: Cendes, UCV.

Argones, Nelson
1985   *El juego del poder: De Rodríguez Lara a Febres Cordero*. Quito: Corporación Financiera Nacional.

Arízaga Vega, Rafael
1985   *Velasco Ibarra: El rostro del caudillo*. Quito: Ediciones Culturales UNP.
1990   *Memoria histórica, 1920–1989*. Vol. 1. Quito: Editorial Voluntad.

Arroyo del Río, Carlos
1946   *Bajo el Imperio del Odio: Las Sanciones en el Ecuador, primera parte*. Bogotá: Editorial El Gráfico.
1948   *En Plena Vorágine*. Bogotá: Editorial el Gráfico.

Arteaga, Rosalía
1997   *La presidenta: El secuestro de una protesta*. Quito: EDINO.

Auyero, Javier
1998   "Todo por amor, o lo que quedó de la herejía: 'Clientelismo populista' en la Argentina de los noventa." In *El fantasma del populismo: Aproximación a un tema (siempre) actual*, edited by Felipe Burbano, 81–119. Caracas: Nueva Sociedad.
2001   *Poor People's Politics: Peronist Survival Networks and the Legacy of Evita*. Durham: Duke University Press.

Avritzer, Leonardo
2002   *Democracy and the Public Sphere in Latin America*. Princeton: Princeton University Press.

Báez, René, ed.
  1997 *¿Y ahora qué?* Quito: Eskeletra.

Bakhtin, Mikhail
  1984 *Rabelais and His World*. Bloomington: Indiana University Press.

Barozet, Emmanuelle
  2006 "Relecturas de la noción de clientelismo: Una forma diversificada de intermediación política y social." *Ecuador Debate* 69 (December): 77–102.

Barr, Robert
  2009 "Populists, Outsiders and Anti-Establishment Politics." *Party Politics* 15 (1): 29–48.

Barra, Ximena de la, and Richard Dello Buono
  2009 *Latin America after the Neoliberal Debacle: Another Region Is Possible*. Lanham, Md.: Rowman and Littlefield.

Barrios, Franz Xavier
  2008 "The Weakness of Excess: The Bolivian State in an Unbounded Democracy." In *Unresolved Tensions: Bolivia Past and Present*, edited by John Crabtree and Laurence Whitehead, 125–41. Pittsburgh: University of Pittsburgh Press.

Benites Vinueza, Leopoldo
  1986 *Ecuador: Drama y paradoja*. Quito: Banco Central del Ecuador and Corporación Editora Nacional. Original edition, 1950.

Betz, Hans-Georg
  1994 *Radical Right-Wing Populism in Western Europe*. New York: St. Martin's Press.

Bethell, Leslie, and Ian Roxborough
  1988 "Latin America between the Second World War and the Cold War: Some Reflections on the 1945–48 Conjuncture." *Journal of Latin American Studies* 20:167–89.

Blanksten, George
  1951 *Ecuador: Constitutions and Caudillos*. Berkeley: University of California Press.

Boas, Taylor
  2005 "Television and Neopopulism in Latin America: Media Effects in Brazil and Peru." *Latin American Research Review* 40 (2): 27–50.

Bobbio, Norberto
  1987 *The Future of Democracy*. Minneapolis: University of Minnesota Press.

REFERENCES

Brader, Ted
  2006   *Campaigning for Hearts and Minds: How Emotional Appeals in Political Ads Work.* Chicago: University of Chicago Press.
Braun, Herbert
  1985   *The Assassination of Gaitán: Public Life and Urban Violence in Colombia.* Madison: University of Wisconsin Press.
Bucaram, Abdalá
  1990   *Las verdades de Abdalá.* Quito: Editorial El Duende.
  1998   *Golpe de estado.* Guayaquil: PREdiciones.
Burbano, Felipe
  1992   "Populismo, democracia, y política: El caso de Abdalá Bucaram." In *Populismo,* edited by Juan Paz y Miño, 119–41. Quito: ILDIS.
  1997   "Reflexiones a propósito de 'un loco que ama.'" *Íconos* 1 (February–April): 43–52.
  1998   "A modo de introducción: El impertinente populismo." In *El fantasma del populismo: Aproximación a un tema (siempre) actual,* edited by Felipe Burbano, 9–25. Caracas: Nueva Sociedad.
Burbano, Felipe, and Carlos de la Torre, eds.
  1989   *El populismo en el Ecuador: Antología de textos.* Quito: ILDIS.
Burgwal, Gerrit
  1995   "Struggle of the Poor: Neighborhood Organization and Clientelist Practice in a Quito Squatter Settlement." Ph.D. diss., University of Amsterdam.
Butler, Judith
  1995   "Contingent Foundations." In *Feminist Contentions: A Philosophical Exchange,* edited by Seyla Benhabib, Judith Butler, Drucilla Cornell, and Nancy Fraser, 35–57. New York: Routledge.
Buxton, Julia
  2005   "Venezuela's Contemporary Political Crisis in Historical Context." *Bulletin of Latin American Research* 24 (3): 328–47.
Canessa, Andrew
  2006   "Todos somos indígenas: Toward a New Language of National Political Identity." *Bulletin of Latin American Research* 25, 2:241–63
  2007   "Who Is Indigenous? Self-Identification, Indigeneity, and Claims to Justice in Contemporary Bolivia." *Urban Anthropology and*

Studies of Cultural Systems and World Economic Development 36 (3): 195–238.

Canovan, Margaret

1981   *Populism.* New York: Harcourt Brace Jovanovich.

1999   "Trust the People! Populism and the Two Faces of Democracy." *Political Studies* 47:2–16.

2002   "Taking Politics to the People: Populism as the Ideology of Democracy." In *Democracies and the Populist Challenge,* edited by Yves Mény and Yves Surel, 25–45. New York: Palgrave.

2005   *The People.* Cambridge: Polity Press.

Cárdenas Reyes, María Cristina

1991   *Velasco Ibarra: Ideología, poder, y democracia.* Quito: Corporación Editora Nacional.

Carrión, Andrés

1997   "Y llegó el comandante y mandó a parar." In *¿Y ahora qué?* edited by René Báez, 117–44. Quito: Eskeletra.

Castañeda, Jorge

2006   "Latin America's Left Turn." *Foreign Affairs* 85 (3): 28–42.

Chevigny, Paul

1995   *The Edge of the Knife: Police Violence in the Americas.* New York: New Press.

Cohen, Jean, and Andrew Arato

1992   *Civil Society and Political Theory.* Cambridge, Mass.: MIT Press.

Collier, David

1979   "The Bureaucratic-Authoritarian Model: Synthesis and Priorities for Future Research." In *The New Authoritarianism in Latin America,* edited by David Collier, 19–33. Princeton: Princeton University Press.

Collins, Randal

2004   *Interaction Ritual Chains.* Princeton: Princeton University Press.

Conaghan, Catherine

1987   "Party Politics and Democratization in Ecuador." In *Authoritarians and Democrats: Regime Transition in Latin America,* edited by James M. Malloy and Mitchell A. Seligson, 145–67. Pittsburgh: University of Pittsburgh Press.

1988   *Restructuring Domination: Industrialists and the State in Ecuador.* Pittsburgh: University of Pittsburgh Press.

1995   "Politicians against Parties: Discord and Disconnection in Ecuador's Party System." In *Building Democratic Institu-*

tions: Party Systems in Latin America, edited by Scott Mainwaring and Timothy R. Scully, 434–59. Stanford: Stanford University Press.

2005   *Fujimori's Peru: Deception in the Public Sphere.* Pittsburgh: University of Pittsburgh Press.

2008a   "Bucaram en Panamá: Las secuelas del populismo en Ecuador." In *El retorno del pueblo: Populismo y nuevas democracias en América Latina,* edited by Carlos de la Torre and Enrique Peruzzotti, 239–67. Quito: FLACSO Ecuador.

2008b   "Ecuador: Correa's Plebiscitary Democracy." In *Latin America's Struggle for Democracy,* edited by Larry Diamond, Marc Plattner, and Diego Abente Brun, 199–217. Baltimore: Johns Hopkins University Press.

Conaghan, Catherine, and Carlos de la Torre

2008   "The Permanent Campaign of Rafael Correa: Making Ecuador's Plebiscitary Presidency." *International Journal of Press/Politics* 13 (3): 267–84.

Conniff, Michael, ed.

1982   *Latin American Populism in Comparative Perspective.* Albuquerque: University of New Mexico Press.

1999   *Populism in Latin America.* Tuscaloosa: University of Alabama Press.

Cornejo Menacho, Diego

1996   *Crónica de un delito de blancos.* Quito: Ojo de Pez.

——, ed.

1997   *¡Que se Vaya! Crónica del Bucaramato.* Quito: Edimpres-Hoy.

Coronil, Fernando

1997   *The Magical State: Nature, Money, and Modernity in Venezuela.* Chicago: University of Chicago Press.

Coronil, Fernando, and Julie Skurski

1991   "Dismembering and Remembering the Nation: The Semantics of Political Violence in Venezuela." *Comparative Studies in Society and History* 33 (2): 288–337.

Crawford de Roberts, Louis

1997   *Los Libaneses en el Ecuador. Una Vida de Éxitos.* Guayaquil: Fundación Cultural Ecuatoriano-Libanesa Nicasio Safadi.

Cremieux, Robert

1946   *Geografía económica del Ecuador.* Guayaquil: Publicaciones de la Universidad de Guayaquil.

Cross, John

1998 *Informal Politics: Street Vendors and the State in Mexico City.* Stanford: Stanford University Press.

Cueva, Agustín

1988 *El proceso de dominación política en el Ecuador.* 2d ed. Quito: Editorial Planeta. (First edition in Spanish, 1972; First edition in English, 1982.)

Cuvi, María, and Alexandra Martínez

1997 "Los códigos ocultos del poder masculino." *Íconos* 1 (February-April): 34–43.

Davis, Natalie

1975 *Society and Culture in Early Modern France.* Stanford: Stanford University Press.

Degregori, Carlos Iván

1991 "El aprendiz de brujo y el curandero chino." In *Demonios y redentores en el nuevo Perú,* edited by Carlos Iván Degregori and Romeo Grompone, 71–137. Lima: IEP.

De Ípola, Emilio

1979 "Populismo e ideología." *Revista mexicana de sociología* 41: 925–60.

1983 *Ideología y discurso político.* Buenos Aires: Folios Ediciones.

de la Torre, Carlos

1992 "The Ambiguous Meanings of Latin American Populisms." *Social Research* 59 (2): 385–414.

1993 *La seducción velasquista.* Quito: FLACSO and Libri-Mundi.

1994a "Las imágenes contradictorias de Abdalá: Discursos y culturas políticas en las elecciones de 1992," *Ecuador Debate* 32 (August 1994): 54–64.

1994b "Velasco Ibarra and 'La Revolución Gloriosa': The Social Production of a Populist Leader in Ecuador in the 1940s." *Journal of Latin American Studies* 26 (3): 286–311.

1996 *¡Un sólo toque!: Populismo y cultura política en Ecuador.* Quito: CAAP.

1997 "Populism and Democracy: Political Discourses and Cultures in Contemporary Ecuador." *Latin American Perspectives* 24 (3): 12–25.

1998 "Populist Redemption and the Unfinished Democratization of Latin America." *Constellations* 5 (1): 85–95.

2006   "Populismo, democracia, protestas y crisis políticas recurrentes en Ecuador." *Europa América Latina,* no. 21. Rio de Janeiro: Fundación Konrad Adenauer.

de la Torre, Carlos, and Catherine Conaghan
2009   "The Hybrid Campaign: Tradition and Modernity in Ecuador's 2006 Presidential Election." *International Journal of Press, Politics* 14 (3): 335-52.

de la Torre, Carlos, and Enrique Peruzzotti, eds.
2008   *El retorno del pueblo: Populismo y nuevas democracias en América Latina.* Quito: FLACSO Ecuador.

de la Torre, Carlos María
1944   "Oración Gratulatoria pronunciada por el Exmo. y Rvm. Sr. Dr. D. Carlos María de la Torre Arzobispo de Quito, en la Catedral Metropolitana, el 13 de Abril de 1944 con motivo del Primer Centenario del nacimiento del Exmo. y Rmo. Monseñor Federico González Suárez." Quito: Imprenta del Clero.

1954   "La Masonería: Discurso en la Catedral de Riobamba, el 5 de Julio de 1925, Día de la Fé." In *Problemas religiosos y problemas nacionales,* edited by Francisco Miranda Ribadeneira, 228-41. Quito: La Prensa Católica.

Deler, Jean Paul
1987   *Ecuador: Del espacio al estado nacional.* Quito: Banco Central del Ecuador.

De Lima, Venicio A.
1993   "Brazilian Television in the 1989 Presidential Campaign: Constructing a President." In *Television, Politics, and the Transition to Democracy in Latin America,* edited by Thomas E. Skidmore, 97–118. Washington and Baltimore: Woodrow Wilson Center Press and Johns Hopkins University Press.

Demmers, Jolle, A. E. Fernández Jilberto, and Barbara Hogenboom, eds.
2001   *Miraculous Metamorphoses: The Neoliberalization of Latin American Populism.* London: Zed Books.

Diamond, Larry, Marc Plattner, and Diego Abente Braun, eds.
2008   *Latin America's Struggle for Democracy.* Baltimore: Johns Hopkins University Press.

Dieterich, Heinz

2007   "Diálogo con el Presidente Rafael Correa." In *Ecuador y América Latina: El socialismo del siglo XXI,* edited by Edgar Ponce, 39–67. Quito: NINA.

Dirección Nacional de Estadísticas

1944   *Ecuador en cifras: 1938 a 1942.* Quito: Imprenta del Ministerio de Hacienda.

di Tella, Torcuato

1973   "Populismo y Reformismo." In *Populismo y contradicciones de clase en Latinoamérica,* edited by Octavio Ianni, 38–83. Mexico City: Ediciones ERA.

Domínguez, Jorge

2008   "Three Decades since the Start of the Democratic Transitions." In *Constructing Democratic Governance,* edited by Domínguez and Michael Shifter, 323–53. Baltimore: Johns Hopkins University Press.

Domínguez, Jorge, and Michael Shifter, eds.

2008   *Constructing Democratic Governance in Latin America.* 3rd ed. Baltimore: Johns Hopkins University Press.

Dornbusch, Rudiger, and Sebastian Edwards, eds.

1991   *The Macroeconomics of Populism in Latin America.* Chicago: University of Chicago Press.

Douglas, Mary

1966   *Purity and Danger: An Analysis of the Concepts of Pollution and Taboo.* New York: Routledge.

Drake, Paul

1982   "Conclusion: Requiem for Populism?" In *Latin American Populism in Comparative Perspective,* edited by Michael L. Conniff, 217–47. Albuquerque: University of New Mexico Press.

Dunkerley, James

2007   "Evo Morales, the 'Two Bolivias' and the Third Bolivian Revolution." *Journal of Latin American Studies* 39 (1): 133–66.

Edelman, Murray

1988   *Constructing the Political Spectacle.* Chicago: University of Chicago Press.

Ellner, Steve

2005   "Revolutionary and Non-Revolutionary Paths of Radical Populism: Directions of the *Chavista* Movement in Venezuela." *Science and Society* 69 (2): 160–90.

2008   *Rethinking Venezuelan Politics: Class, Conflict, and the Chávez Phenomenon.* Boulder: Lynne Rienner.

Fernández, Iván, and Gonzalo Ortiz

1988   *¿La agonía del populismo?* Quito: Editorial Plaza Grande.

Fernández-Kelly, Patricia, and Jon Shefner, eds.

2006   *Out of the Shadows: Political Action and the Informal Economy in Latin America.* University Park: Pennsylvania State University Press.

Figueroa, V. M.

2006   "The Bolivarian Government of Hugo Chávez: Democratic Alternative for Latin America?" *Critical Sociology* 32 (1): 187–212.

Fischer, Sabine

1983   *Estado, clases, e industria.* Quito: Editorial El Conejo.

Franco, Carlos

1990   "La plebe urbana, el populismo, y la imagen del 'alumbramiento.'" *Socialismo y participación* 52 (December): 43–52.

Franco, Carlos, Julio Cotler, and Guillermo Rochabrún

1991   "Populismo y modernidad." *Pretextos* 2 February: 103–20.

Frank, Erwin, Ninfa Patiño, and Marta Rodríguez

1992   *Los políticos y los indígenas: Diez entrevistas a candidatos presidenciales y máximos representantes de partidos políticos del Ecuador sobre la cuestión indígena.* Quito: Abya-Yala and ILDIS.

Franklin, Albert

1984   *Ecuador: Retrato de un pueblo.* Quito: Corporación Editora Nacional. Original edition, 1944.

Fraser, Nancy

1999   "Repensando la esfera pública: Una contribución a la crítica de la democracia actualmente existente." *Ecuador Debate* 46:139–74.

Freidenberg, Flavia

2003   *Jama, caleta y camello: Las estrategias de Abdalá Bucaram y del PRE para ganar elecciones.* Quito: Corporación Editora Nacional.

2008   "El flautista de Hammelin: Liderazgo y populismo en la democracia ecuatoriana." In *El retorno del pueblo: Populismo y nuevas democracias en América Latina,* edited by Carlos de la Torre and Enrique Peruzzotti, 189–239. Quito: FLACSO Ecuador.

French, John D.
1989   "Industrial Workers and the Birth of the Populist Republic in Brazil, 1945–1946." *Latin American Perspectives* 16, 4 (issue 63): 5–27.
2009   "Understanding the Politics of Latin America's Plural Lefts (Chávez/Lula): Social Democracy, Populism and Convergence on the Path to a Post-neoliberal World." *Third World Quarterly* 30 (2): 349–70.

Furet, François
1985   *Interpreting the French Revolution.* Cambridge: Cambridge University Press.

Gamarra, Eduardo
2008   "Bolivia: Evo Morales and Democracy." In *Constructing Democratic Governance in Latin America,* edited by Jorge Domínguez and Michael Shifter. Baltimore: Johns Hopkins University Press.

García Canclini, Nestor
1995   *Hybrid Cultures: Strategies for Entering and Leaving Modernity.* Minneapolis: University of Minnesota Press.

García-Guadilla, María Pilar.
2003   "Civil Society: Institutionalization, Fragmentation, Autonomy." In *Venezuelan Politics in the Chávez Era: Class, Polarization, and Conflict,* edited by Steve Ellner and Daniel Hellinger. Boulder: Lynne Rienner.
2007   "Ciudadanía y autonomía en las organizaciones sociales bolivarianas: Los Comités de Tierra Urbana como movimientos sociales." *Cuadernos del CENDES,* 24 (6): 47–73.

García Linera, Álvaro
2001   *Tiempos de rebelión.* La Paz: Muela del Diablo Editores.
2004   "La crisis del estado y las sublevaciones indígeno plebeyas." In *Memorias de octubre,* edited by Luis Tapia, Alvaro García Linera, and Raúl Prada Alcoreza, 27–86. La Paz: Muela del Diablo Editores.
2005   *Democracia en Bolivia: Cinco análisis temáticos del segundo Estudio Nacional sobre Democracia y Valores Democráticos.* La Paz: Corte Nacional Electoral, República de Bolivia.

Gay, Robert
1994   *Popular Organization and Democracy in Rio de Janeiro: A Tale of Two Favelas.* Philadelphia: Temple University Press.

Geertz, Clifford
1985   "Centers, Kings, and Charisma: Reflections on the Symbols of
       Power." In *Rites of Power: Symbolism, Ritual, and Politics
       since the Middle Ages,* edited by Sean Wilentz, 13–38. Phila-
       delphia: University of Pennsylvania Press.

Germani, Gino
1971   *Política y sociedad en una epoca de transición.* Buenos Aires: Edi-
       torial Paidos.
1978   *Authoritarianism, Fascism, and National Populism.* Brunswick,
       N.J.: Transaction Books.

Girón, Sergio Enrique
1945   *La Revolución de Mayo.* Quito: Editorial Atahualpa.

Guerrero, Andrés
1997   "The Construction of a Ventriloquist's Image: Liberal Discourse
       and the 'Miserable Indian Race' in Late Nineteenth Century
       Ecuador." *Journal of Latin American Studies* 29: 555–90.
1998   "Ciudadanía, frontera étnica, y compulsión binaria." *Íconos* (Re-
       vista de FLACSO-Ecuador) 4 (December-March): 112–24.

Guerrero Bargos, Rafael
1994   *Regionalismo y democracia social en los orígenes del "CFP."*
       Quito: CAAP Diálogos.

Guevara Moreno, Carlos
1946   *Del 28 de Mayo de 1944 al 30 de Marzo de 1946.* Quito: Talleres
       Gráficos Nacionales.

Hawkins, Kirk, and David Hansen
2006   "Dependent Civil Society: The Círculos Bolivarianos in
       Venezuela." *Latin American Research Review* 41 (1): 102–32.

Held, David
1987   *Models of Democracy.* Stanford: Stanford University Press.

Hermet, Guy, Soledad Loaeza, and Jean François Prud'homme, eds.
2001   *Del populismo de los antiguos al populismo de los modernos.* Mex-
       ico City: El Colegio de México.

Herrera Aráuz, Francisco
2001   *Los golpes del poder—al aire: El 21 de enero a través de la radio.*
       Quito: Abya-Yala.

Hurtado, Osvaldo
1988   *El poder político en el Ecuador.* Quito: Planeta.

1990   *La política democrática: Los últimos veinte y cinco años.* Quito: Corporación Editora Nacional.

Hylton, Forrest, and Sinclair Thomson
2007   *Revolutionary Horizons: Past and Present in Bolivian Politics.* London: Verso

Ianni, Octavio
1973   "Populismo y contradicciones de clase." In *Populismo y contradicciones de clase en Latinoamérica,* edited by Octavio Ianni, 83–150. Mexico City: Editorial ERA.
1975   *La formación del estado populista en América Latina.* Mexico City: Editorial ERA.

Ibarra, Hernán
1996   "Las elecciones de 1996 o la costeñización de la política ecuatoriana." *Ecuador Debate* 38 August: 33–39.
1997   "La caída de Bucaram y el incierto camino de la reforma política." *Ecuador Debate* 40 (April): 21–33.

INIESEC
1984   *El 28 de Mayo y la fundación de la CTE.* Quito: Corporación Editora Nacional.

Informe Confidencial
1997   Encuestas sobre imagen y labor de Abdalá Bucaram.

Ionescu, Ghiţa, and Ernest Gellner, eds.
1969   *Populism: Its Meaning and National Characteristics.* New York: Macmillan.

Isaacs, Anita
1991   "Problems of Democratic Consolidation in Ecuador." *Bulletin of Latin American Research* 10 (2): 221–39.
1993   *Military Rule and Transition in Ecuador, 1972–92.* Pittsburgh: University of Pittsburgh Press.

Jackman, Mary
1994   *The Velvet Glove: Paternalism and Conflict in Gender, Class, and Race Relations.* Berkeley: University of California Press.

James, Daniel
1988a   "October Seventeenth and Eighteenth, 1945: Mass Protest, Peronism, and the Argentinean Working Class." *Journal of Social History* (Spring): 441–61.
1988b   *Resistance and Integration: Peronism and the Argentine Working Class, 1946–1976.* Cambridge: Cambridge University Press.

Kimmel, Michael
1994 "Masculinity as Homophobia: Fear, Shame, and Silence in the Construction of Gender Identity." In *Theorizing Masculinities,* edited by Harry Brod and Michael Kaufman, 119–41. Thousand Oaks, Calif.: Sage Publications.

Knight, Alan
1998 "Populism and Neopopulism in Latin America, Especially Mexico." *Journal of Latin American Studies* 30:223–48.

Krauze, Enrique
2008 *El poder y el delirio.* Barcelona: Tusquets Editores.

Laclau, Ernesto
1977 *Politics and Ideology in Marxist Theory.* London: Verso.
2005a *On Populist Reason.* London: Verso.
2005b "Populism: What's in a Name?" In *Populism and the Mirror of Democracy,* edited by Francisco Panizza, 32–50. London: Verso.
2006 "Consideraciones sobre el populismo latinoamericano." *Cuadernos del CENDES* 23 (64): 115–20.

Lander, Edgardo
2005 "Venezuelan Social Conflict in a Global Context." *Latin American Perspectives* 32 (2): 20–39.
2007 "Venezuelan Social Conflict in a Global Context." In *Venezuela: Hugo Chávez and the Decline of an "Exceptional Democracy,"* edited by Steve Ellner and Miguel Tinker Salas, 16–33. Lanham, Md.: Rowman and Littlefield.

Larrea, Tatiana
2007 *¿En qué pensamos los ecuatorianos al hablar de democracia?* Quito: Participación Ciudadana.

Larrea Maldonado, Ana María
2008 "La plurinacionalidad: Iguales y diversos en busca del Sumak Kawsay." In *Constitución 2008: Entre el quiebre y la realidad,* edited by Kintto Lucas, 77–87. Quito: Abya-Yala.

Laserna, Roberto
2003 "Bolivia: Entre populismo y democracia." *Nueva sociedad,* no. 188:4–14.

Lazar, Sian
2008 *El Alto, Rebel City: Self and Citizenship in Andean Bolivia.* Durham: Duke University Press.

Le Bon, Gustave
1983   *Psicología de las masas.* Madrid: Ediciones Morata. Original edition, 1895.

Lefort, Claude
1986   "The Image of the Body and Totalitarianism." In *The Political Forms of Modern Society: Bureaucracy, Democracy, Totalitarianism,* edited by John B. Thompson. Cambridge, Mass.: MIT Press.
1988   *Democracy and Political Theory.* Minneapolis: University of Minnesota Press.

Lentz, Carola
1997   *Migración e identidad étnica: La transformación histórica de una comunidad en la sierra ecuatoriana.* Quito: Abya-Yala.

León, Jorge, and Juan Pablo Pérez Sáinz
1986   "Crisis y movimiento sindical en Ecuador: Las huelgas nacionales del FUT (1981–1983)." In *Movimientos sociales en el Ecuador,* edited by Luis Vedesoto, 93–151. Quito: CLACSO.

Levitsky, Steve
2001   "An 'Organized Disorganization': Informal Organization and the Persistence of Local Party Structures in Argentine Peronism." *Journal of Latin American Studies* 33 (1): 29–65.

Lincoln, Bruce
1989   *Discourse and the Construction of Reality: Comparative Studies of Myth, Ritual, and Classification.* Oxford: Oxford University Press.

López Maya, Margarita
2003   "Hugo Chávez Frías: His Movement and His Presidency." In *Venezuelan Politics in the Chávez Era,* edited by Steve Ellner and Daniel Hellinger, 73–93. Boulder: Lynne Rienner.
2005   *Del viernes negro al referendo revocatores.* Caracas: Alfadil.
2008   "Examining Participatory Innovations in Bolivarian Caracas: The Cases of the TWRs and SMCOs." Unpublished manuscript; photocopy in possession of the author.

Loveman, Brian
1994   "'Protected Democracies' and Military Guardianship: Political Transitions in Latin America, 1978–1993." *Journal of Interamerican Studies and World Affairs* 36 (2): 105–91.

Lucas, Kintto
2000   *La rebelión de los indios.* Quito: Abya-Yala.

Lynch, Nicolás
1997   "New Citizens and Old Politics in Peru." *Constellations* 4 (1): 124–41.
Macas, Luis, Linda Belote, and Jim Belote
2003   "Indigenous Destiny in Indigenous Hands." In *Millennial Ecuador: Critical Essays on Cultural Transformations and Social Dynamics,* edited by Norman Whitten, 216–42. Iowa City: University of Iowa Press.
Machado, Decio
2009   "Ecuador ante los comicios del próximo 26 de abril." *Rebelión.* http://jbcs.blogspot.com/2009/04/ecuador-ante-los-comicios-del-proximo.html.
Mackinnon, María Moira, and Mario Alberto Petrone
1998   "Los complejos de la Cenicienta." In *Populismo y neopopulismo en América Latina: El problema de la Cenicienta,* edited by María Moira Mackinnon and Mario Alberto Petrone, 13–59. Buenos Aires: Editorial Universitaria de Buenos Aires.
Maiguashca, Juan
1991   "Los sectores subalternos en los años treinta y el aparecimiento del velasquismo." In *Las crisis en el Ecuador: Los treinta y los ochenta,* edited by Rosemary Thorp, 75–95. Quito: Corporación Editora Nacional.
Maiguashca, Juan, and Liisa North
1991   "Orígenes y significados del velasquismo: Lucha de clases y participación política en el Ecuador, 1920–1972." In *La cuestión regional y el poder,* edited by Rafael Quintero, 89–161. Quito: Corporación Editora Nacional.
Maldonado Tamayo, Luis
1947   *Traición a la democracia en el Ecuador.* Quito: n.p.
Malloy, James
1977   "Authoritarianism and Corporatism in Latin America." In *Authoritarianism and Corporatism in Latin America,* edited by James Malloy, 3–23. Pittsburgh: University of Pittsburgh Press.
1987   "The Politics of Transition in Latin America." In *Authoritarians and Democrats: Regime Transition in Latin America,* edited by James Malloy and Mitchell Seligson, 235–59. Pittsburgh: University of Pittsburgh Press.
Malloy, James, and Eduardo Gamarra
1987   "The Transition to Democracy in Bolivia." In *Authoritarians and Democrats: Regime Transition in Latin America,* edited

by James Malloy and Mitchell Seligson, 93–121. Pittsburgh: University of Pittsburgh Press.

March, Luke
2007   "From Vanguard of the Proletariat to Vox Populi: Left-Populism as a Shadow of Contemporary Socialism." *SAIS Review* 27 (1): 63–78.

Marchán, Carlos
1987   "Crisis nacional, aprovechamiento regional, y discriminación social de sus efectos económicos (1920–1927)." In *Crisis y cambios de la economía ecuatoriana en los años veinte,* edited by Carlos Marchán, 221–85. Quito: Banco Central del Ecuador.

Marshall, T. H.
1963   *Class, Citizenship, and Social Development.* Chicago: University of Chicago Press.

Martín Arranz, Raul
1987   "El liderazgo carismático en el contexto del estudio del liderazgo." In *Populismo, caudillaje, y discurso demagógico,* edited by José Álvarez Junco, 73–101. Madrid: Centro de Investigaciones Sociológicas.

Martz, John D.
1987   *Politics and Petroleum in Ecuador.* New Brunswick, N.J.: Transaction Books.
1989   "La expresión regionalista del populismo: Guayaquil y el CFP, 1948–60." In *El populismo en el Ecuador,* edited by Felipe Burbano and Carlos de la Torre, 323–51. Quito: ILDIS.

Matta, Roberto da
1987   "The Quest for Citizenship in a Relational Universe." In *State and Society in Brazil: Continuity and Change,* edited by John D. Wirth, Edson de Oliveira Nunes, and Thomas E. Bogenschild, 308–35. Boulder: Westview Press.
1991   *Carnivals, Rogues, and Heroes: An Interpretation of the Brazilian Dilemma.* Notre Dame, Ind.: University of Notre Dame Press.

Mayorga, Fernando
1998   "Compadres y padrinos: El rol del neopopulismo en la consolidación democrática y la reforma estatal en Bolivia." In *El fantasma del populismo: Aproximación a un tema (siempre) actual,* edited by Felipe Burbano, 119–31. Caracas: Nueva Sociedad.

Mayorga, René Antonio

2009 "Sociedad civil y estado bajo un populismo plebiscitario y autoritario." In *La nueva izquierda en América Latina: Derechos humanos, participación política, y sociedad civil,* edited by Cynthia Arnson, 109–19. Washington, D.C.: Woodrow Wilson International Center for Scholars.

McCoy, Jennifer, and David Myers, eds.

2004 *The Unraveling of Representative Democracy in Venezuela.* Baltimore: Johns Hopkins University Press.

Menéndez-Carrión, Amparo

1986 *La conquista del voto en el Ecuador: De Velasco a Roldós.* Quito: Corporación Editora Nacional.

1992 "El populismo en el Ecuador: ¿Tiene sentido seguirlo 'Descubriendo'?" In *Populismo,* edited by Juan Paz y Miño, 197–213. Quito: ILDIS.

Mény, Yves, and Yves Surel

2002a "The Constitutive Ambiguity of Populism." In *Democracies and the Populist Challenge,* edited by Mény and Surel, 1–25. New York: Palgrave.

2002b *Democracies and the Populist Challenge.* New York: Palgrave.

Miño, Edison Ramiro, and Luis Macas

1997 *Por qué cayó Bucaram: Entretelones y actores.* Quito: n.p.

Moisés, José Álvaro

1993 "Elections, Political Parties, and Political Culture in Brazil: Changes and Continuities." *Journal of Latin American Studies* 25:575–611.

Morales, Evo

2006 *La revolución democrática y cultural: Diez discursos de Evo Morales.* La Paz: Editorial Malatesta.

Moscovici, Serge

1985 *La era de las multitudes: Un tratado histórico de psicología de las masas.* Mexico City: Fondo de Cultura Económica.

Mosse, George

1975 *The Nationalization of the Masses.* New York: Howard Fertig, 1975.

Mouffe, Chantal
2005a "The 'End of Politics' and the Challenge of Right Wing Populism." In *Populism and the Mirror of Democracy,* edited by Francisco Panizza, 50–72. London: Verso.
2005b *On the Political.* London: Routledge.

Muñoz Vicuña, Elias, ed.
1984 *El 28 de Mayo de 1944: Testimonio.* Guayaquil: Universidad de Guayaquil.

Murmis, Miguel, and Juan Carlos Portantiero
1971 *Estudios sobre los orígenes del peronismo.* Buenos Aires: Siglo Veintiuno.

Naranjo Campaña, José Antonio
1945 *Verdades sobre la Revolución de Mayo: El Batallón de Infantería "Carchi" en la Gloriosa efemérides del 28 y 29 de Mayo de 1944 en Guayaquil.* Quito: Editorial Escuela Técnica.

Nascimento, Elimar Pinheiro do
1994 "Adiós Señor Presidente: Análisis del proceso de la renuncia de Collor de Mello." *Ecuador Debate* 33 (December): 64–85.

Navarro, Marysa
1982 "Evitas's Charismatic Leadership." In *Latin American Populism in Comparative Perspective,* edited by Michael Conniff, 47–67. Albuquerque: University of New Mexico Press.

Novaro, Marcos
1994 *Pilotos de tormentas: Crisis de representación y personalización de la política en Argentina (1989–1993).* Buenos Aires: Ediciones Letra Buena.
1996 "Los populismos latinoamericanos transfigurados." *Nueva sociedad* 144 (July-August): 90–104.
1998 "Populismo y gobierno: Las transformaciones en el peronismo y la consolidación democrática argentina." In *El fantasma del populismo: Aproximación a un tema (siempre) actual,* edited by Felipe Burbano, 25–49. Caracas: Nueva Sociedad.

Novaro, Marcos, and Vicente Palermo
1996 *Política y poder en el gobierno de Menem.* Buenos Aires: FLACSO-Norma.

Nun, José
1994 "Populismo, representación, y menemismo." *Sociedad* 5:93–121.

O'Donnell, Guillermo

1973   *Modernization and Bureaucratic Authoritarianism: Studies in South American Politics.* Berkeley: University of California Press.

1994   "Delegative Democracy." *Journal of Democracy* 5, 1 (January): 55–69.

1999   "Polyarchies and the (Un)Rule of Law in Latin America: A Partial Conclusion." In *The (Un) Rule of Law and the Underprivileged in Latin America,* edited by Juan Méndez, Guillermo O'Donnell, and Paulo Sérgio Pinheiro, 303–39. Notre Dame: University of Notre Dame Press.

Offe, Claus

1984   *Contradictions of the Welfare State.* Cambridge, Mass.: MIT Press.

Ojeda, Lautaro

1971   *Mecanismos y articulaciones del caudillismo velasquista.* Quito: JUNAPLA.

Oliveira, Francisco de

1992   "Fernando Collor de Mello: Perfil de un prestidigitador." *Nueva sociedad* 118 (March-April): 99–109.

Ornstein, Norman J., and Thomas E. Mann

2000   "The Permanent Campaign and the Future of American Democracy." Conclusion to *The Permanent Campaign and Its Future,* edited by Ornstein and Mann. Washington, D.C.: American Enterprise Institute.

Ortiz, Benjamín

1997   "La negociación: Un sánduche en el Hotel Quito." In *¡Que se vaya! Crónica el Bucaramato,* edited by Diego Cornejo, 73–84. Quito: Edimpres-Hoy.

Ospina, Pablo

2008   "Ecuador al ritmo de la iniciativa política del gobierno de la revolución ciudadana." In *Constitución 2008: Entre el quiebre y la realidad,* edited by Kintto Lucas, 125–43. Quito: Abya-Yala.

Ostiguy, Pierre

2007   "Syncretism in Argentina's Party System and Peronist Political Culture." In *Reconfiguring Institutions across Time and Space: Syncretic Responses to Challenges of Political and Economic Transformation,* edited by Dennis Galvan and Rudra Sil, 83–113. New York: Palgrave.

Oxhorn, Philip
1998   "The Social Foundation of Latin America's Current Populism:
        Problems of Popular Class Formation and Collective Action."
        Journal of Historical Sociology 11, 2 (June): 212–46.
Pachano, Simón
1997   "¡Bucaram Fuera! ¿Fuera Bucaram?" In ¿ *Y ahora qué?* edited by
        René Báez, 229–64. Quito: Eskeletra.
2002   "Partidos políticos y clientelismo en Ecuador." In *Dadme un bal-
        cón y el país es mío: Liderazgo político en América Latina,*
        edited by Wilhem Hofmeister, 117–43. Rio de Janeiro: Konrad
        Adenauer.
2007   *La trama de Penélope: Procesos políticos e instituciones en el
        Ecuador.* Quito: FLACSO Ecuador.
Palacio, Emilio
2008   *El libro blanco de las bestias salvajes: La polémica sobre la libertad
        de expresión con Rafael Correa.* Guayaquil: Emilio Palacio.
Pallares, Martín, and Marcia Cevallos
1997   "El tema de la corrupción: Comedia de escándalos." In *¡Que
        se vaya! Crónica el Bucaramato,* edited by Diego Cornejo,
        21–28. Quito: Edimpres-Hoy.
Panfichi, Aldo
1997   "The Authoritarian Alternative: 'Anti-Politics' in the Popular
        Sectors of Lima." In *The New Politics of Inequality in Latin
        America,* edited by Douglas Chalmers, Carlos Vilas, Kather-
        ine Hite, Scott B. Martin, Karianne Piester, and Monique
        Segarra, 217–37. Oxford: Oxford University Press.
Panizza, Francisco
2005a   *Populism and the Mirror of Democracy.* London: Verso.
2005b   "Unarmed Utopia Revisited: The Resurgence of Left-of-Centre
        Politics in Latin America." *Political Studies* 53 (4): 716–34.
2007   "Parties, Democracy and Grounded Utopias: A Reply to Sara
        Motta." *Political Studies* 55 (4): 885–92.
2008   "Fisuras entre populismo y democracia en América Latina." In
        *El retorno del pueblo: Populismo y nuevas democracias en
        América Latina,* edited by Carlos de la Torre and Enrique
        Peruzzotti, 77–97. Quito: FLACSO Ecuador.
Patzi Paco, Félix
2004   *Sistema comunal: Una propuesta alternativa al sistema liberal:
        Una discusión teórica para salir de la colonialidad y del liber-
        alismo.* La Paz: Comunidad de Estudios Alternativos.

Paz y Miño, Juan, ed.
1992   *Populismo*. Quito: ILDIS.

Pérez Castro, Franklin
1990   *Así fue el 28 de Mayo: Conversaciones con Jaime Galarza Zavala*. Guayaquil: Escuela Superior Politécnica del Litoral.

Pérez Sáinz, Juan Pablo
1985   *Clase obrera y democracia en el Ecuador*. Quito: Editorial El Conejo.
1986   *Entre la fábrica y la ciudad*. Quito: Editorial El Conejo.

Peri, Yoram
2004   *Telepopulism: Media and Politics in Israel*. Stanford: Stanford University Press.

Perruci, Gamaliel, and Steven Sanderson
1989   "Presidential Succession, Economic Crisis, and Populist Resurgence in Brazil." *Studies in Comparative International Development* 24, 3 (Fall): 30–50.

Peruzzotti, Enrique
2008   "Populismo y representación democrática." In *El retorno del pueblo: Populismo y nuevas democracias en América Latina*, edited by Carlos de la Torre and Enrique Peruzzotti, 97–125. Quito: FLACSO Ecuador.

Petras, James
1997   "Alternatives to Neoliberalism in Latin America." *Latin American Perspectives* 24 (1): 80–91.

Pinheiro, Paulo Sérgio
1994   "The Legacy of Authoritarianism in Democratic Brazil." In *Latin American Development and Public Policy*, edited by Stuart S. Nagel, 237–53. New York: St. Martin's Press.
1997   "Popular Responses to State-Sponsored Violence in Brazil." In *The New Politics of Inequality in Latin America*, edited by Douglas Chalmers, Carlos Vilas, Katherine Hite, Scott B. Martin, Karianne Piester, and Monique Segarra, 261–80. Oxford: Oxford University Press.

Plotke, David
1997   "Representation Is Democracy." *Constellations* 4 (1): 19–35.

Ponce Enríquez, Camilo
1944   "Es el desvío del orden moral la causa remota y múltiple de la ruina de la patria." *La patria* (Quito), 1 May 1944, pp. 2–3.

Poole, Deborah, and Gerardo Rénique

1992   *Peru: Time of Fear.* London: Latin American Bureau.

Popular Memory Group

1982   "Popular Memory: Theory, Politics, Method." In *Making Histories,* edited by Richard Johnson, Greg McLennan, Bill Schwarz, and David Sutton, 205–53. Minneapolis: University of Minnesota Press.

Porto, Mauro

2000   "La crisis de confianza en la política y sus instituciones: Los medios y la legitimidad de la democracia en Brasil." *América Latina hoy* 25:23–34.

2007   "Framing Controversies: Television and the 2002 Presidential Election in Brazil." *Political Communication* 24 (19): 19–36.

Quijano, Aníbal

1998   "Populismo y fujimorismo." In *El fantasma del populismo: Aproximación a un tema [siempre] actual,* edited by Felipe Burbano, 171–207. Caracas: Nueva Sociedad.

Quintero, Rafael

1980   *El mito del populismo en el Ecuador.* Quito: FLACSO.

2005   *Electores contra partidos en un sistema político de mandos.* Quito: Abya-Yala/ILDIS.

Quintero, Rafael, and Erika Silva

1991   *Una nación en ciernes.* 3 vols. Quito: FLACSO and Abya-Yala.

Raby, D. L.

2006   *Democracy and Revolution: Latin America and Socialism Today.* London: Pluto.

Radcliffe, Sarah, and Sallie Westwood

1996   *Remaking the Nation: Place, Identity, and Politics in Latin America.* New York: Routledge.

Ramírez Gallegos, Franklin

2005   *La insurrección de abril no fue sólo una fiesta.* Quito: Abya-Yala.

Ramírez Gallegos, Franklin, and Analía Minteguiaga

2007   "El nuevo tiempo del estado: La política posneoliberal del correísmo" *Observatorio social de América Latina* (Buenos Aires: CLACSO) 7 (22): 87–103.

Reygadas, Luis.

2005   "Imagined Inequalities: Representations of Discrimination and Exclusion in Latin America." *Social Identities* 11 (5): 489–508.

Rivera Cusicanqui, Silvia.
1990   "Liberal Democracy and Ayllu Democracy in Bolivia: The Case of Northern Potosí." *Journal of Developmental Studies* 26 (4): 97–121.

Roberts, Kenneth
1995   "Neoliberalism and the Transformation of Populism in Latin America: The Peruvian Case." *World Politics* 48 (October): 82–116.
2003 "Social Polarization and the Populist Resurgence in Venezuela." In *Venezuelan Politics in the Chávez Era,* edited by Steve Ellner and Daniel Hellinger, 55–73. Boulder: Lynne Rienner.
2008   "El resurgimiento del populismo latinoamericano." In *El retorno del pueblo: Populismo y nuevas democracias en América Latina,* edited by Carlos de la Torre and Enrique Peruzzotti, 55–77. Quito: FLACSO Ecuador.

Roberts, Kenneth, and Moisés Arce
1998   "Neoliberalism and Lower-Class Voting Behavior in Peru." *Comparative Political Studies* 31 (2): 217–46.

Rock, David, ed.
1994   *Latin America in the 1940s: War and Postwar Transitions.* Berkeley: University of California Press.

Rodríguez, Linda
1985   *The Search for Public Policy: Regional Politics and Government Finances in Ecuador, 1830–1940.* Berkeley: University of California Press.

Rojas, Milton, and Gaitán Villavicencio
1988   *El proceso urbano de Guayaquil.* Quito: ILDIS and CER-G.

Roseberry, William
1989   *Anthropologies and Histories: Essays in Culture, History, and Political Economy.* New Brunswick, N.J.: Rutgers University Press.

Rowe, William, and Vivian Schelling
1991   *Memory and Modernity: Popular Culture in Latin America.* London: Verso.

Roxborough, Ian
1984   "Unity and Diversity in Latin American History." *Journal of Latin American Studies* 16:1–26.

Salcedo, José María
1995   *Terremoto: ¿Por qué ganó Fujimori?* Lima: Editorial Brasa.

Sánchez Parga, José

1996 *Población y pobreza indígenas*. Quito: CAAP.

1998 "Encubrimientos sociopolíticos del populismo." In *El fantasma del populismo: Aproximación a un tema [siempre] actual*, edited by Felipe Burbano, 149–71. Caracas: Nueva Sociedad.

Sarlo, Beatriz

1995 "Argentina under Menem: The Aesthetics of Domination." In *Free Trade and Economic Restructuring in Latin America: A NACLA Reader*, edited by Fred Rosen and Deidre McFadyen, 253–63. New York: Monthly Review Press.

Sartori, Giovanni

1998 *Homo videns: La sociedad teledirigida*. Madrid: Taurus.

Schedler, Andreas

1996 "Anti-Political-Establishment Parties." *Party Politics* 2, 3: 291–312.

1997 "Antipolitics-Closing and Colonizing the Public Sphere." Introduction to *The End of Politics? Explorations into Modern Antipolitics*, edited by Andreas Schedler, 1–21. New York: St. Martin's Press.

Sigal, Silvia, and Eliseo Verón

1986 *Perón o muerte: Los fundamentos discursivos del fenómeno peronista*. Buenos Aires: Editorial Legasa.

Silva, Carlos Eduardo Lins da

1993 "The Brazilian Case: Manipulation by the Media?" In *Television, Politics, and the Transition to Democracy in Latin America*, edited by Thomas E. Skidmore, 137–45. Washington and Baltimore: Woodrow Wilson Center Press and Johns Hopkins University Press.

Skidmore, Thomas E.

1993 "Politics and the Media in a Democratizing Latin America." In *Television, Politics, and the Transition to Democracy in Latin America*, edited by Thomas E. Skidmore, 1–23. Washington and Baltimore: Woodrow Wilson Center Press and Johns Hopkins University Press.

Skurski, Julie

1994 "The Ambiguities of Authenticity in Latin America: *Doña Bárbara* and the Construction of National Identity." *Poetics Today* 15 (4): 605–42.

Sommer, Doris
  1990   "Irresistible Romance: The Foundational Fictions of Latin
         America." In *Nation and Narration,* edited by Homi Bhabha,
         71–98. New York: Routledge.

Sosa, Arturo
  2007   "Reflexiones sobre el poder comunal." In *Ideas para debatir el
         socialismo del siglo XXI,* edited by Margarita López Maya,
         41–59. Caracas: Editorial Alfa.

Spalding, Hobart
  1977   *Organized Labor in Latin America.* New York: Harper and Row.
Stefanoni, Pablo, and Hervé do Alto.
  2006   *La revolución de Evo Morales: De la coca al palacio.* Buenos
         Aires: Capital Intelectual.

Stein, Stanley J., and Barbara H. Stein
  1970   *The Colonial Heritage of Latin America.* New York: Oxford Uni-
         versity Press.

Stein, Steve
  1980   *Populism in Peru.* Madison: University of Wisconsin Press.

Straubhaar, Joseph, Organ Olsen, and Maria Cavaliari Nunes
  1993   "The Brazilian Case: Influencing the Voter." In *Television, Poli-
         tics, and the Transition to Democracy in Latin America,*
         edited by Thomas E. Skidmore, 118–37. Washington and Bal-
         timore: Woodrow Wilson Center Press and Johns Hopkins
         University Press.

Stutzman, Ronald
  1981   "El Mestizaje: An All-Inclusive Ideology of Exclusion." In *Cul-
         tural Transformations and Ethnicity in Modern Ecuador,*
         edited by Norman Whitten Jr., 45–94. Urbana: University of
         Illinois Press.

Taguieff, Pierre-André
  1995   "Political Science Confronts Populism: From a Conceptual Mi-
         rage to a Real Problem." *Telos* 103 (Spring): 9–43.

Talmon, Jacob
  1991   *Myth of the Nation and Vision of Revolution: Ideological Polari-
         sation in the Twentieth Century.* New Brunswick: Transac-
         tion Books.

Tapia Mealla, Luis
2004   *La condición multisocietal: Multiculturalidad, pluralismo, modernidad.* La Paz: Muela del Diablo Editores.
2006   *La invención del núcleo común: Ciudadanía y gobierno multisocietal.* La Paz: Muela del Diablo Editores.
Tapia Mealla, Luis, Alvaro García Linera, and Raúl Prada Alcoreza
2004   *Memorias de octubre.* La Paz: Muela del Diablo Editores.
Thompson, E. P.
1971   "The Moral Economy of the English Crowd in the Eighteenth Century." *Past and Present* 50 (February): 76–136.
Ticona Alejo, Esteban, comp.
2006   "El racismo intelectual en el Pachakuti: Algunas consideraciones simbólicas del ascenso de Evo Morales a la presidencia de Bolivia." In *El Pachakuti ha empezado (Pachakutixa qalltiwa): Democracia y cultura política en Bolivia,* edited by Ticona, 155–91. La Paz: Corte Nacional Electoral.
Tilly, Charles
1995   "Democracy Is a Lake." In *The Social Construction of Democracy, 1870–1990,* edited by George Reid Andrews and Herrick Chapman, 365–88. New York: New York University Press.
Tismaneanu, Vladimir
1998   *Fantasies of Salvation: Democracy, Nationalism, and Myth in Post-communist Europe.* Princeton: Princeton University Press.
Tocqueville, Alexis de
1961   *La democracia en América.* 2 vols. Madrid: Alianza Editorial.
Torre, Juan Carlos, ed.
1995   *El 17 de Octubre de 1945.* Buenos Aires: Ariel.
Torres Ballesteros, Sagrario
1987   "El Populismo: Un concepto escurridizo." In *Populismo, caudillaje, y discurso demagógico,* edited by José Álvarez Junco, 159–81. Madrid: Centro de Investigaciones Sociológicas.
Touraine, Alain
1989   *América Latina: Política y sociedad.* Madrid: Espasa-Calpe.
Unión Panamericana
1954   *Ecuador: Hacienda pública y política fiscal.* Washington, D.C.: Unión Panamericana.

Urbinati, Nadia
1998   "Democracy and Populism." *Constellations* 5 (1): 110–25.

Vaca, Fermín
1997   "¿Qué pasó en el Congreso?" In *¡Que se vaya! Crónica el Bucaramato,* edited by Diego Cornejo, 20. Quito: Edimpres-Hoy.

Vargas Llosa, Mario
1995   *A Fish in the Water: A Memoir.* New York: Penguin.

Vega Ugalde, Silvia
1987   *La Gloriosa: De la revolución del 28 de Mayo de 1944 a la contrarrevolución velasquista.* Quito: Editorial El Conejo.

Velasco Ibarra, José María
1937   *Conciencia o barbarie.* Quito: Editorial Moderna.
1943   *Expresión política hispanoamericana.* Vols. 6, 7 of *Obras completas,* edited by Juan Velasco Espinosa. Quito: Ediciones Lexigrama.
1946   *El 28 de Mayo en Guayaquil: Balance de una revolución popular: Documentos para la historia.* Quito: Talleres Gráficos Nacionales.
1974   *Discursos.* Vol. 12 of *Obras completas,* edited by Juan Velasco Espinosa. Quito: Editorial Santo Domingo.

Vera, Alfredo
1948   *Anhelo y pasión de la democracia ecuatoriana.* Guayaquil: Imprenta de la Universidad and Talleres Municipales.

Vilas, Carlos
1992–93   "Latin American Populism: A Structural Approach." *Science and Society* 56 (4): 389–420.
1995a   "Entre la democracia y el neoliberalismo: Los caudillos electorales de la posmodernidad." *Socialismo y participación* 69 (March): 31–43.
1995b   "Estudio preliminar: El populismo o la democratización fundamental de América Latina." In *La democratización fundamental: El populismo en América Latina,* 11–118. Mexico City: Consejo Nacional para la Cultura y las Artes.
1997   "Participation, Inequality, and the Whereabouts of Democracy." In *The New Politics of Inequality in Latin America,* edited by Douglas Chalmers, Carlos Vilas, Katherine Hite, Scott B. Martin, Karianne Piester, and Monique Segarra, 3–43. Oxford: Oxford University Press.

1998   "Buscando al leviatán: Hipótesis sobre ciudadanía, desigualdad, y democracia." In *Democracia sin exclusiones ni excluidos,* edited by Emir Sader, 115–35. Caracas: Nueva Sociedad.

Villavicencio, Gaitán
1988   "Las ofertas electorales y los límites del clientelismo." In *Ecuador 88: Elecciones, economía, y estrategias,* 11–33. Quito: Editorial El Conejo.

Waisbord, Silvio
1996   "Farewell to Public Spaces? Electoral Campaigns and Street Spectacle in Argentina." *Studies in Latin American Popular Culture* 15.

Waters, William
1997   "The Road of Many Returns: Rural Bases of the Informal Urban Economy in Ecuador." *Latin American Perspectives* 24 (3): 50–65.

Webber, Jeffery
2008   "Rebellion to Reform in Bolivia. Part 2: Revolutionary Epoch, Combined Liberation and the December 2005 Elections." *Historical Materialism* 16 (3): 55–76.

Weber, Max
1968   *Max Weber on Charisma and Institution Building: Selected Papers,* edited by S. N. Eisenstadt. Chicago: University of Chicago Press.

Weffort, Francisco
1998   "El populismo en la política brasileña. In *Populismo y neopopulismo en América Latina: El problema de la Cenicienta,* edited by María Moira Mackinnon and Mario Alberto Petrone, 135–52. Buenos Aires: Editorial Universitaria de Buenos Aires. Original edition, 1967.

Weyland, Kurt
1993   "The Rise and Fall of President Collor and Its Impact on Brazilian Democracy." *Journal of Interamerican Studies and World Affairs* 35 (1): 1–37.
1996   "Neopopulism and Neoliberalism in Latin America: Unexpected Affinities." *Studies in Comparative International Development* 31 (3): 3–31.
1998   "Swallowing the Bitter Pill: Sources of Popular Support for Neoliberal Reform in Latin America." *Comparative Political Studies* 31 (5): 539–68.

2001   "Clarifying a Contested Concept." *Comparative Politics* 34 (1): 1–22.

2003   "Neopopulism and Neoliberalism in Latin America: How Much Affinity?" *Third World Quarterly* 24 (6): 1095–1116.

2009   "The Rise of Latin America's Two Lefts: Insights from Rentier State Theory." *Comparative Politics* 41 (2): 145–64.

Weyland, Kurt, et al.

2004   *Releer los Populismos.* Quito: Centro Andino de Acción Popular.

Wiles, Peter

1969   "A Syndrome, Not a Doctrine." In *Populism: Its Meaning and National Characteristics,* edited by Ghiţa Ionescu and Ernest Gellner, 166–80. New York: Macmillan.

Williams, Raymond

1976   *Keywords: A Vocabulary of Culture and Society.* New York: Oxford University Press.

Willner, Ann Ruth

1984   *The Spellbinders: Charismatic Political Leadership.* New Haven: Yale University Press.

Wilpert, Gregory

2007   *Changing Venezuela by Taking Power: The History and Policies of the Chávez Government.* London: Verso.

Wolfe, Joel

1994   "'Father of the Poor' or 'Mother of the Rich'? Getúlio Vargas, Industrial Workers, and Constructions of Class, Gender, and Populism in São Paulo, 1930–1954." *Radical History Review* 58: 80–112.

Ycaza, Patricio

1991   *Historia del movimiento obrero ecuatoriano.* 2 vols. Quito: CEDIME and CIUDAD.

Zamosc, Leon

1994   "Agrarian Protest and the Indian Movement in the Ecuadorian Highlands." *Latin American Research Review* 29 (3): 37–69.

Zanatta, Loris

2008   "El populismo, entre la religión y la política: Sobre las raíces históricas del antiliberalismo en América Latina." *Estudios interdisciplinarios de América Latina y el Caribe* 19 (2): 29–45.

Zavaleta Mercado, René
1983   *Las masas en noviembre*. La Paz: Librerí¬a Editorial "Juventud."
Zirker, Daniel
1998   "Jose Nun's 'Middle-Class Military Coup' in Contemporary Perspective: Implications of Latin America's Neoliberal Democratic Coalitions." *Latin American Perspectives* 25 (5): 76–86.
Zúquete, José Pedro
2007   *Missionary Politics in Contemporary Europe*. Syracuse: Syracuse University Press.
2008   "The Missionary Politics of Hugo Chávez." *Latin American Politics and Society* 50 (1): 91–122.

Index

Acosta, Alberto, 191, 194
AD (Democratic Action), 160
Alarcón, Fabián, 80, 106
Albornoz, Miguel, 36, 49 53
Alianza Democrática Ecuatoriana (ADE),
    29, 37, 51–52, 59, 68, 69, 70, 78
Alianza Popular Revolucionaria Americana
    (APRA), 6, 15–16
Alliance for a Proud and Sovereign Home-
    land (AP), 174, 179
Arroyo del Río, Carlos, 35, 36 53, 61, 62, 63,
    70, 75
Arteaga, Rosalía, 80, 89–90

Borja, Rodrigo, xviii, 178
Bucaram, Abdalá, xviii, 80–112, 131–32; base
    of support, 95–98, 101–4, 108–9; and
    Congress, 105–6; corruption, 101,
    106–7, 111–12, 117; demonstrations
    against, 80, 98–101; discourse, 91–95,
    115–16; economic plan, 81–82, 84–85,
    89, 98–100, 101; electoral strategy,
    89–98, 123; government, 98–103; mas-
    culinity and sexuality, 89–90, 94–95,
    102, 109–10; media, 108, 110, 112–13,
    117, 129; military, 108, 110; overthrow,
    138; political spectacle, 102–5, 113–15;
    regionalist tensions, 90–91, 103, 104;
    relations with upper classes, 101, 105;
    religion, 93, 109, 116, 207; return of,
    111–18; studies of, 219n; U.S. Em-
    bassy, 106

Cavallo, Domingo, 99
charisma, 10–12. *See also* populist leadership
Chávez Hugo, vii, xi, 146, 164, 171, 173; Boli-
    varian circles, 150; communal coun-
    cils, 151; constitution 1999, 203–4;
    coup against, xi, 150; democracy,
    149–52; discourse, 165–66
Caracazo, 163–64, 221n

citizenship, xxiii, xxiv, 9, 87, 93, 124
citizens' revolution. *See under* Correa,
    Rafael
clientelism, 20–21, 85–86, 96–97, 125, 134,
    169–71, 183, 209–10
Collor de Mello, Fernando, 119, 120, 129–30,
    135, 220–21n; election, 132, 133, 134;
    media, 129–30; overthrow, 137–38
communal and assembly democracy, xii,
    154–60
Concentración de Fuerzas Populares
    (CFP), 20
Confederation of Indigenous Nationalities
    of Ecuador (CONAIE), 100, 153, 154,
    191
COPEI (Christian Political Electoral Inde-
    pendent Organization), 160
Correa, Rafael, vii, xiii, 146, 166, 171, 173,
    174–97, 210; 2006 election, 176–87;
    citizens' revolution, 175, 194–96;
    clientelism, 184, 190–91; Con-
    stituent Assembly, 175, 187, 191–92,
    203–4; democracy, 187, 192–94,
    196–97; discourse, 166–67, 183–84,
    190; media, xii, 180, 181, 187,
    196–97; permanent campaign,
    187–92; relations with social move-
    ments, 173, 191, 194–97, 215

Dahik, Alberto, 107
delegative democracy, xxiv, 110, 141, 143–49
democratizing traditions, vii–viii; liberal-re-
    publican, vii–viii, ix, x, 125, 138–39;
    Marxist, viii, 202; populist, vii, 125,
    149, 152
discourse: anti-Velasquista, 56–57; Aprista,
    14, 15, 17; Bucaram's, 91–95, 115–16,
    207–10; Conservative, Ecuador,
    1930s–1940s, 47–50; Chávez, 165–66;
    Correa's, 166–67, 183–84, 190, 210–11;
    discourse analysis, 12–14, 34–35, 204;